I0901025

POSTCARD HISTORY SERIES

Navajo Weavers of the American Southwest

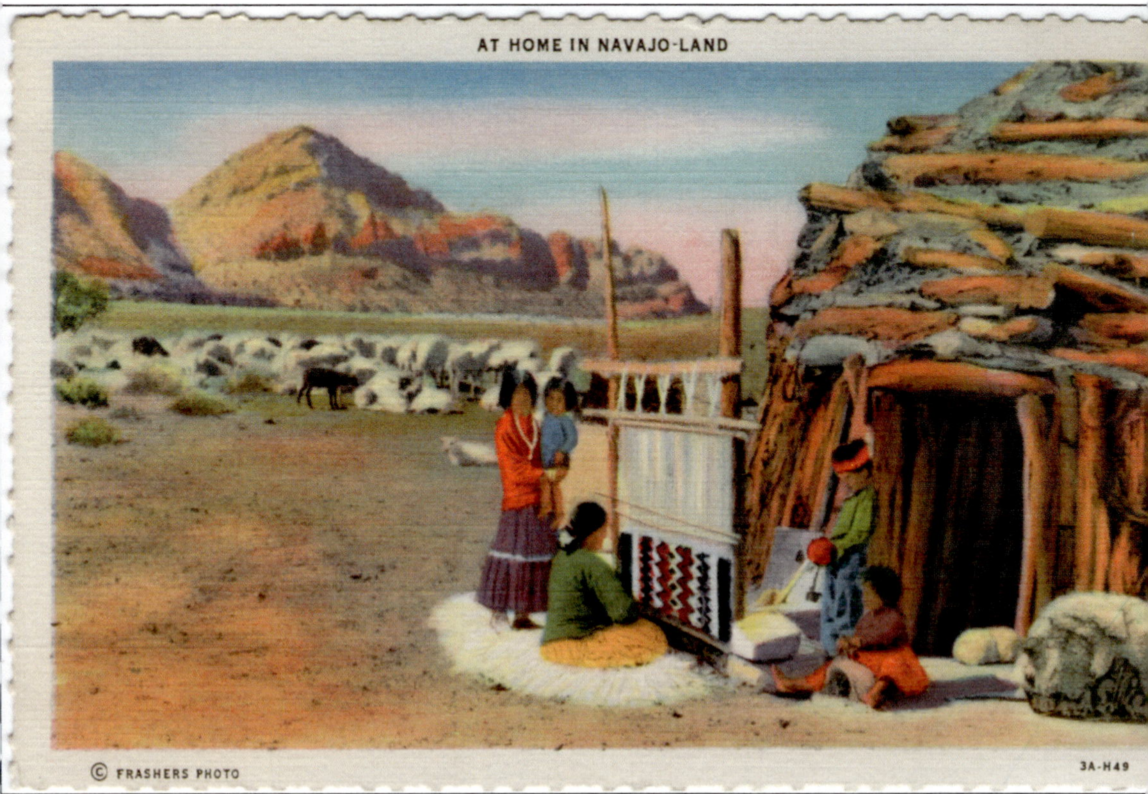

Burton Frasher Sr. (1888–1955) was one of the West's most prolific photographers. During his 40-year career in commercial photography, he produced over 60,000 negatives, which were used to print thousands of postcards. Black-and-white images were made first (see back cover); hand-colored versions like this followed shortly after. This postcard is reproduced with permission from the Burton Frasher family. (Courtesy of the Peter Hiller Collection.)

ON THE FRONT COVER: A weaver publicly known only as "Elle of Ganado" and her family demonstrated handicrafts in the "Indian Village" at the 1915 Panama-California Exposition in San Diego. The caption notes, "The Navaho [*sic*] Indians . . . are the most skilled Indian weavers in the world." The photographer of this image was J.R. Willis; the publisher was the Fred Harvey Company. This postcard is reproduced with permission from Walter Haussamen and the J.R. Willis Collection. (Courtesy of the Peter Hiller Collection.)

ON THE BACK COVER: Burton Frasher specialized in photographing weavers' homes throughout Navajo country. This postcard is aptly titled "At Home in Navajo-Land," for it shows the essentials of traditional life—a family, a *hogan* ("house" in the Diné language), a flock of sheep, and the surrounding landscape. Then, as today, weaving represented an important livelihood for one's family. See page 76 for additional information about this image and the one shown above. This postcard is reproduced with permission from the Burton Frasher family. (Courtesy of the Peter Hiller Collection.)

POSTCARD HISTORY SERIES

Navajo Weavers of the American Southwest

Peter Hiller, Ann Lane Hedlund, and Ramona Sakiestewa

ARCADIA PUBLISHING

ISBN 978-1-4671-2972-5

Published by Arcadia Publishing
Charleston, South Carolina

Printed in the United States of America

Library of Congress Control Number: 2018945931

For all general information contact Arcadia Publishing at:
Telephone 843-853-2070
Fax 843-853-0044
E-mail sales@arcadiapublishing.com
For customer service and orders:
Toll-Free 1-888-313-2665

Visit us on the Internet at www.arcadiapublishing.com

To the Diné weavers and their families who appear in these photographs, although most remain unidentified by name or locale; to today's Native American weavers who will never let that happen again.

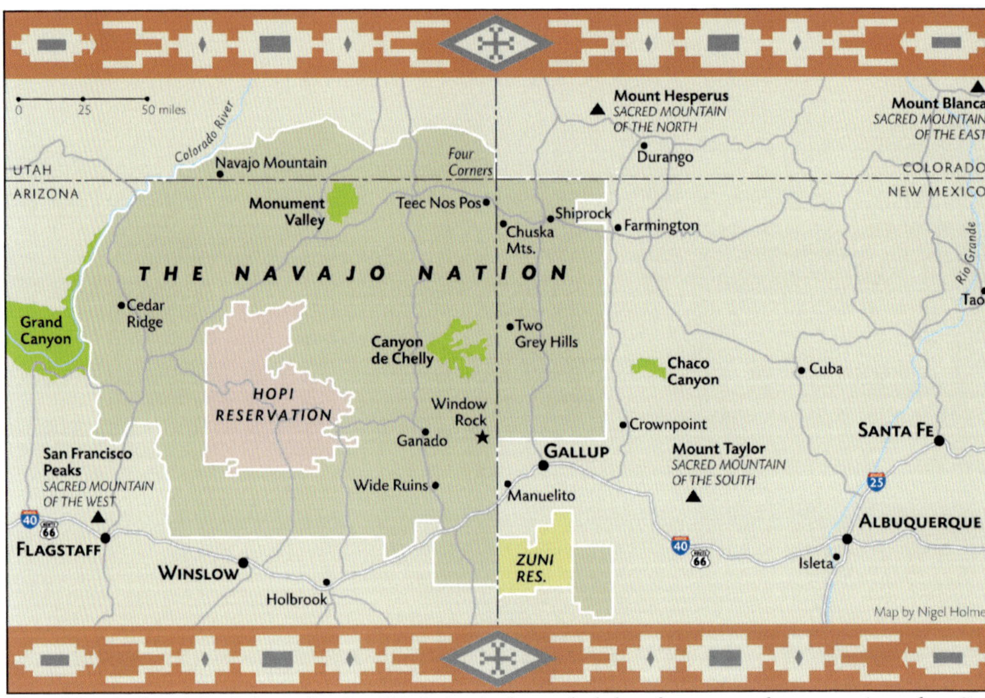

The Navajos' original homeland—*Dinétah*—is bounded by four sacred mountains: the San Francisco Peaks (*Dook'o'oosłííd*), Mount Hesperus (*Dibé Ntsaa*), Mount Blanca (*Sisnaajiní*), and Mount Taylor (*Tsoodził*). This map of Navajo country was designed by Nigel Holmes.

Contents

Foreword

In October 2017, while examining a half-dozen 19th-century Navajo blankets with several Arizona State Museum colleagues, I said out loud, "If we could spend more time looking at historic pictures of Navajo weavers at their looms, we might better answer the technical questions we're pondering." Those questions concerned how Navajo weavers handled blankets larger than their loom frames and how they kept their working areas close to hand. The answers lay, we felt, in the blankets' physical traits that are called lazy lines, stitch-downs, and loom-turns—little documented or understood by textile analysts. One week after that museum conversation and totally out of the blue, Peter Hiller called me, introduced himself, and asked if I would like to see his collection of 200-plus historic photographs and postcards of Navajo weaving. In fact, he queried, would I consider doing a book with him and Ramona Sakiestewa, our mutual friend and colleague who had the insight to introduce us? As they say, "The rest is history."

This book is intended for a wide audience with broad interests, even though the project started with questions about technical traits. Looking closely at these pictures, living inside them for several months, has brought out many stories about Navajo families, homes, livestock, and, most importantly, weaving's relationship to Diné life and beliefs. Our original questions were not all answered; new ones have arisen. Our collaborative captions offer commentary on weaving's many facets—artistic design, history, material sources, economy, and, most importantly, stories about real people. We hope the book illustrates, informs, and entertains readers who are, or might become, weavers, artists, collectors, curators, and others interested in Native American lifestyles and worldviews.

Ranging from the 1880s to 1980s, our coverage falls short of trends in contemporary Navajo weaving, although we mention present practices and anticipate the future. The movements from floor rugs to wall art, weavers' training in university art programs, rug sales in galleries and museum shops, asymmetrical abstraction, and European-style pictorial realism all come later. What remain most significant—as threads through past, present, and future—are the weavers' strong and individual identities.

—Ann Lane Hedlund

Acknowledgments

Peter Hiller's collection began in 1995, when he and his son, Jake, purchased a 1940s fruit crate label at a California flea market. Drawn to that stylized Navajo weaver and handspinner (see page 122), he began searching for similar imagery. Over time, postcards proved accessible and cost-efficient, and they form the basis of this book. Without Peter's persistent collecting, we (Ann, Ramona, and Peter) would never have had the joy of putting our words to these pictures. Moreover, our research proved that only a few of his photographs have appeared in other publications.

Peter acknowledges his parents, Ann Mayer and Wally Hiller: Through them I grew up surrounded by Navajo and Hopi material. The cultural aesthetic has remained in my heart to this day. My wife, Celeste, shares my interest in the same, making it hers, as have our two sons, Sam and Jake. Thanks to Nigel Holmes, for your gift of map making and great patience. To my co-authors, Ramona and Ann—your expertise has enriched this project beyond words; you made a dream flourish and come true.

Ramona and Ann are grateful to Peter for inviting us to participate in this book: It has been fun working with you and your collection. All of us have learned much from the images and each other.

We credit Lindsey Givens, Stacia Bannerman, and Sara Miller for moving us adroitly through the Arcadia Publishing production process. We are grateful to Will Wroth, Rebecca Valette, James B. Klein, Alan Ferg, and Jonathan Batkin for several helpful identifications. Thanks to Kathy Howard and Diana Pardue, whose research and book, *Inventing the Southwest: The Fred Harvey Company and Native American Art*, proved instrumental in understanding the lives and work of the people known as "Elle and Tom of Ganado," whose full names remain unknown.

All postcards, photographs, and objects pictured here belong to Peter Hiller's personal collection except those noted as owned by the Ocotillo Trust. We are most grateful to the individuals, families, and institutions who provided permission to use images under their supervision or copyright. The families of Robert Bradshaw, Richard Erdoes, Burton Frasher, Bernard Glasgow, Teresa Harbaugh, George H. Hight, Jerome E. Milord, and Bob Petley were especially helpful, as were Virginia Couse Leavitt and Davison Koenig for E.I. Couse, Stefanie Bell (ACMAA) for Laura Gilpin, Teako Nunn for L.H. Larsen, Peter Runge (NAU-CL) for Josef Muench, the Nello Guadagnoli family for the Mullarky Studios, Nathan Sowry (NMAI) for George Pepper, Frank Dzousa for Eric J. Seaich, and Walter Haussamen for the J.R. Willis Collection. We want to recognize the images' original sources, producers, and publishers wherever possible and include the following abbreviations, which appear in parentheses at the end of their respective captions:

Amon Carter Museum of American Art: ACMAA
Audio-Visual Designs: AVD
Bradshaw Color Studios: BCS
Camera Shop of New Mexico CSNM
Curt Teich & Company: CTC
Detroit Publishing Company DPC
E.C. Kropp: ECK
Frank S. Thayer: FST
Flying W Ranch: FWR
Frashers [Fotos] Studios: FFS
Fred Harvey Company: FHC
H.H. McNeil: HHM
H.S. Crocker: HSC
Keystone View Company: KVC
L.H. Larsen: LHL
Milner Photography Studios: MPS
Mullarky Studios: MS
National Museum of the American Indian: NMAI
Navajo Marketing Company: NMC
New Mexico State Tourism: NMST
Newman Post Card: NPC
Northern Arizona University, Cline Library: NAU-CL
Petley Studios: PS
Rembrant Pikes Peak Litho: RPPL
Rembrant W.E. Noble: RWEN
Seaich Corporation: SC
Santa Fe Railway: SFR
S.W. Post Card: SWPC
Tichnor Brothers: TB
Williamson-Haffner: W-H
William Pennington Studio: WPS
Underwood & Underwood: UU
Unidentified source: US

Introduction

Traditional *Diné* narratives describe how the Holy People known as Spider Woman and Spider Man brought weaving and its tools to the Navajo people. ("Diné" is the indigenous name for the Navajo people and translates as "The People." Generally considered interchangeable with "Navajo," it is used here when traditional, philosophical, linguistic, and spiritual aspects of the culture are emphasized. Diné words appear first in italics.) The Holy People gave weaving to the Navajos to clothe their families and sustain them, as they say, "with all the good things in life."

The first Diné loom was an object of beauty and utility made from sacred elements such as sunrays, precious stones, and lightning. The upright loom's structure and function closely relate to looms used for centuries by the Ancient Puebloan people (prehistoric societies known archaeologically and through oral histories) and by Hopi and other Pueblo communities (with cultures that are historically known and still vital today). Technical details in early Diné blankets, dresses, and shawls resemble those made by indigenous Pueblo weavers. Native fibers and cultivated cotton yarns preceded sheep's wool, which arrived on the hoof with Spaniards beginning in the mid-1500s. Spanish reports attest to Diné weaving as well-established in the American Southwest by the 1650s.

Navajo women were responsible for sheep, preparation of weaving materials, and creation of designs on their woven garments and blankets. Men constructed looms and hand tools—combs, battens, and spindles—as some still do today. Several Navajo male weavers were historically known, and this trend has grown, with several men playing strong roles in the weaving arts.

Children helped with livestock, prepared wool, and performed tasks that led some to become weavers. Ramona Sakiestewa recalls:

> Children herded many flocks of sheep. At age 10, my Navajo aunt and her two younger brothers herded sheep from Window Rock, Arizona, over the Chuska Mountains to Crystal Trading Post. It took them most of the summer and they carried their own food. At the end of a day of herding, she made biscuits and bacon. Every ten days, her mother and father intercepted them in a buckboard to check on their progress and bring supplies. Beginning at age five, a Navajo friend was sent by bus from Shiprock, Arizona, south to the dirt road at the Two Grey Hills turn off. He was told to start walking west until his aunt met him in a wagon. He spent many summers herding sheep to Crystal with his cousins.

Weaving blankets and garments continued through classic (1750–1850) and late classic (1850–1875) periods, but was gravely disrupted during the 1860s by the United States' forced transfer of Navajo families from their homeland to Fort Sumner in eastern New Mexico. The so-called Long Walk and imprisonment at Bosque Redondo took a toll on human lives. Survivors who eventually returned home lost substantial livestock and livelihoods.

The Navajos' original homeland—Dinétah—extended across the Four Corners region, where Arizona, New Mexico, Colorado, and Utah meet. In 1868, the US government established the Navajo Reservation, with boundaries adjusted over time. Today, the Navajo Nation (see map on page 4) covers over 27,000 square miles and is home to more than 350,000 Navajo citizens.

By the 1880s, with the arrival of the transcontinental railroad, the building of trading posts, a barter-cash economy, and increased access to manufactured goods, Navajo weavers switched from making utilitarian items, wearing blankets, and textiles for intertribal trade to weaving decorative rugs for outsiders. The railway also brought curious travelers and photographers. Trying to please East Coast and Midwestern consumers, weavers began using Oriental carpets and linoleum patterns as models, wove borders around their rugs, and combined natural colors with bright, sometimes garish, synthetically colored yarns. Thus, Navajo weaving began to become a driving force in popular culture and an iconic image of the West.

The earliest photographs of Navajo people were taken during the Long Walk and incarceration at Fort Sumner during the late 1860s. At that time, photography was time-consuming and cumbersome. Cameras were large, the processing was technical, and the work primarily remained with professionals. Posing for a picture meant the model sat still in a contrived studio setting. The results were far from spontaneous or natural.

In 1889, Kodak cameras with roll film became available, moving photography from studios to natural settings. Black-and-white photographs appeared in books, magazines, postcards, calendars, and curio items. Non-professionals (the general public) gained access to photographers' tools, which opened up picture-taking opportunities for tourists.

Photography represented a two-way dilemma for many Native Americans who became its subjects and objects. The belief that cameras held the power to steal one's spirit made many reluctant to be captured on film. In public and private gatherings, individuals shied away from candid shots, shielding their faces and those of their children. This consideration continues today among some Diné people. As photography became common, posed photograph sessions in picturesque settings, however, supplemented families' incomes between periodic rug sales and seasonal jobs. Despite this objectifying and stereotyping trend, weavers also treasure photographs of themselves, their families, and their rugs. Today, historic photographs and family albums represent glimpses into Diné heritage for Navajo people and observers.

Ranging from the 1880s to 1980s, the postcards and photographs in Peter Hiller's collection feature many notable photographers and publishers. In 1876, English émigré Fred H. Harvey established a restaurant concession with the Atchison, Topeka & Santa Fe Railway. He and his family built a company that eventually provided food service to over 20 stops along the transcontinental train routes and provisioned a growing tourist trade. The Fred Harvey Company published picture postcards to promote tourism in the American West. Led by Herman Schweizer and J.F. Huckel, the company established an Indian Department, amassed an extensive artifact collection, constructed the Indian Building (with naturalistic displays) in Albuquerque's Alvarado Hotel, and participated in major expositions across the United States.

From 1878 until a fatal rattlesnake bite in 1903, Ben Wittick worked out of Albuquerque, Santa Fe, Gallup, and Fort Wingate. He made studio portraits and traveled throughout the backcountry with backdrops and artifacts serving as props. George Wharton James summarized his Southwest experiences in 1914: "For upwards of thirty years I have . . . bought many hundreds of blankets, known personally scores of the best weavers of the tribe, and as late as the winter of 1912–13 spent over three months visiting them, watching them work, engaging in their ceremonies, sleeping in their hogans, eating their food, riding their ponies, and listening to their legends." In 1892, B.L. Singley founded Keystone View Company, which, by 1905, was the world's largest manufacturer of stereographic images. Mounting two identical photographs side-by-side and using a special viewfinder produced three-dimensional effects. Keystone drew from hundreds of photographers and published thousands of images between 1892 and 1963. The Detroit Photographic Company (renamed Detroit Publishing in 1904) flourished from 1895 to 1924, producing thousands of postcard images, often in collaboration with Fred Harvey.

In 1887, Edward S. Curtis arrived in Seattle from Minnesota, became a partner in a photographic studio, and began his life's work documenting indigenous life in the American West; his career peaked with the publication of the 20-volume *The North American Indian* (1907–1930), based on 1,500 photographs and partially funded by J.P. Morgan. E.O. Richmond had a Durango studio in the 1890s. George Pepper accompanied museum expeditions to the Southwest beginning in 1896, extensively documenting Navajo weaving. In 1900, W.H. Simpson became an advertising agent for the Santa Fe Railway; he purchased art for its corporate collection and started an annual calendar series. In 1903, Karl Moon established a photography studio in Albuquerque and, like Simpson and others, worked for the Fred Harvey Company from 1906 until 1914. In 1904, William Pennington had a studio in Albuquerque and later opened one in Durango, Colorado. J.R. Willis arrived in Arizona in 1917 to photograph the Hopi villages, but he documented Navajo weavers at the 1915 Panama-Pacific Exposition in San Diego while working as a Hollywood backdrop painter. Willis established a studio in Gallup, then moved to Albuquerque in 1931. Tom Mullarky took over Willis' studio in 1927. During 33 years in Gallup, he recorded the Gallup Intertribal Ceremonial Fair and held prominent civic positions. Mullarky's Camera Shop was sold to Shan and Nello Guadagnoli in 1960. George C. Hight continued Mullarky and Willis's legacy in Gallup.

Burton Frasher Sr. documented the Navajo weaving process more thoroughly than any other photographer, yet this comprised a small part of his business established in Pomona, California, in 1914. Combining his love of travel with an interest in small town life, local people, and spectacular landscapes, he produced some 1,500 glass plates and more than 60,000 negatives during his 40 years working in commercial photography under the names Frashers Fotos; Frasher's, Inc.; and other permutations. From 1930 to 1939, Frasher made repeated trips to the Southwest, where he filmed Navajo families, homes, crafts, and landscapes. His early postcards had handwritten legends; later forms included typescript captions. Popular hand-tinted versions followed. Frasher traveled with a portable darkroom and produced orders on demand for local stores. In 1948, its top year, the studio sold over 3.5 million postcards.

Alabama Milner and her brother Algernon Milner maintained a commercial photography studio in Albuquerque from 1919 to 1955. Professionally trained in art and photography, Laura Gilpin became known for her Southwest work during the mid-20th century. Her 1968 retrospective book, *The Enduring Navaho*, championed a harmonious and upbeat view of Navajo life even as the New Deal changed Diné lives for both better and worse.

Some photographers represented here made significant impact on the pages of *Arizona Highways* magazine. Josef (alternately Joseph) Muench came from Germany and landed in Detroit in 1928. By 1936, he had arrived in Arizona, where he made his name with his natural and cultural photographs. Esther Henderson was a Tucson activist and professional photographer during the 1930s and 1940s. Bob Bradshaw opened his first studio in Sedona in 1949 and for several decades continued the tradition of Southwest photography, publishing his own books and regularly appearing in the magazine. The commercial photographs of Ray Manley graced the pages of many magazines and art books beginning in the 1950s.

In 1943, Bob Petley established his Arizona company that became "the nation's largest publisher and distributor of scenic color postcards, with an annual sales exceeding 25 million pieces through 3,500 dealers in Arizona, New Mexico, West Texas, southwestern Colorado, and eastern California," as noted in the *Arizona Republic* on July 11, 2006. Photo-documentarian Richard Erdoes studied at the Berlin Academy of Art and lived in Paris, London, and New York before moving to Santa Fe in 1975.

Over the years, Navajo weaving and the field of photography have each flourished in the American Southwest. The enjoyment they provide to tourists and local communities has never waned—witness the thousands who return each year to the Santa Fe Indian Market and the popularity of weaving demonstrations, exhibitions, and *Arizona Highways* illustrations. Rather than documenting a dying art, historic photographs and postcards provide lasting and vital lessons for weavers, other artists, and collectors of the future.

One

Pueblo Antecedents and Early Navajo Weavers

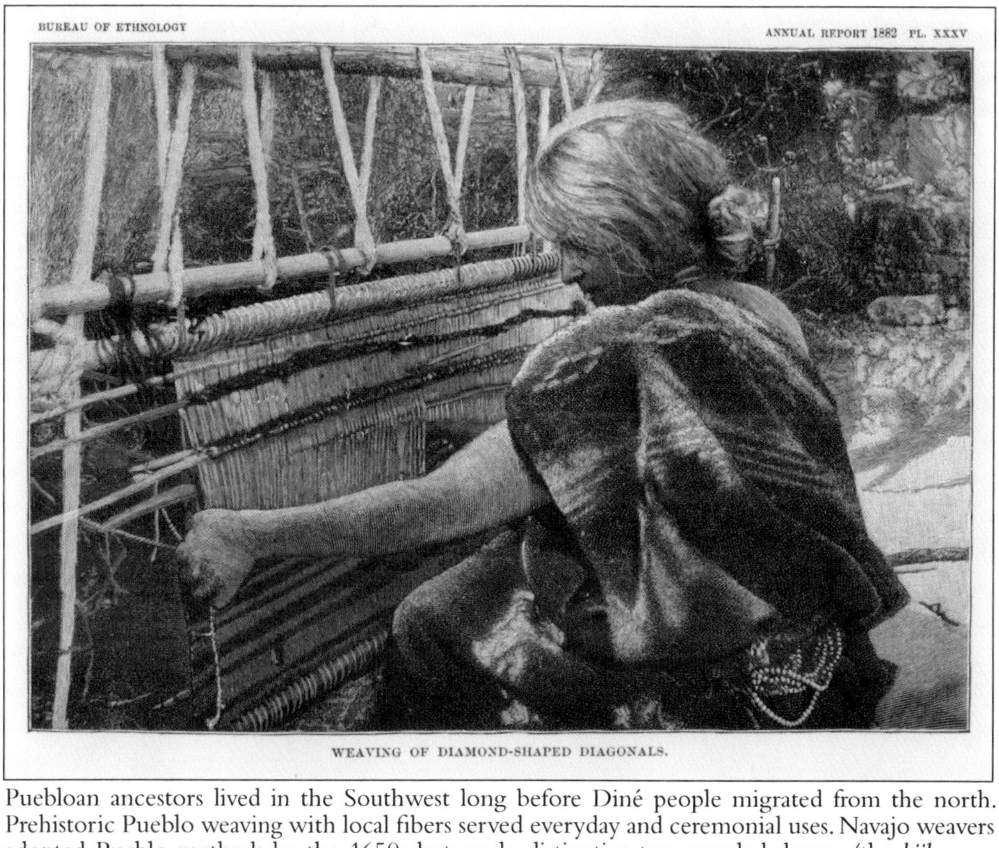

Puebloan ancestors lived in the Southwest long before Diné people migrated from the north. Prehistoric Pueblo weaving with local fibers served everyday and ceremonial uses. Navajo weavers adopted Pueblo methods by the 1650s but made distinctive two-paneled dresses (the *biil* worn here) and shawls (on the loom). This photogravure is Plate XXV in Washington Matthews' 1881–1882 report to the Bureau of American Ethnology.

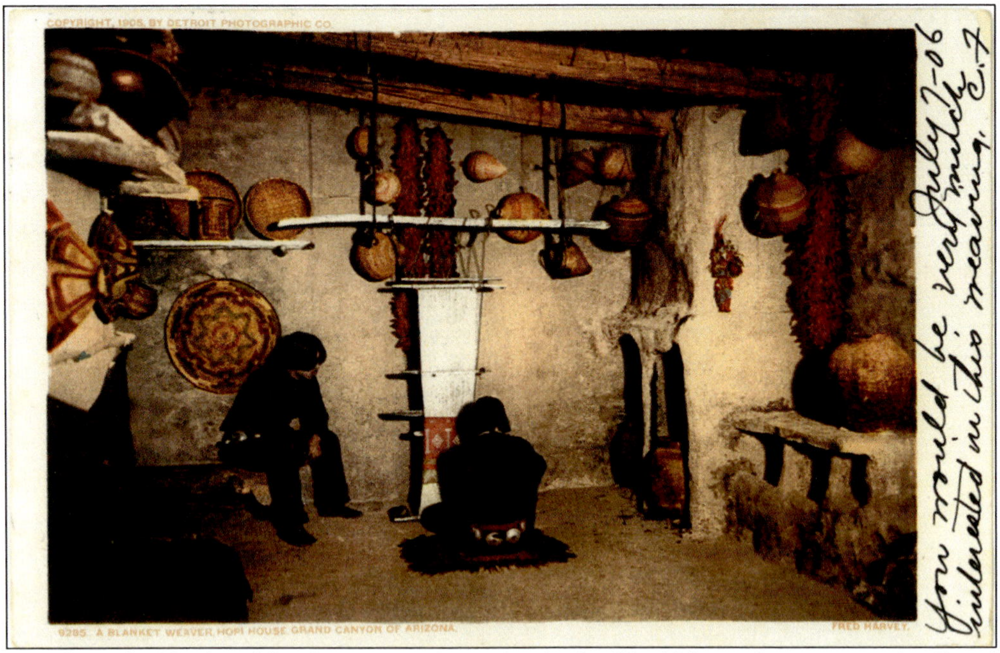

Men from the Hopi pueblos demonstrated weaving in the Hopi House showroom at the Grand Canyon. This room replicates a Hopi household storeroom, where corn, chiles, and other foods were stowed. This weaver is making one panel of a fringed ceremonial dance sash with white cotton and colorful wool brocading. This card was mailed from the Grand Canyon in 1906. (DPC and FHC.)

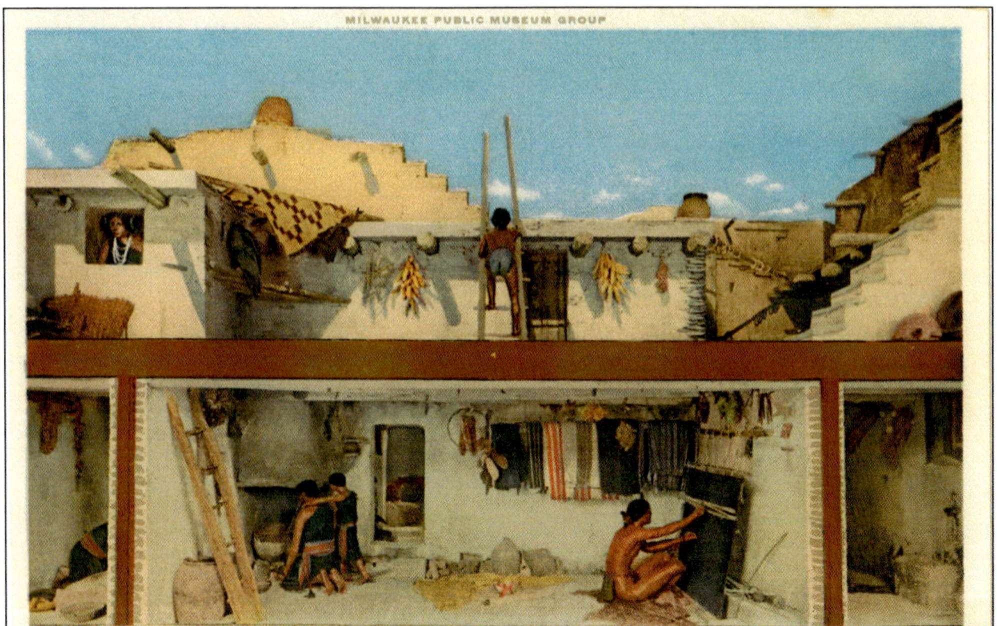

A museum diorama reveals the interior and rooftop of a Hopi two-story home. Striped blankets hang over a "rug pole" on the back wall, while a male weaver makes a dress or *manta* (shawl) in blue and black wool. Pueblo manta-dresses are wrapped around the wearer and under one arm in the manner worn by the three women in the images on page 13. (Milwaukee Public Museum.)

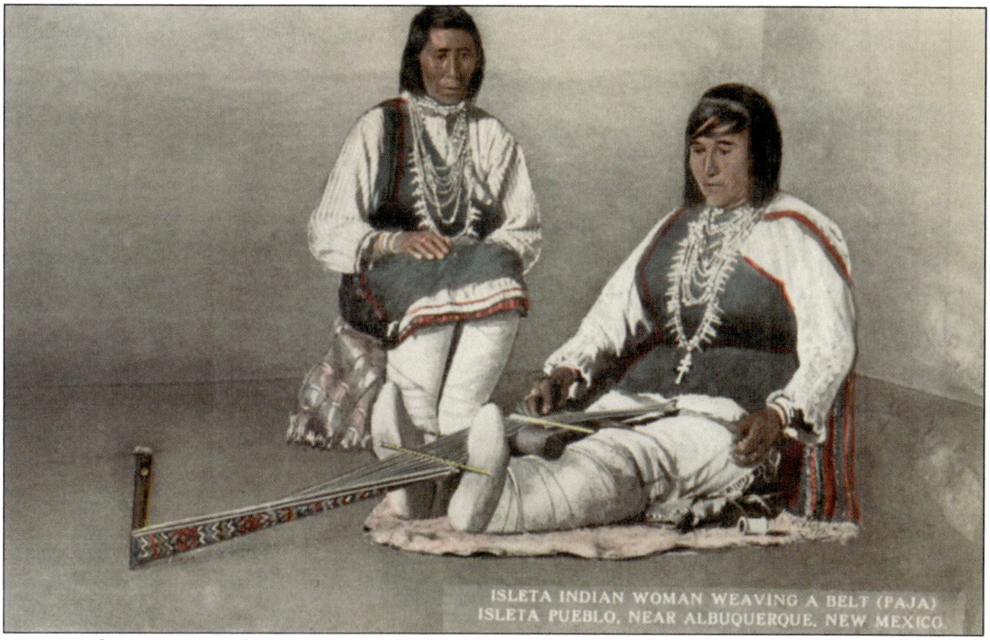

Weavers from Hopi and Rio Grande Pueblos, including Isleta and Zuni, made narrow belts on backstrap- and foot-tensioned looms. In contrast, Navajos used an upright frame for weaving belts and blankets. Karl Moon made the original glass plate sometime between 1904 and 1907. For this postcard, the original background—a non-Indian floral carpet and bed with flounced coverlet—was removed, resulting in this starker scene. (US.)

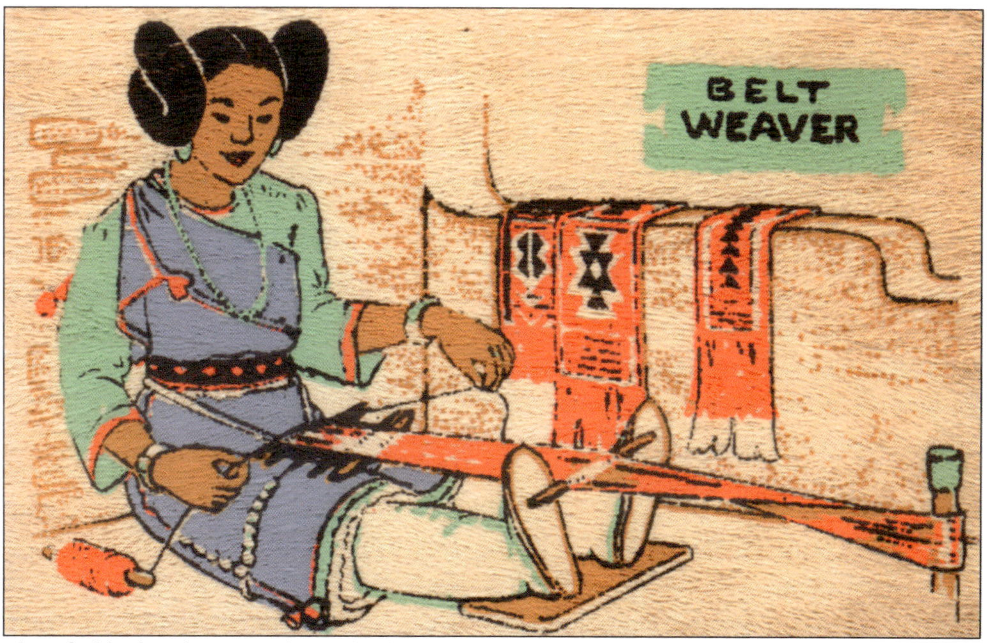

Identified by her distinctive hairstyle, this unmarried Hopi woman works on a backstrap or "waist loom" flanked by fancy sashes. This novelty postcard, postmarked in 1947, was made from a thin sheet of yucca wood laminated to a paper backing. Its caption notes that Pueblo and Navajo weavers make many narrow belts, "all the way from garter and arm bands, to wide sashes and wider ceremonial girdles with long fringe." (US.)

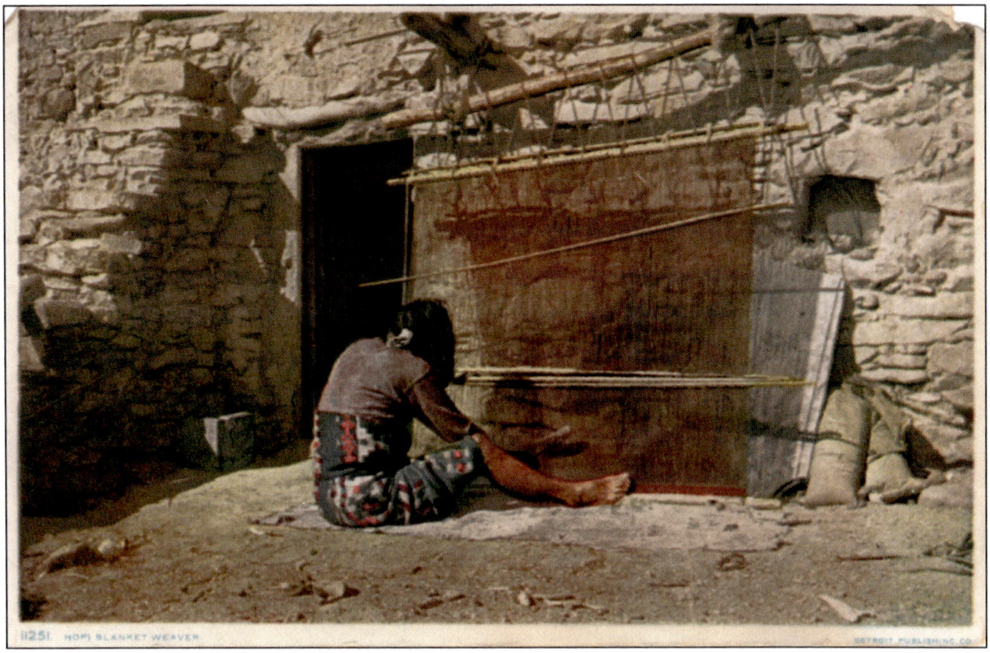

Wrapped in a trade blanket, this Hopi man works at a loom hung from the building's exterior beams. The lower loom bar is fixed in place with hidden "loom blocks" or rag-and-stick bundles inserted into the ground. With four horizontal heddle and shed sticks extending across the dark wool warps (vertical foundation yarns), the weaver is ready to make a twill manta or dress. (DPC.)

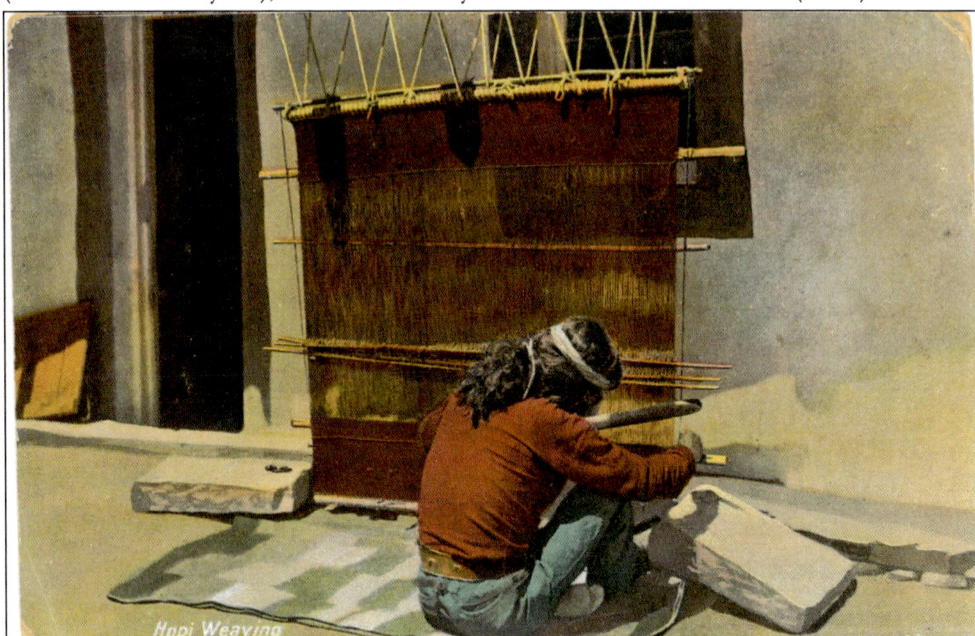

Instead of using underground blocks to anchor his loom, this Hopi weaver used heavy stones. This typical manta has two diamond-twill borders—the first was woven from the bottom, then moved to the top by turning the woven and unwoven web upside down; the second was finished from the bottom up, with a diagonal-twill center panel beginning above a raised line of twining. (M. Reider.)

Although "Navajo weaving a blanket on his handmade loom" is penciled on this card's reverse, the man is clearly Hopi, judging by his hairstyle, the twill weaving sticks, dark wool warps on the loom, and his Pueblo surroundings. He sits, however, on a nearly worn-out Navajo-style rug with a stepped design. Like many neighbors, Hopis and Navajos had friendly long-term trading relationships as well as disputes and rivalries. (US.)

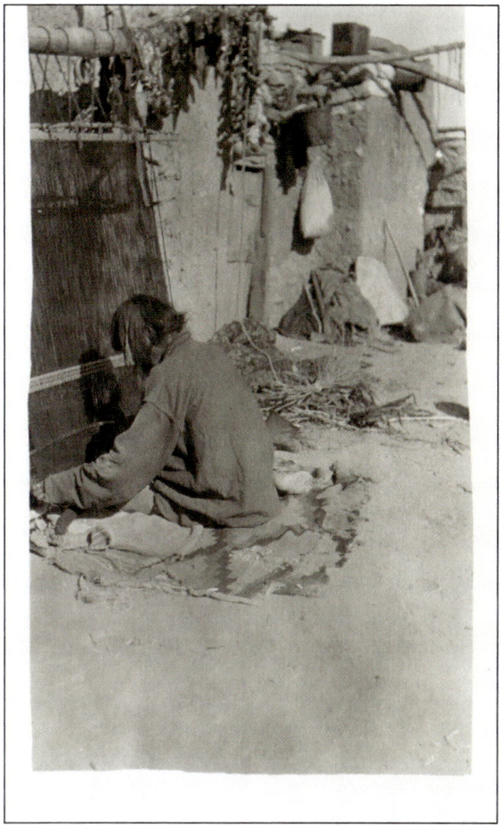

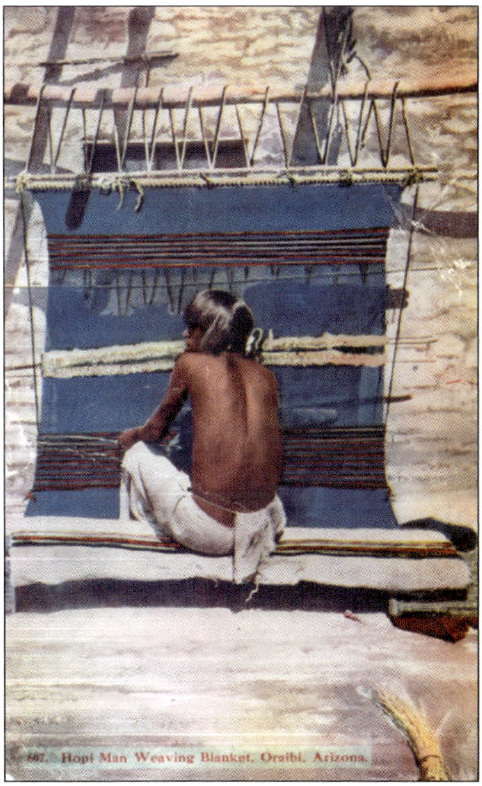

Pueblo weaving appears subtler than Navajo design work. The somber indigo blue and black yarns of a classic manta in the original black-and-white photograph were enlivened by someone who hand-tinted the red stripes and blue background. Oraibi, the site of this well-known 1901 photograph, is a Hopi village in northern Arizona. To publicize the West, the Santa Fe Railway and Fred Harvey Company hired William H. Simpson, the photographer who created this image.

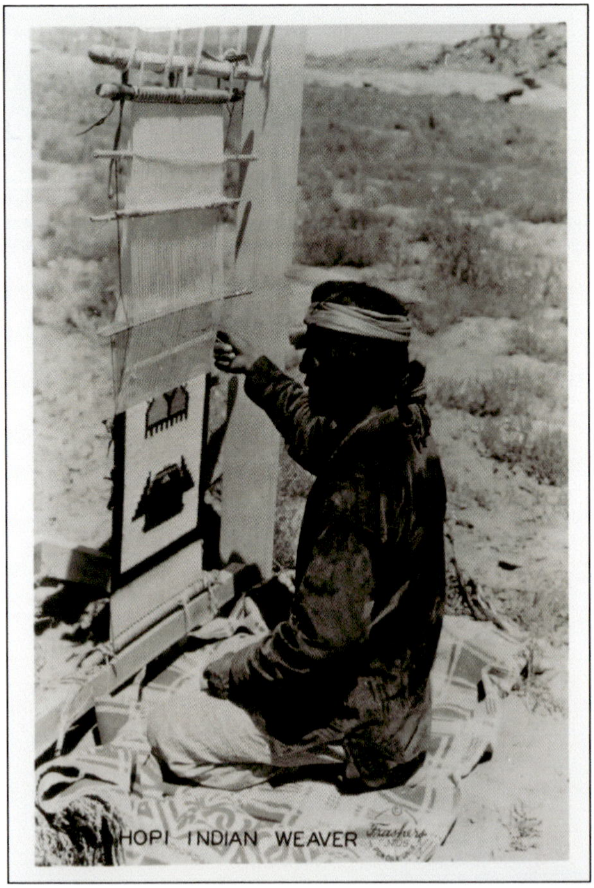

Although Hopi weavers focused on garments for tribal use, they occasionally created pictorial or geometric rugs for sale to outsiders. This Hopi man, pictured around 1932, is making a pictorial panel in tapestry weave, the main technique used by Navajos. In his simply bordered piece with a lower fringe, the visage of a "Crow Mother" kachina is surmounted by an emerging symbol of rain clouds. (FFS.)

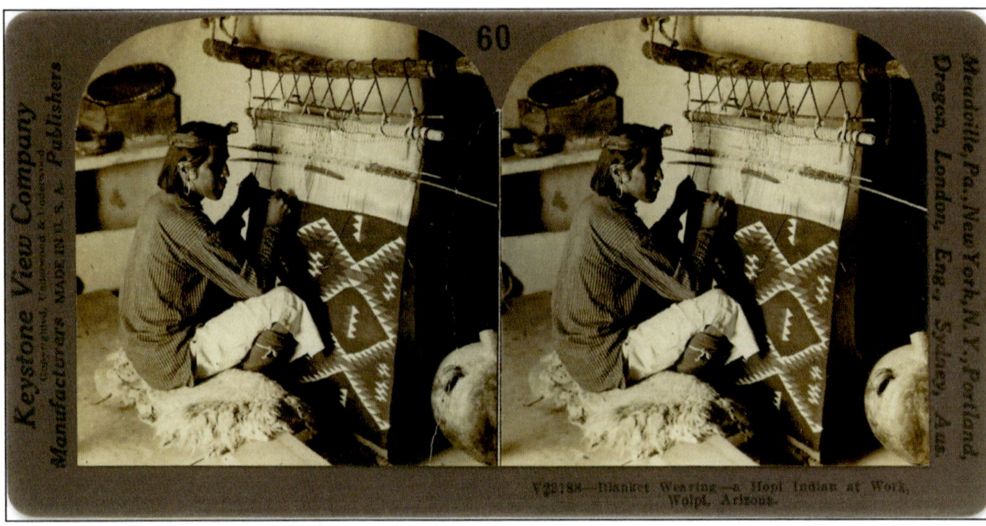

Among Navajos, women are the predominant weavers, but a few men were known to weave as early as the 1880s. In Hopi society, men are the weavers of traditional garments and blankets. Surprisingly, this Hopi man is weaving a Navajo-style blanket with serrate diamonds. In the stereograph's caption, his location is misspelled "Wolpi"—Walpi is an ancient Hopi village still occupied today. (UU and KVC.)

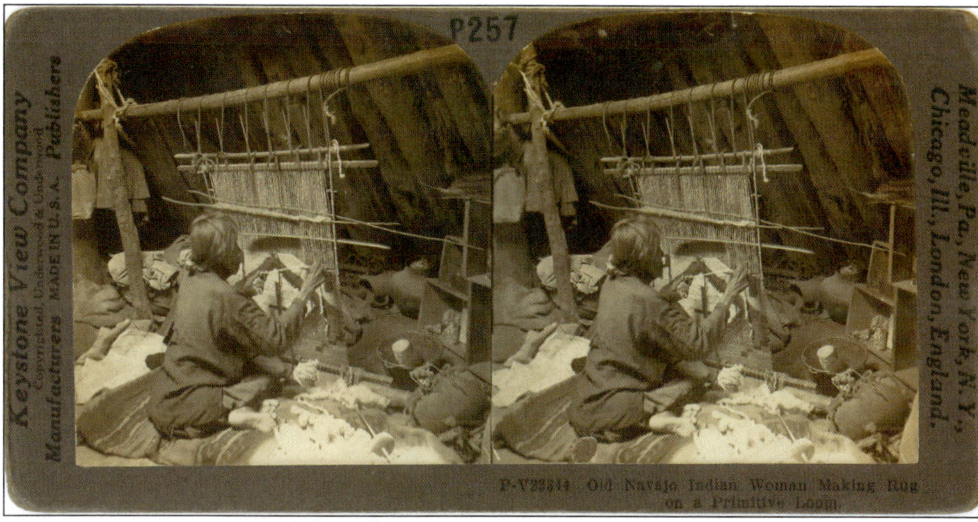

An elder Navajo weaver with bare feet works in her summer shade house of vertical logs. The card's caption mistakes this for a hogan's interior and calls her loom "primitive." The reverse of the stereograph card shown on page 16, however, states that the Navajo heddle system is "a forerunner of the endlessly complicated machinery in modern looms . . . a step ahead of the mere back and forth darning with a needle." (KVC.)

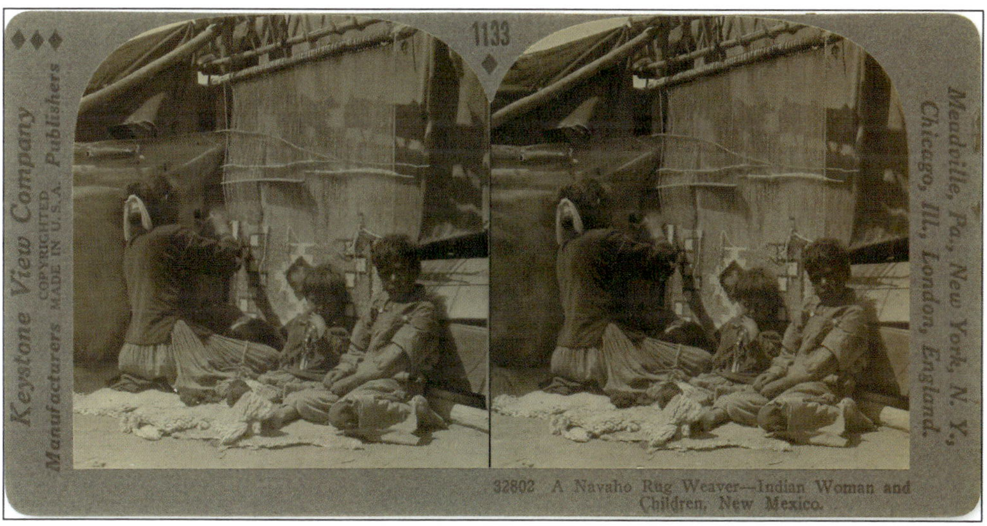

The legend on this stereograph, in which a Navajo weaver works on a geometric-patterned rug, repeats generalizations based in fact but not universally practiced—"The patterns are worked out on the loom and no two are alike. The weavers do not work from a drawing, but plan the design as they weave. The early Navaho [*sic*] blankets were so closely woven that water would not soak through them." (KVC.)

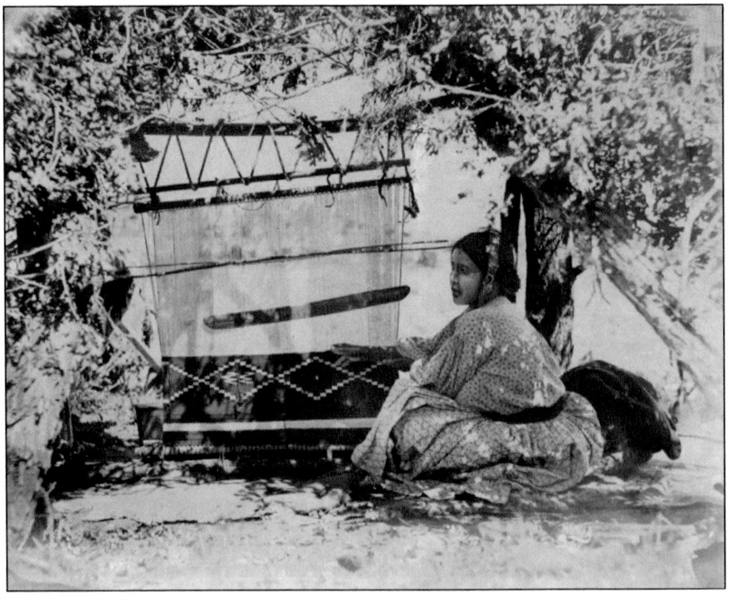

The blanket on this loom has a mix of stepped diamonds of the late classic period and zigzag motifs from the early transitional period. From the early 1800s until the late 1870s, classic and late classic weaving continued the tradition of supple wearing blankets. By the 1880s, when Ben Wittick took this photograph, Diné weaving transitioned from locally used and traded blankets to heavier rugs with enclosing borders fancied by outside buyers.

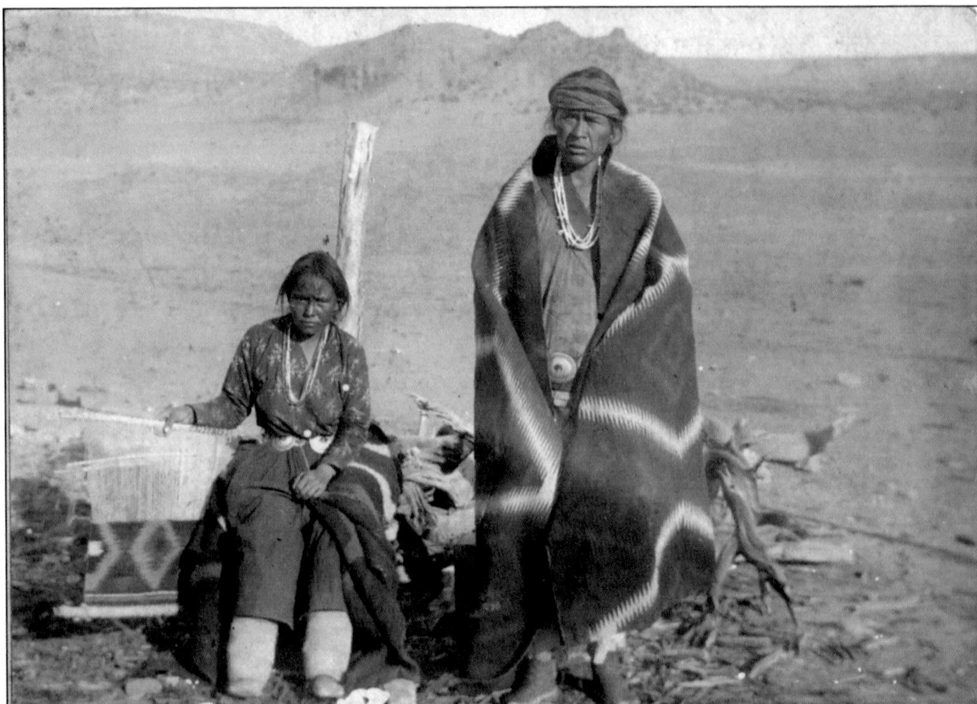

The loom held by this Navajo woman was likely a curio item for the tourist market. Ramona Sakiestewa recalls that her Laguna Pueblo stepmother and her girlfriends made small Navajo-style samplers on miniature looms, which they sold to travelers along Route 66. On the reverse of the original four-by-six-inch photograph is penciled "Heyward J. Watkins, Summerville, SC." An identical image in the Arizona Historical Society collections is titled, "Two Navajos in 1890."

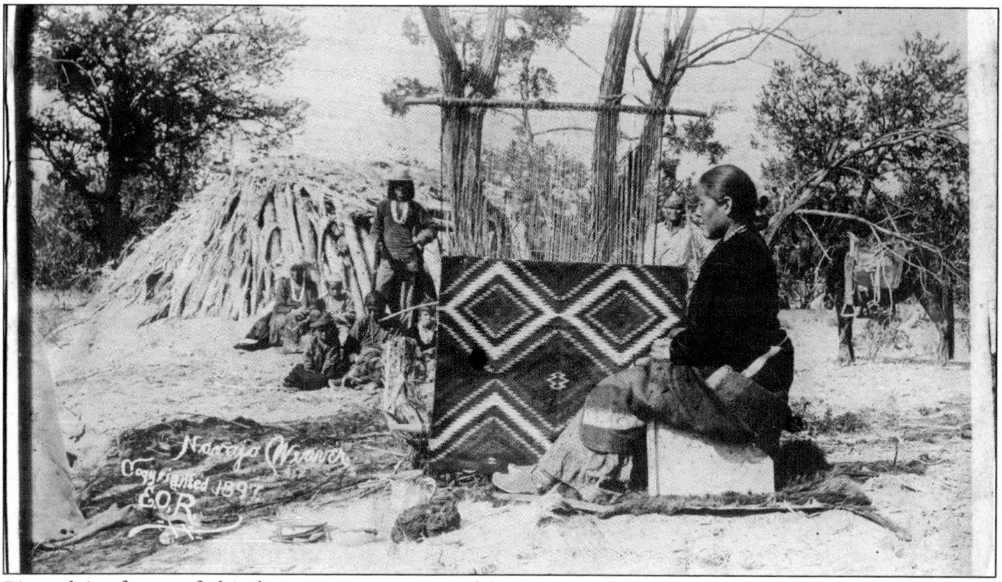

Pinned in front of this loom is a transitional "Eye Dazzler" blanket/rug with yarns milled in Germantown, Pennsylvania. After the Civil War, demand for yarns used in soldiers' socks and sweaters declined; Eastern mills shipped knitting yarns west to emerging Indian markets. Photographer E.O. Richmond copyrighted this image in 1897. "Heyward J. Watkins, Summerville, SC," possibly a previous owner, is penciled on the reverse of the original five-by-eight-inch print.

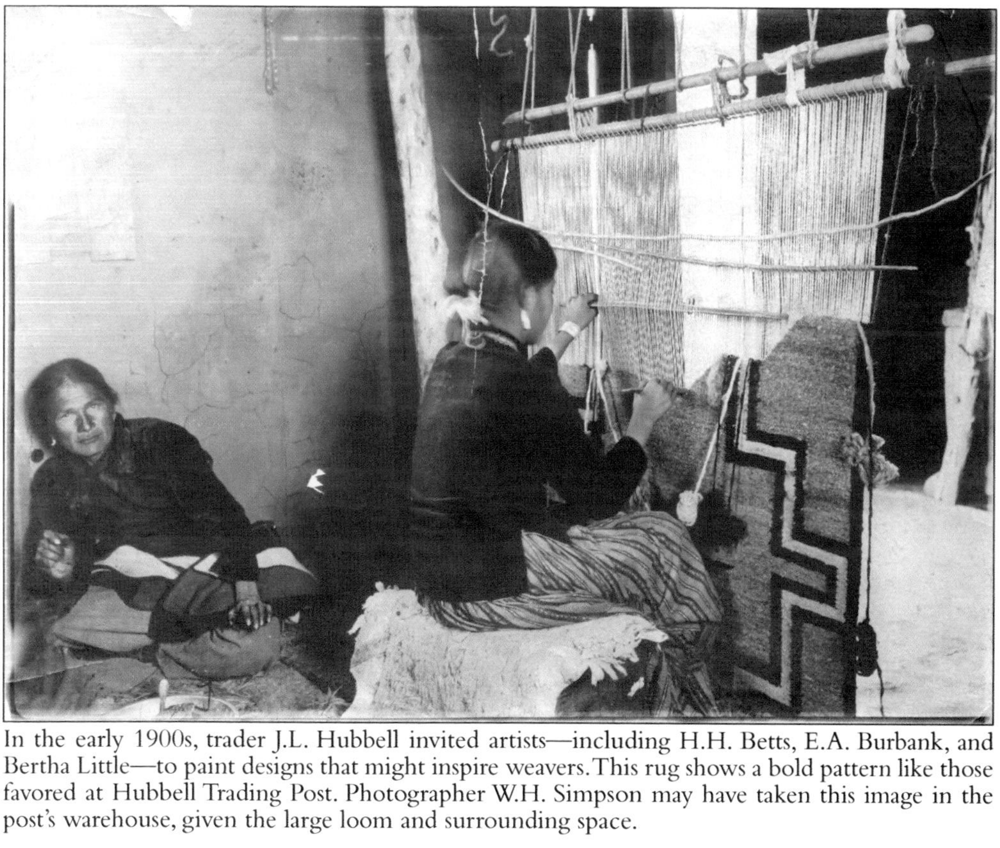

In the early 1900s, trader J.L. Hubbell invited artists—including H.H. Betts, E.A. Burbank, and Bertha Little—to paint designs that might inspire weavers. This rug shows a bold pattern like those favored at Hubbell Trading Post. Photographer W.H. Simpson may have taken this image in the post's warehouse, given the large loom and surrounding space.

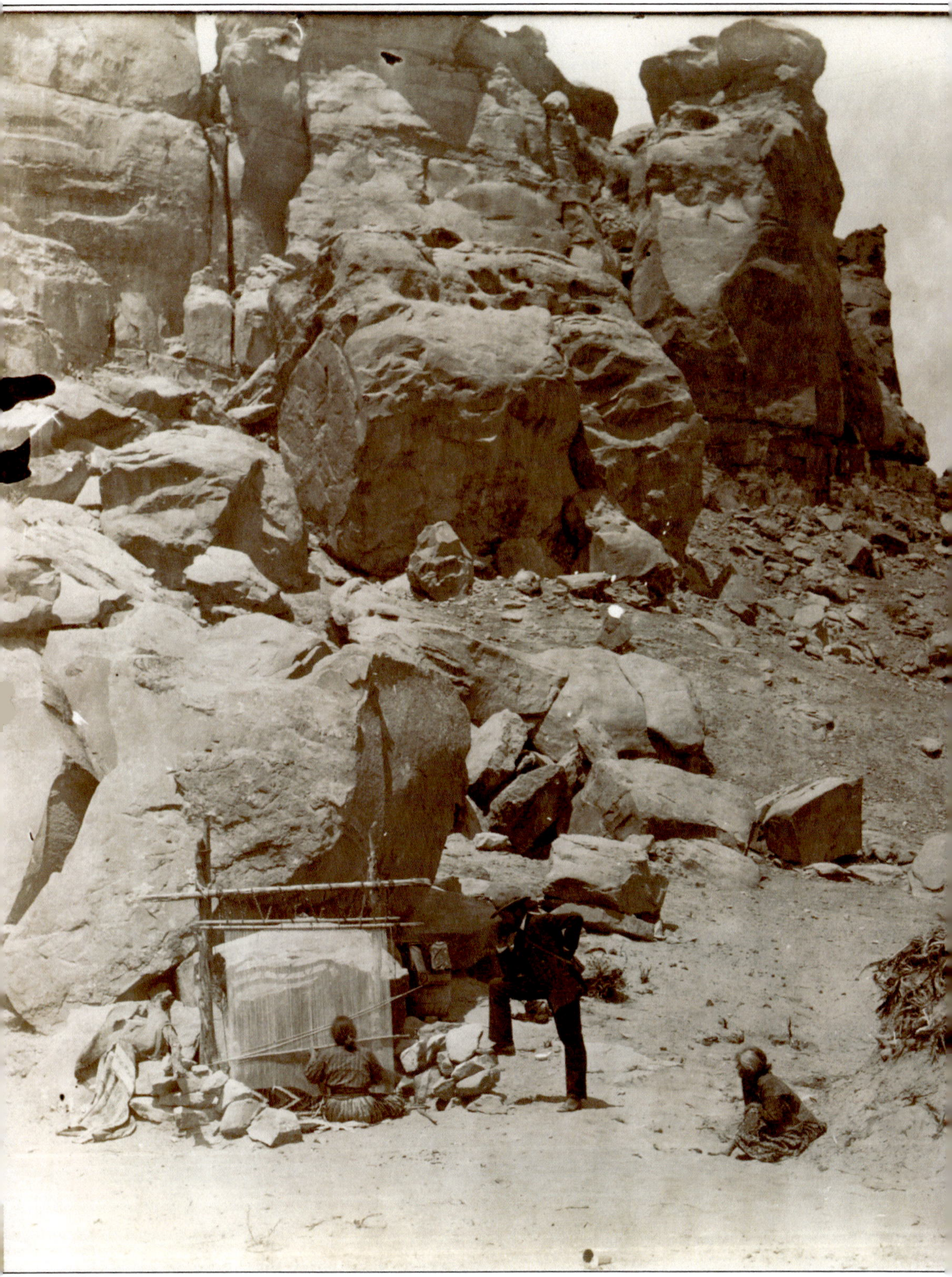

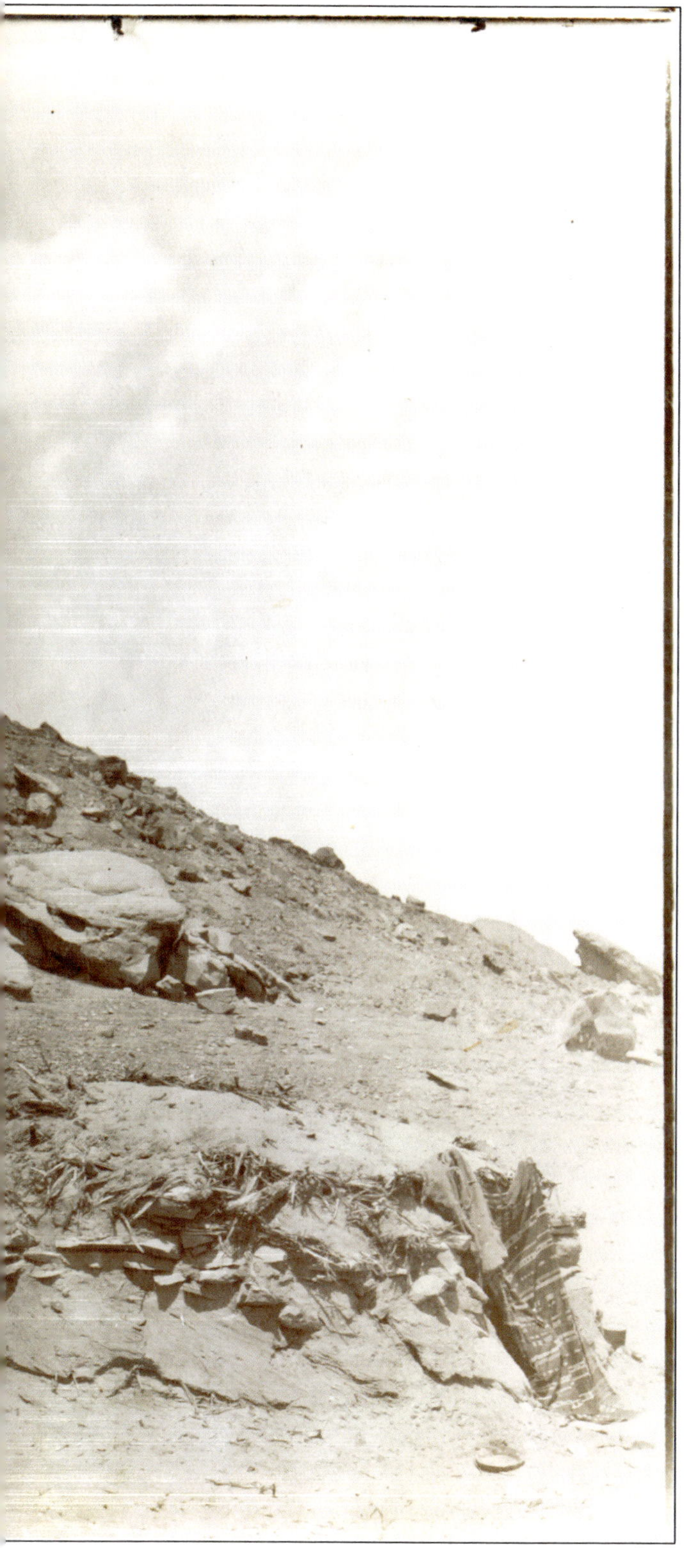

Below Chaco Canyon's massive sandstone formations, a weaver works near a hogan belonging to a man known as Hosteen Jory. In April or May of 1901 she was visited by Samuel J. Holsinger, a geologist and special agent for the Department of the Interior, responsible for proposing federal "land reserves" (future US Forest Service holdings). Pueblo tribes claim Chaco Canyon as their birthright, while Navajos continue living in the area. Today, it is a UNESCO World Heritage Site. The original six-by-eight-inch print from Peter Hiller's collection matches a glass-plate negative, which is labeled "Holsinger taking it in," in the collection of James B. Klein.

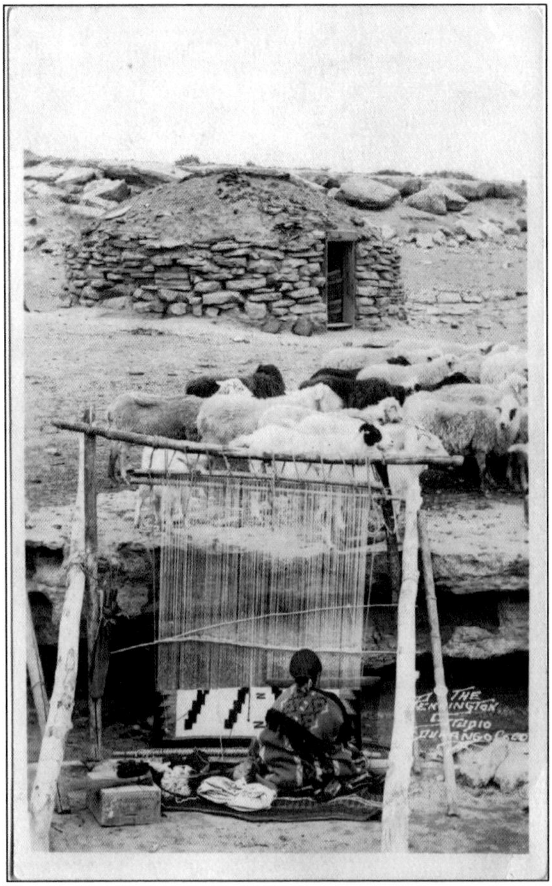

This quintessential view of a Navajo weaver's life, as photographed by William Pennington, shows a rocky landscape, a stone house with a blanket-covered doorway, and a handsome herd of *churro* sheep and goats. A long, narrow sack of weaving tools hangs to her left. Wrapped in a commercial Pendleton blanket and seated on another, she weaves a geometric-patterned rug on her large timber loom. Penciled on the reverse of this card is "Ship Rock N.M." (WPS.)

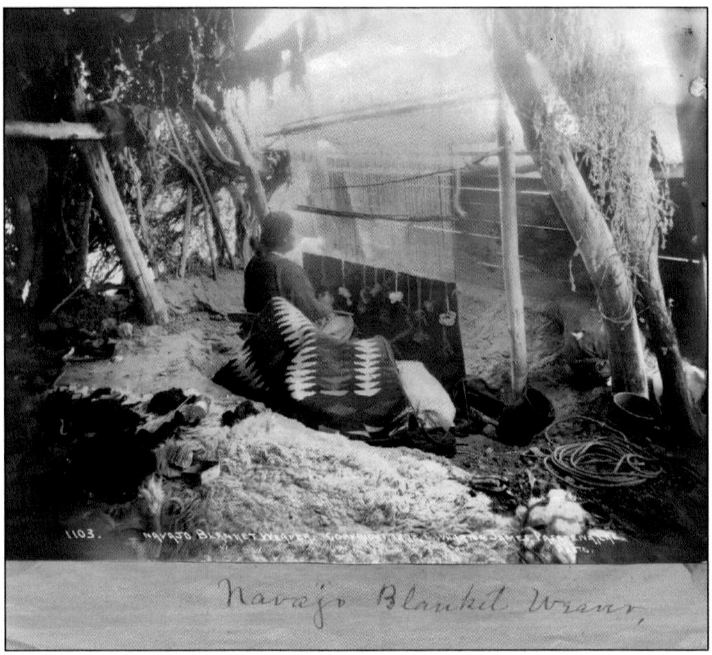

The transitional blanket/rugs on the loom and in the foreground appear made of handspun wool, although mill-spun yarns were available in 1908, when George Wharton James took this photograph. The pot at lower right is a classic Navajo-made vessel of local clay sealed with piñon pitch, whereas fancier Pueblo pots appear in other staged postcard scenes. To view a colorized version of this image, see page 93.

Two

Romance and Realities

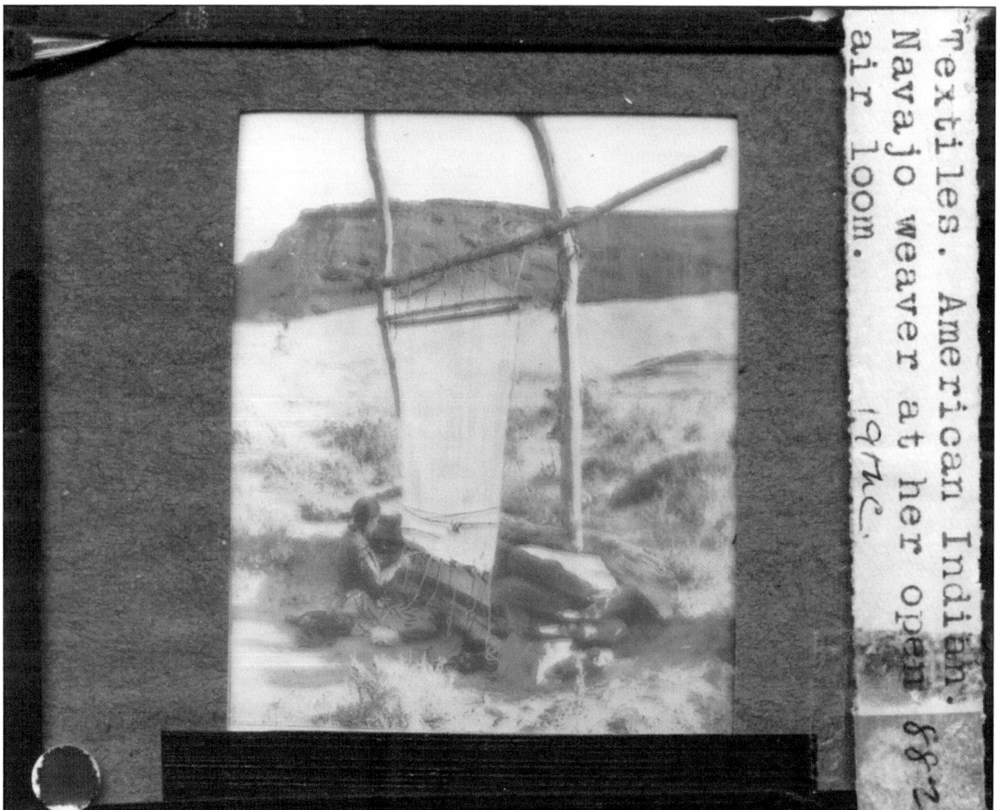

This Navajo weaver at Canyon de Chelly would rarely have worked in such isolation. For the sake of artistry and clarity, her loom was removed from household distractions and photographed by George R. King. The image on this glass plate appeared in George Wharton James' ***Indian Blankets and Their Makers*** and was reprinted in textile histories of the 1920s as an icon of "primitive weaving."

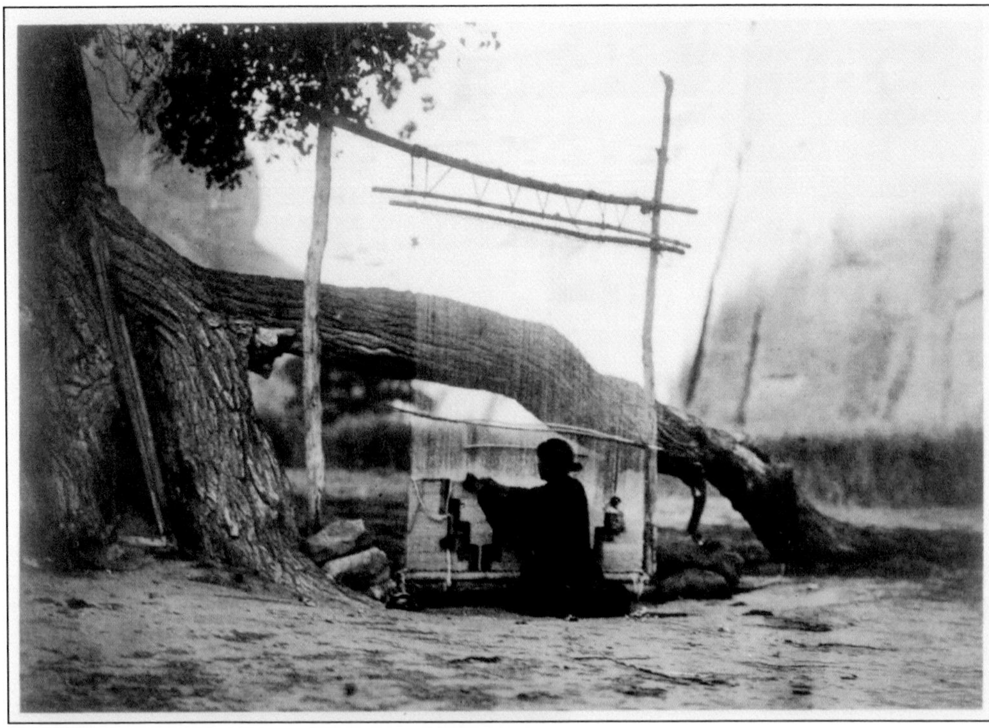

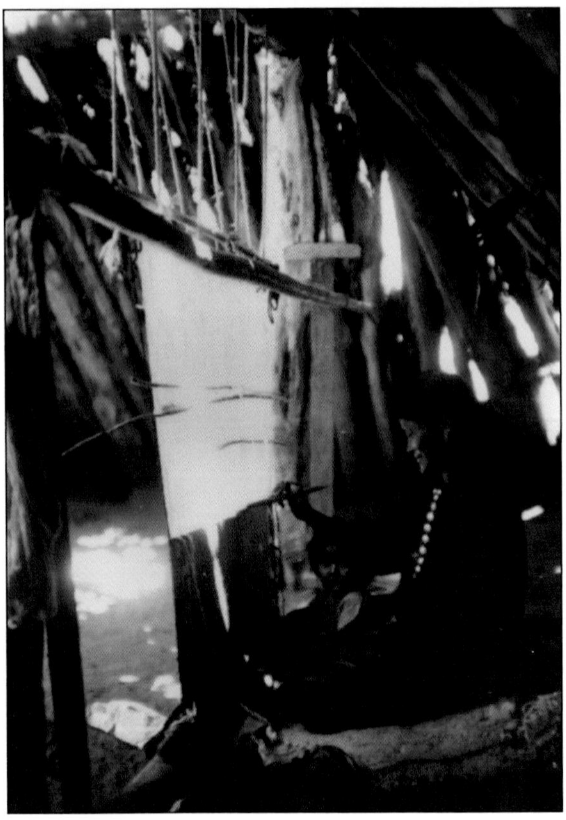

The well-known efforts of Edward S. Curtis to document "disappearing" native lifeways resulted in 20 epic volumes published between 1907 and 1930. His atmospheric photograph, "The Blanket Weaver, Navajo," was made in 1904 and projects a timeless primeval scene. The weaver works on a large blanket in complete isolation from her normal home life. This postcard image is reproduced with permission from Paul Harbaugh and AZUSA Publishing, Englewood, CO, © 1994.

Weaving in the shadows of her summer home, a woman poses with her child. Many Diné children are exposed to their family's weaving practices throughout their young lives, leading some to imitate older weavers. The Diné approach to teaching, as in worldwide craft cultures, is to show through example rather than to explain or instruct verbally. (NAU-CL, the Philip Johnson Collection, NAU. PH.413.747.)

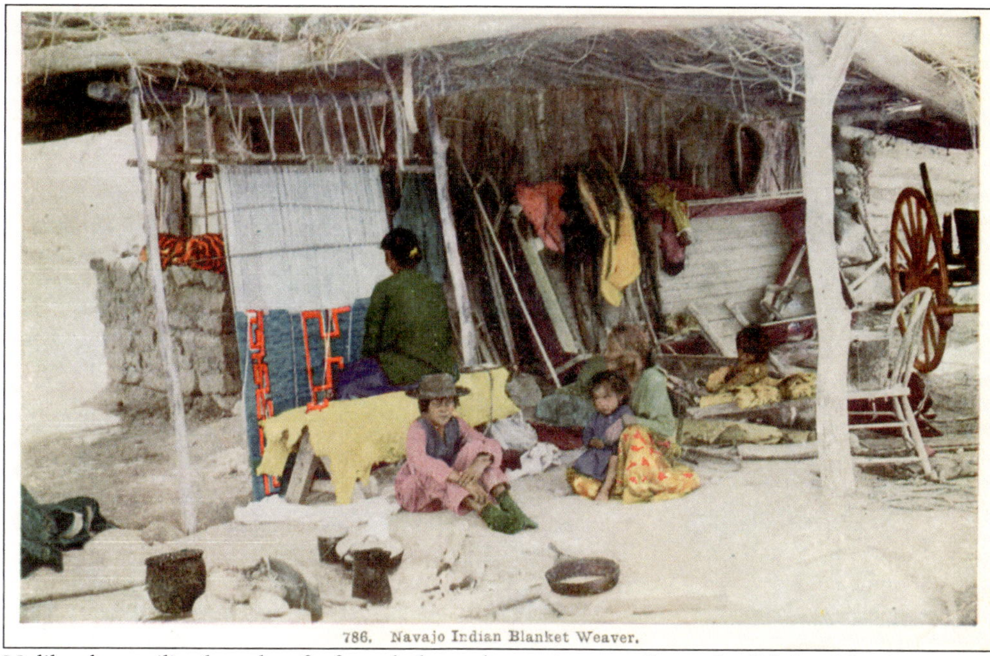

Unlike the sterilized results of a formal photo shoot, pictures of everyday life in a Navajo summer shade house suggest activities such as weaving, cooking, childcare, tool repairing and storage, socializing, sleeping, and many others. Here, although the red and blue in her rug are improbably bright, a weaver's surroundings reflect the roles played within an extended family. For a black-and-white version of this image that dates to 1908, see page 72. (FST.)

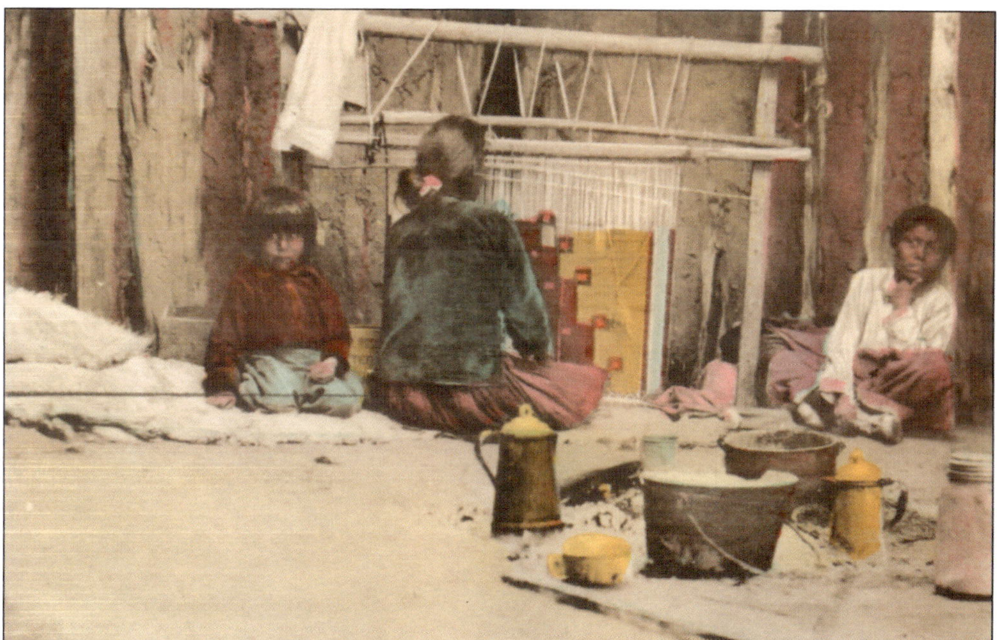

Navajo weavers are typically multitaskers—while they spin and weave, they also monitor children and livestock, cook meals, converse with visitors, and perform other jobs. Real life surrounds the weaver in this hand-colored photograph. The rug on her loom, however, has acquired an improbable background color—yellow was not likely used except in small accents. (R.R. Alton.)

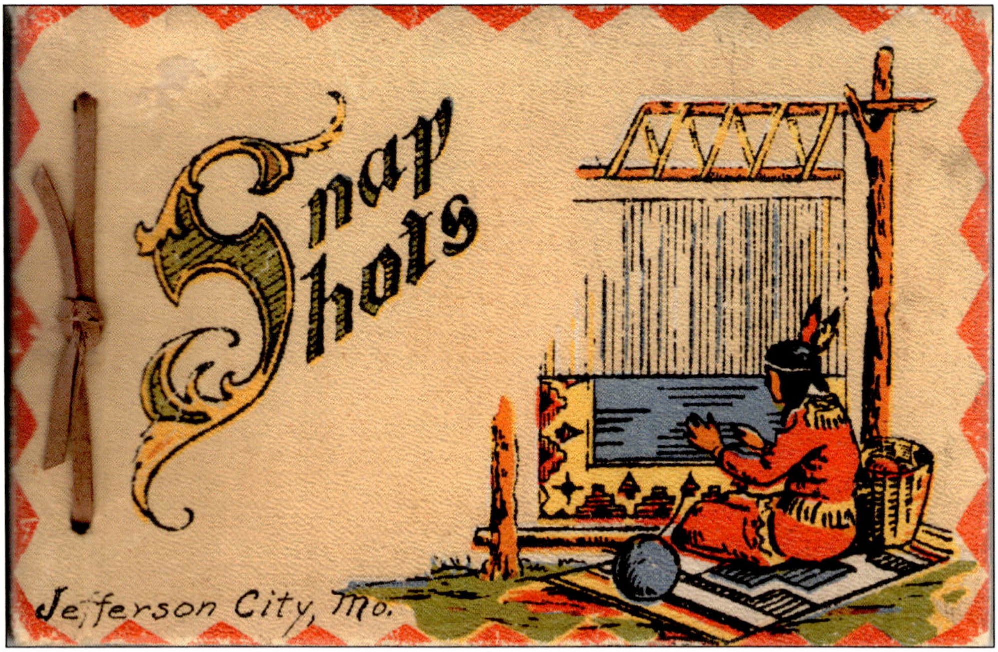

Stereotypical or idealized Native American images abound on 20th-century curio items such as this photograph album. The woman's feathered headdress and fringed garments suggest Plains-style dress—incongruous, because Plains Indians never wove rugs or blankets. The Navajo-style loom is generally accurate in structure but lacks detail and shows a rug of indistinct style. (US.)

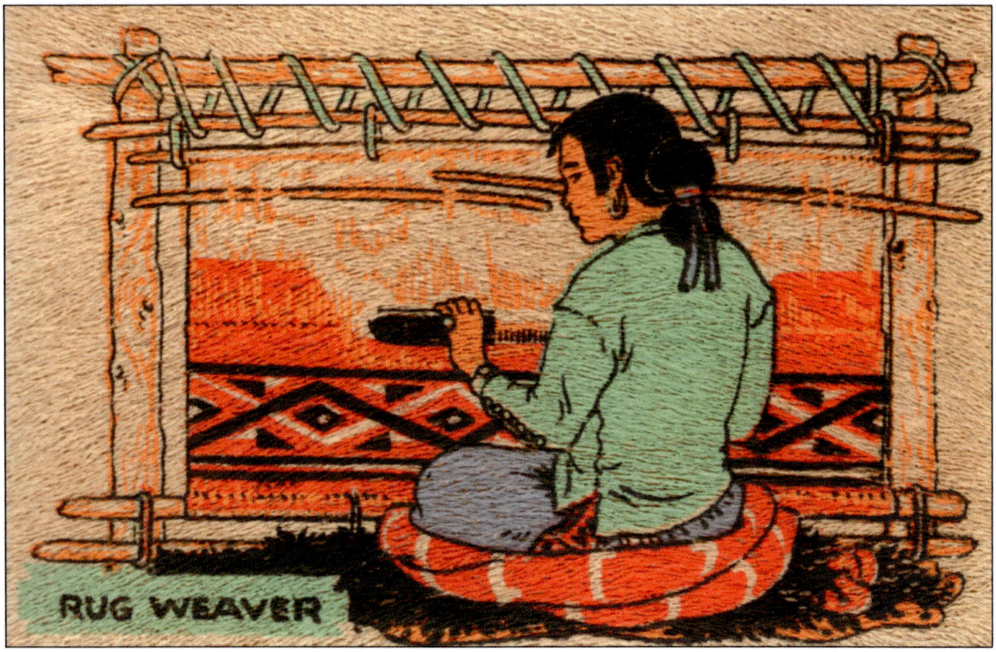

In contrast to the photograph album cover, this postcard, printed on yucca bark paper and postmarked 1946, relays a scene likely drawn from real life. A thoughtful caption notes, in part, "Rug making entails hours of hand labor. The wool is washed in Yucca root suds. Today, commercial dyes supplement vegetable colors formerly used. . . . No two rugs are quite alike. Each piece becomes its own absorbing problem, and the weaver is seldom bored." (US.)

In a storefront window crammed with baskets and other curios, a Navajo woman works on a fancy rug. Several vintage blankets hang overhead. The year of 1903 represented a peak in mail-order catalogs for Indian artifacts and marked an end to the transition from making wearable blankets for local families and intertribal trade to creating decorative floor rugs and curios for sale to outsiders. This card is postmarked 1903; the photographer was H.R. Fitch of San Diego.

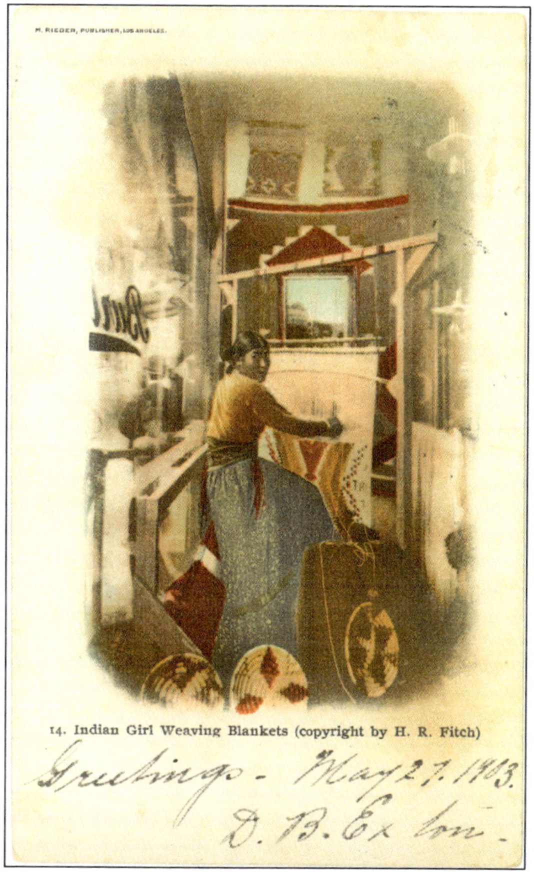

In addition to acquiring vocational training, students learned weaving at the Phoenix Indian School founded in 1891. Here, two girls pose with Germantown-yarn rugs in 1907, while another photograph (published in an online article by Eric Margolis and Jeremy Rowe) shows two boys looking equally unhappy at the same loom. Curiously, the Navajo-style loom's shell-carved ornaments are Hispanic in design. (HHM.)

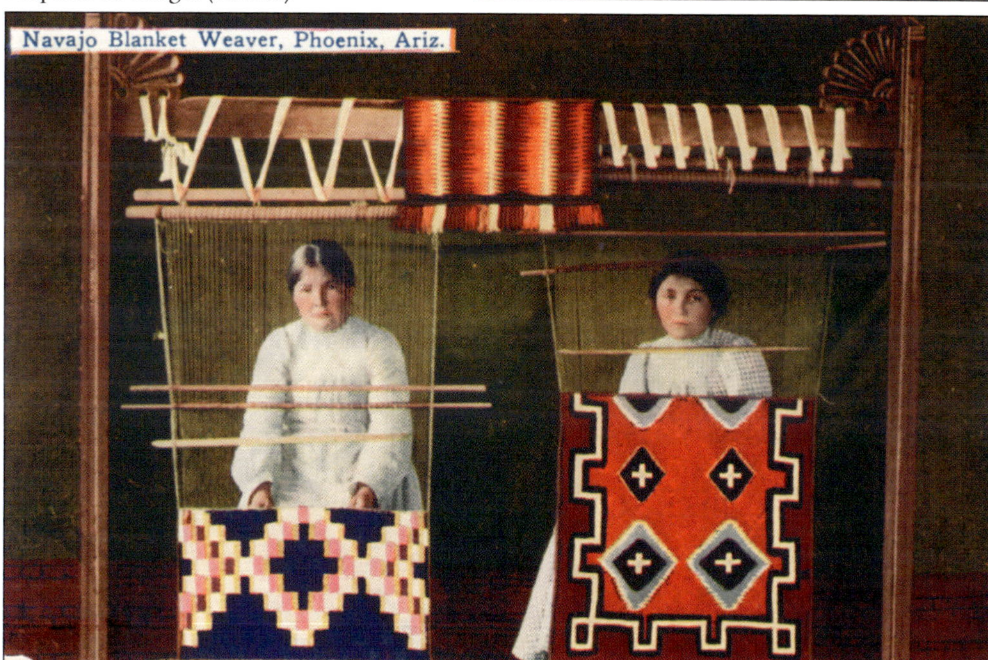

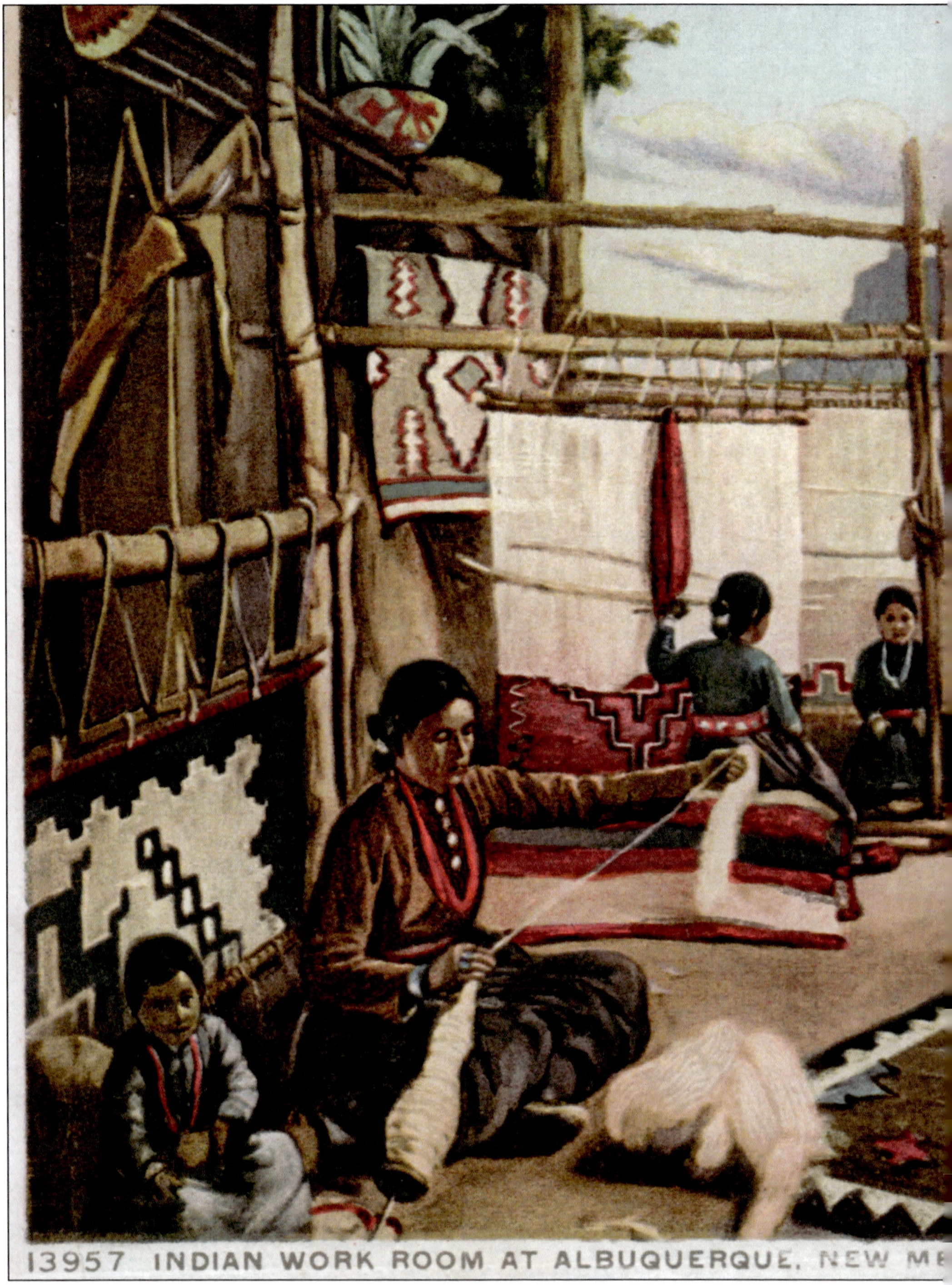

To promote Native American arts and craft, the Fred Harvey Company established its "Indian Building" at the Alvarado Hotel in Albuquerque in 1903. Like a theater set, the room had painted backdrops and staged environments, creating a nostalgic Southwestern atmosphere. During the following two decades, the extended family of Elle and Tom of Ganado frequently demonstrated weaving and silverwork for tourists. In this painting, six women and girls (with Elle carding at

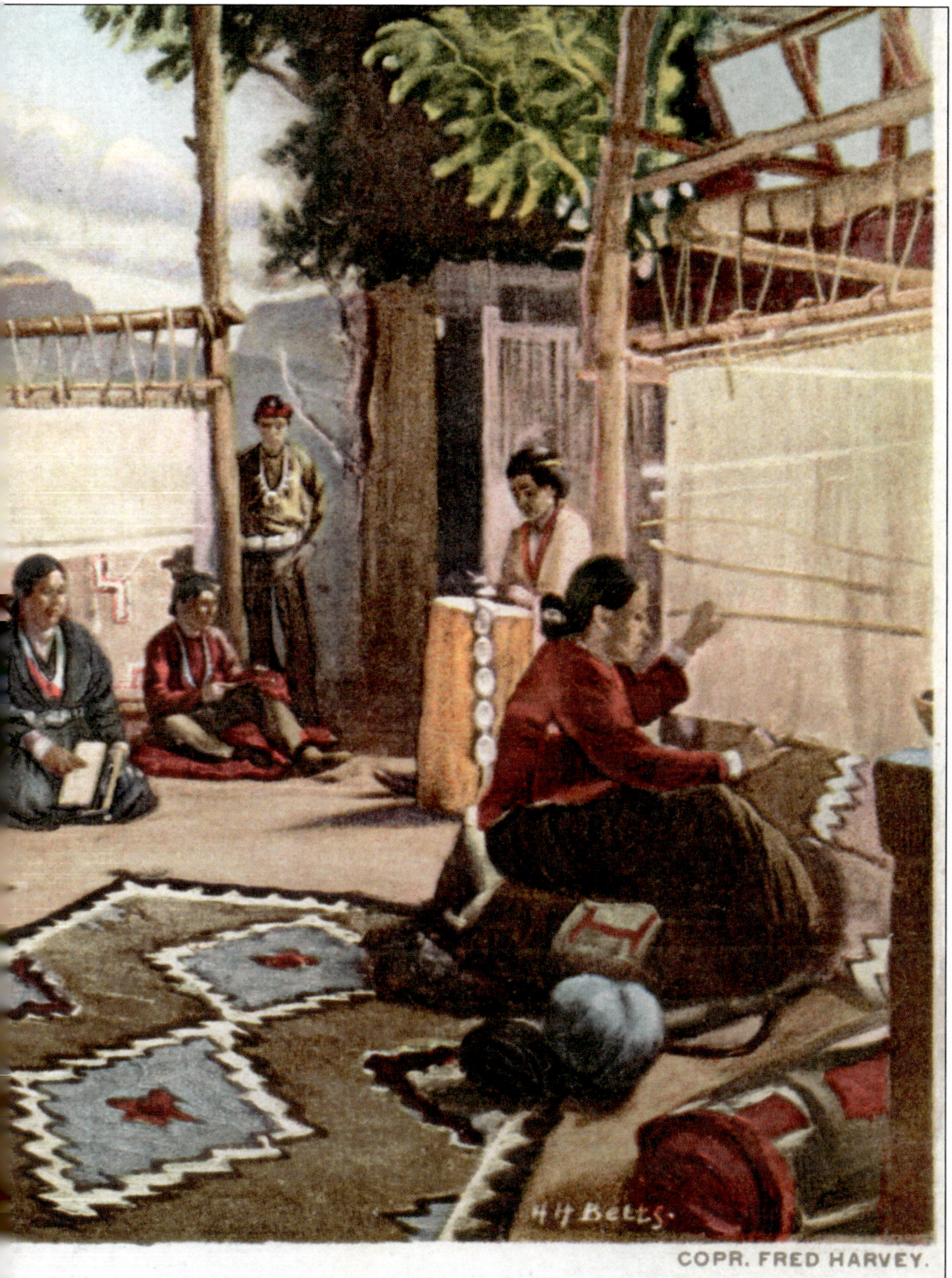

center) showcase various stages of wool processing and weaving, while two of the three men make jewelry. The artist, H.H. Betts, modified an original black-and-white photograph (published in Howard and Pardue's *Inventing the Southwest*, page 56), adding and subtracting various props and radically changing the foreground rug's design. (DPC and FHC.)

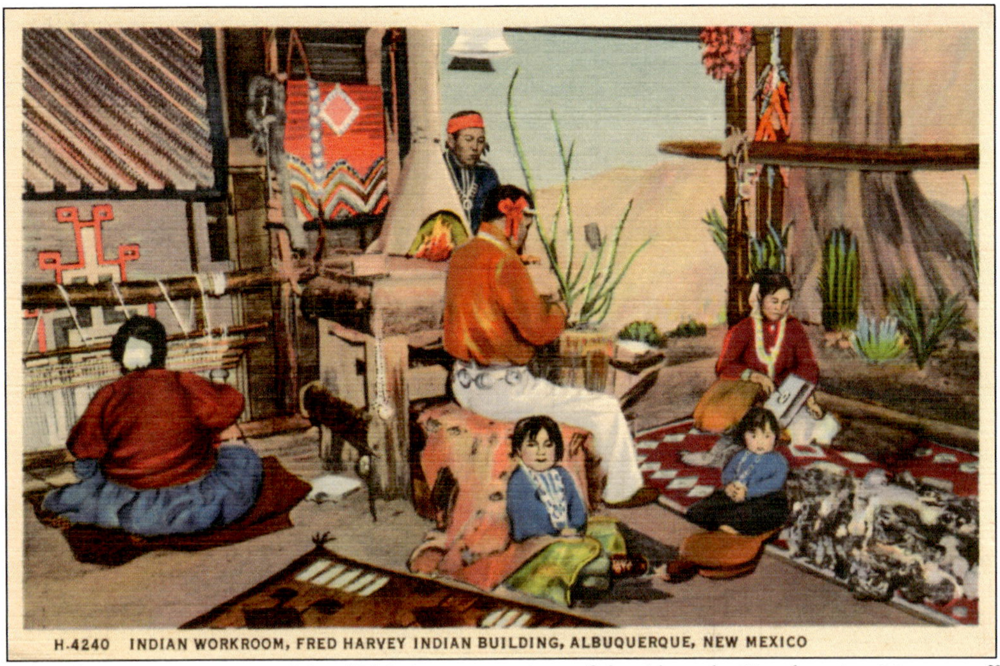

A handwritten message explains, "This is an extension of the Alvarado Hotel station. You get off train and cross a small patio and are in hotel." In the "Indian Workroom," Elle of Ganado is seated at left, and her husband, Tom, works at a forge and silverworking bench made from a tree trunk. This card was mailed from Albuquerque in 1938, but the photograph was taken earlier. (FHC.)

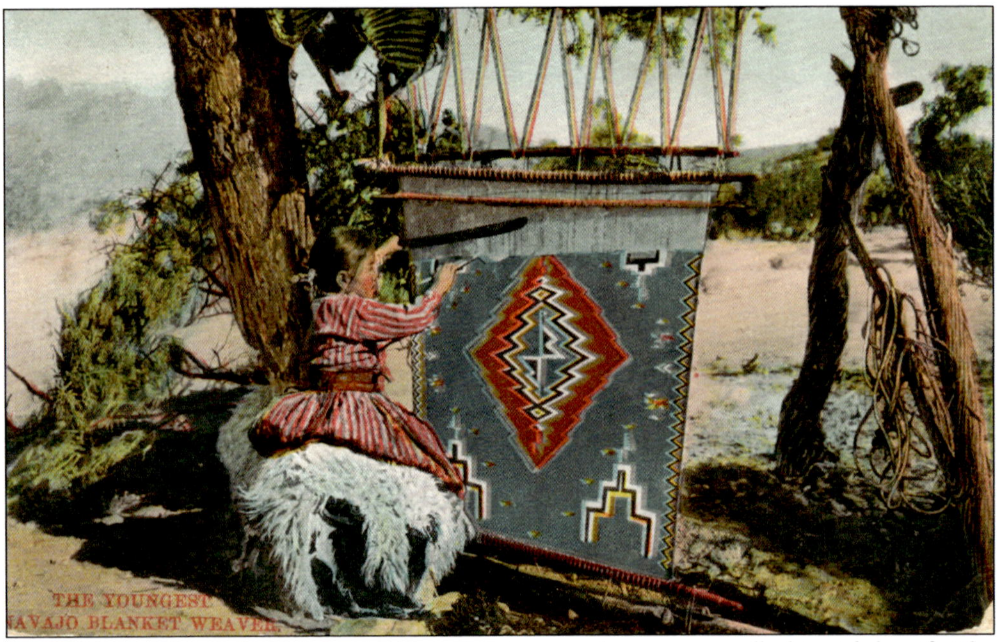

Elle and Tom of Ganado had no children of their own; she was reputedly his eighth wife. The "youngest Navajo Blanket Weaver" was Atlnaba, one of Tom's grandchildren from a previous marriage. The little girl's impressive blanket may have resulted from collaborating with a relative, or possibly not—she had a reputation for precocious talent. This card, printed in Leipzig, Germany, was mailed from Aztec, New Mexico, to Michigan in 1908. (Adolph Selige.)

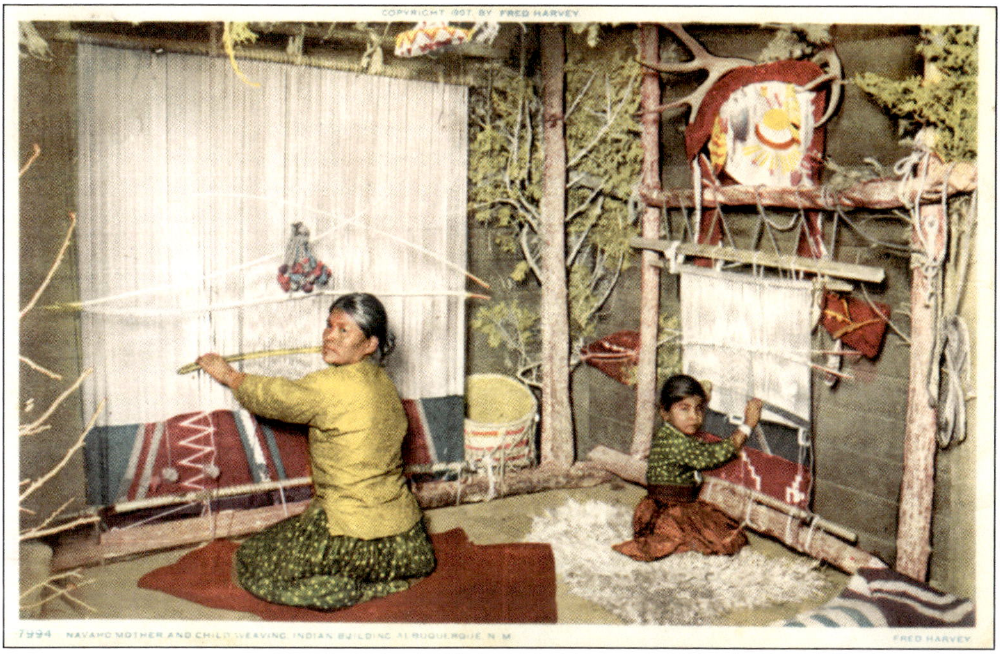

Called "Tsonsi-Pah" when she was photographed at the Alvarado Hotel in 1904, this girl was known as Atlnaba, nicknamed Tuli, when anthropologist Gladys Reichard lived with her family at White Sands near Ganado from 1930 to 1933. Born in 1899, Atlnaba began weaving at four after being taught by an older sister. She rapidly became an accomplished weaver, famed for her exquisite sandpainting tapestries sponsored by J.L. Hubbell. Her father, Miguelito (aka Red Point), was a well-known Diné medicine man and singer. He and his wife, Maria Antonia, and two other daughters (Marie and a woman known as Yilkadezba's Mother) worked at the California expositions for nearly two years. An Apache burden basket sits between the looms; antlers and a painted hide or canvas shield with feathers, possibly Apache or Southern Plains but not Navajo, hang above them. (DPC and FHC.)

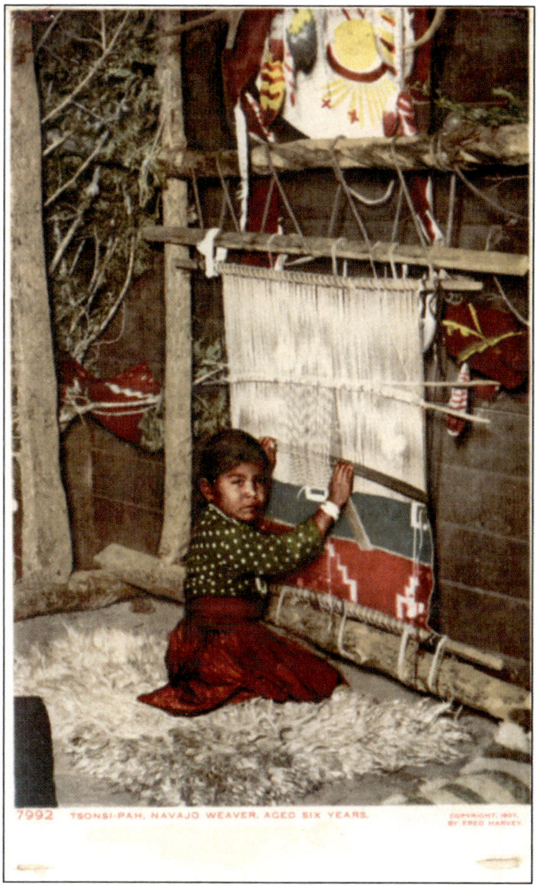

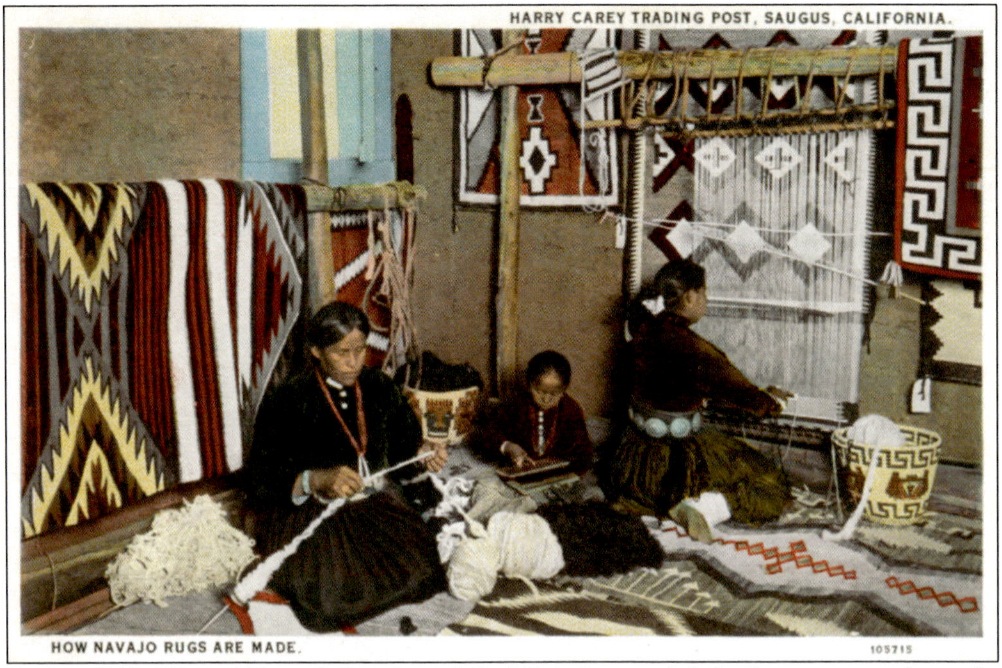

During 1915, Elle and Tom of Ganado and Red Point's extended family spent several months demonstrating at Fred Harvey's "Painted Desert" exhibition at the Panama-California Exposition in San Diego and the Panama-Pacific Exposition in San Francisco. In the image above, she weaves while her younger companions spin and card wool, surrounded by Navajo rugs for sale but not likely made by them. The two large coiled baskets are Hopi-made. On the card below, postmarked "Panama-California Exposition, San Diego—1915," the sender reported, "This is just a greeting from the Exposition grounds. The Indian exhibit is one of the best here. We like San Diego very much. The ocean breeze makes life worthwhile again. Would like to stay here all summer. . ." The photographer of this image was J.R. Willis. (Above, CTC; below, FHC.)

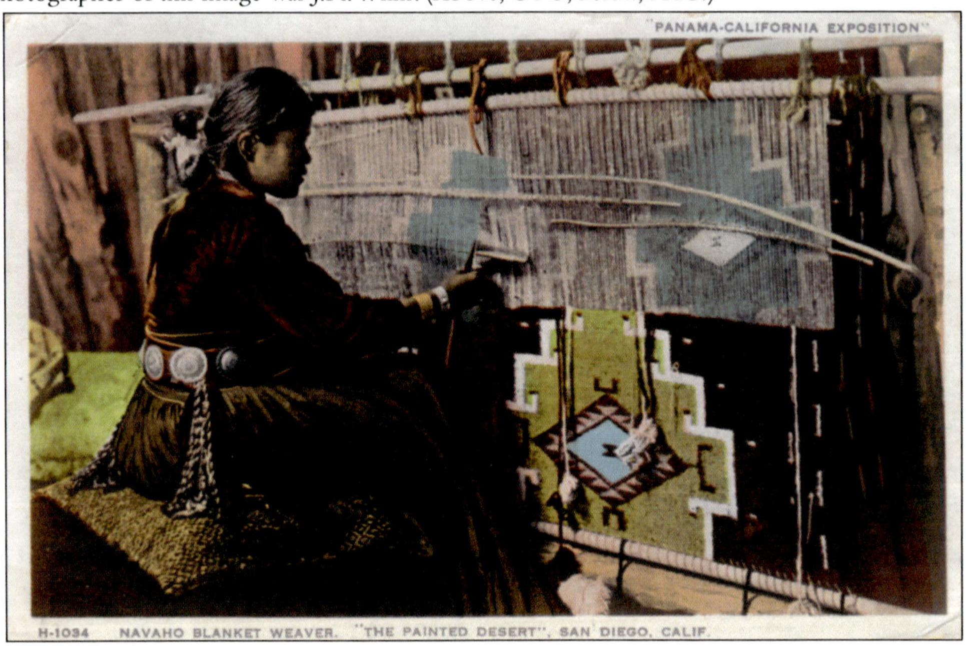

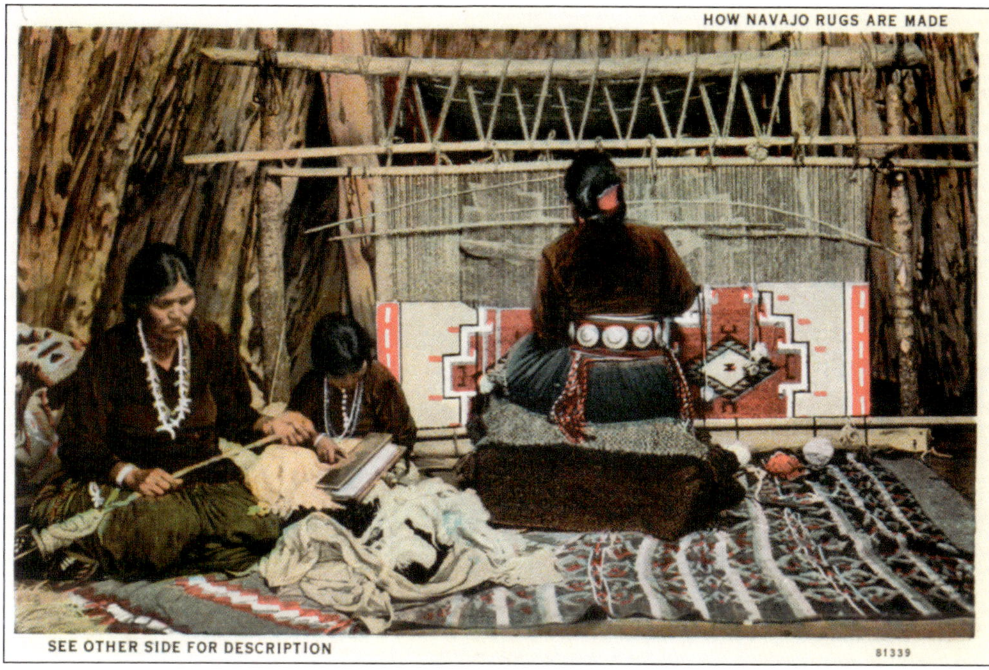

On these two pages, three hand-coloring treatments on photographs taken by J.R. Willis dramatically change how Elle's rug looks; the red version is probably most accurate. Elle is not identified by name, nor is her location in the fabricated "Indian Village" in San Diego mentioned. Instead, one caption describes the carding, spinning, and weaving processes "in the Indians' home or Hogan." (Above, FHC; below, CTC.)

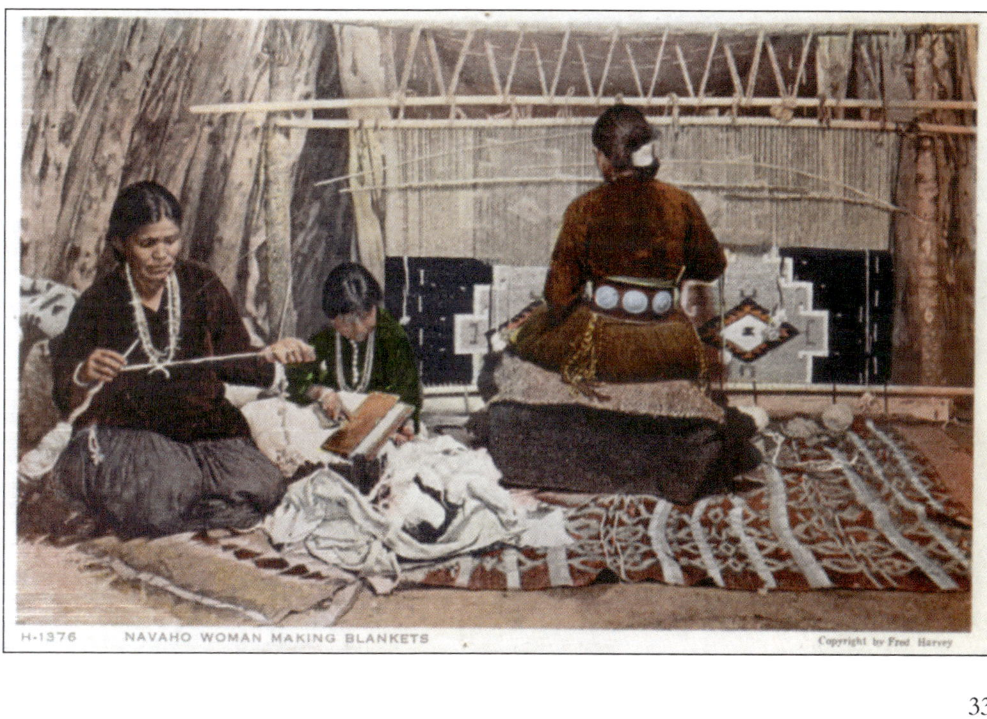

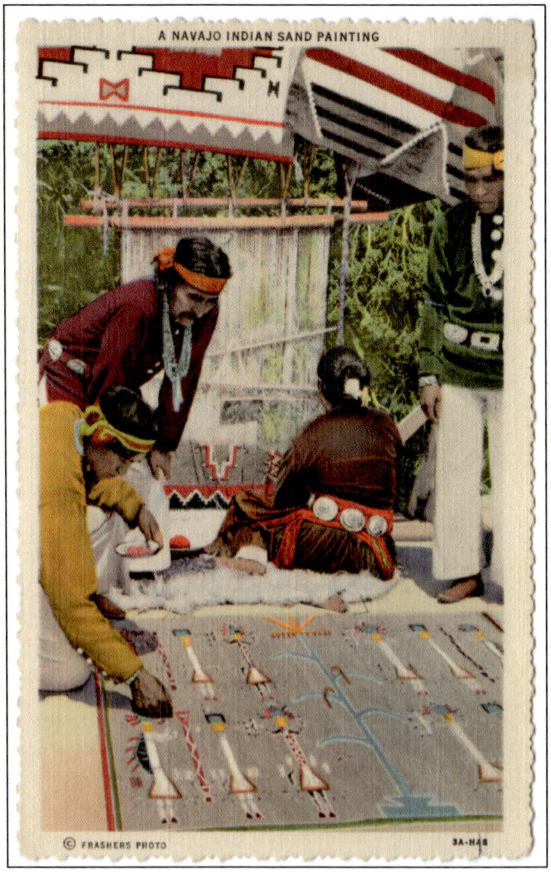

Combining men's ceremonial sandpainting and women's weaving activities into a single scene suggests a theatrical tableau rather than a natural at-home representation. The overhanging Navajo rugs and unusually lush background serve as stage curtains (for other views of this weaver, see pages 91 and 107). Before Burton Frasher ever traveled to the Southwest, he visited the San Diego exposition, where he likely took these photographs sometime between 1915 and 1917. (FFS.)

At home, Elle was known to friends and relations by her Navajo name, *Asdzáán Łichíí'* (Red Woman), born to the *Dibé Łizhiní* (Black Sheep) clan. Her father may have been of Euro-American (*Bilagáana*) or Mexican (*Naakaii dine'é*) descent. Well beyond Ganado, she was famous for having twice woven rugs for US presidents—for Teddy Roosevelt in 1903 and William Howard Taft during the period from 1909 to 1913. (FHC.)

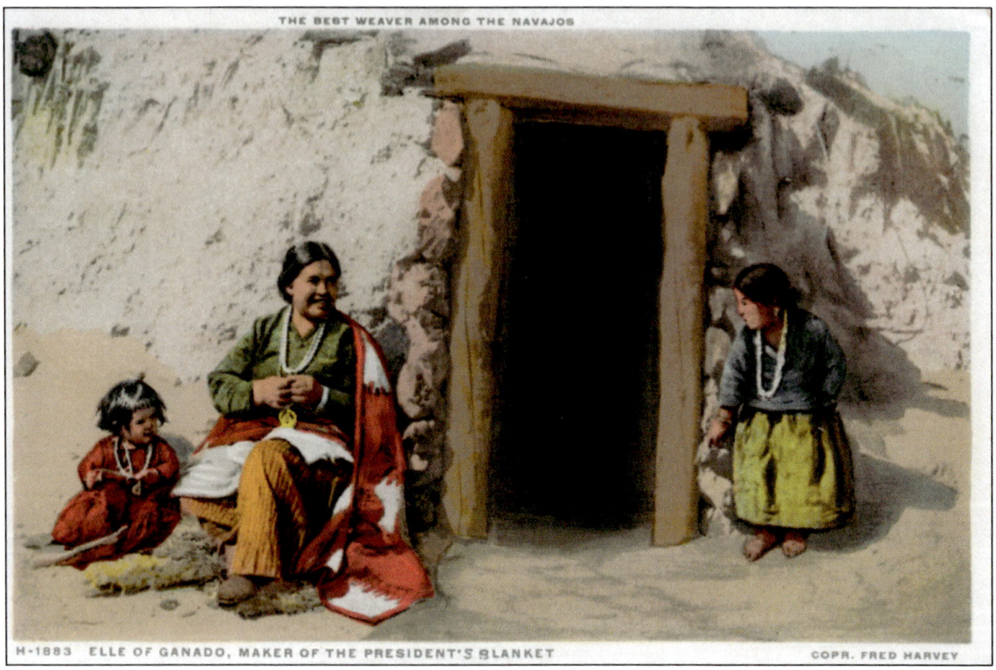

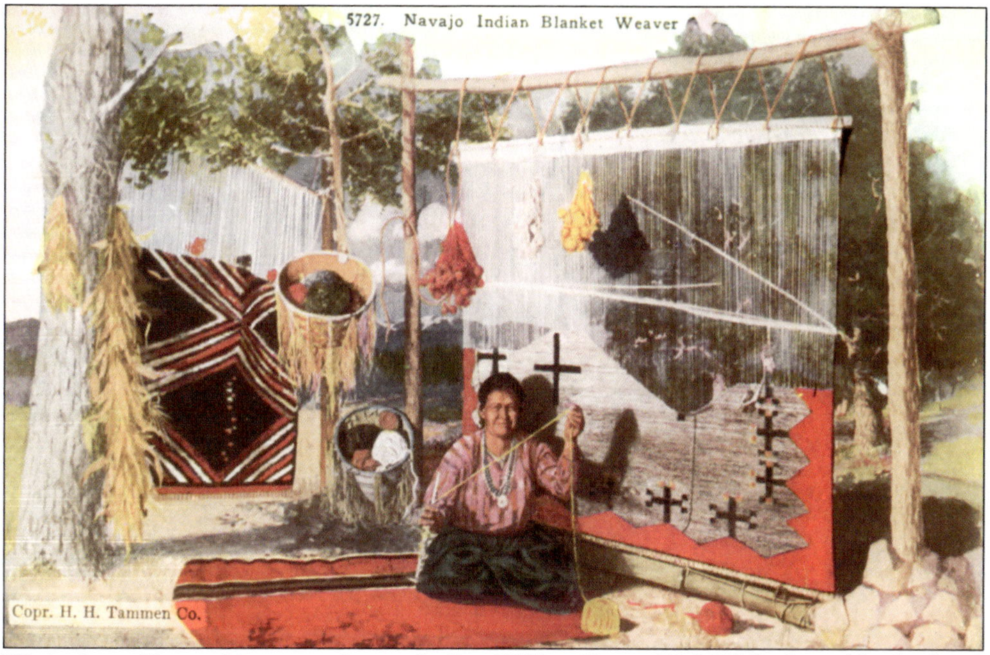

Elle is pictured here with a rug underway for Pres. William Howard Taft. While she and her husband, Tom, were prominent demonstrators at the Alvarado Hotel in Albuquerque from 1903 into the 1920s and spent 1915 and 1916 at the California expositions, they also worked for Fred Harvey and the Santa Fe Railway at the Grand Canyon and as far away as Chicago. (H.H. Tammen.)

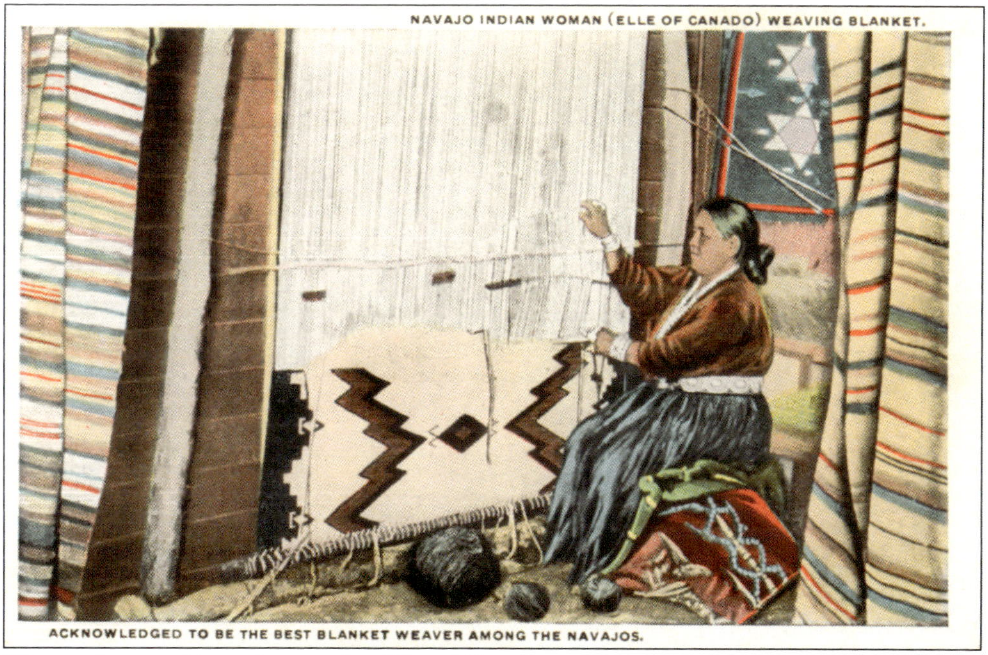

The caption on this card states that Elle of Ganado was "considered quite wealthy as Navajos go, possessing several flocks of sheep, much wampum and the typical Navajo silver jewelry and turquoise. She is daily weaving blankets in the Indian building at Albuquerque. She has been visited by thousands of traveling tourists and is the most widely known Indian woman in the world today." (CTC.)

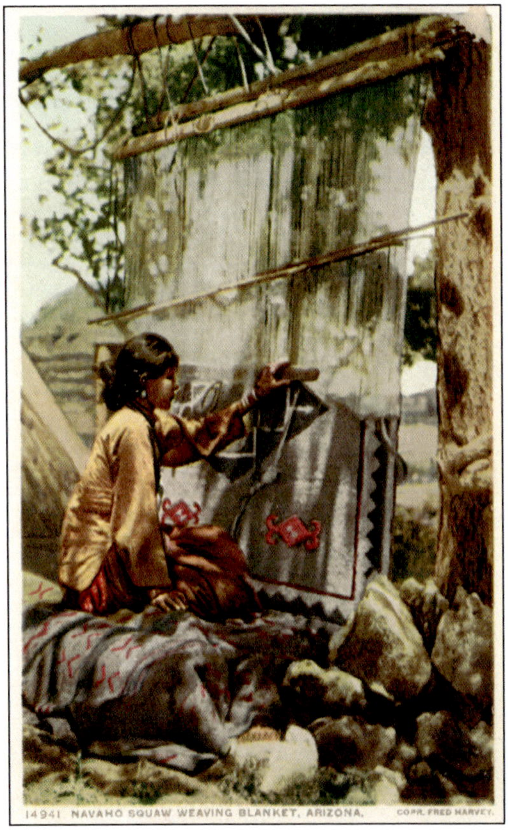

With its use of the archaic moniker "Navaho squaw" in its caption, coupled with the idyllic overpainted setting, this postcard reinforces a romanticized, almost Orientalized, view of Native American women and the Southwest. Tourists were enticed to travel "out West" by images of exotic yet safe surroundings and the promise of experiencing elements of an unchanged past. For a differently colorized version of this photograph that shows a red border on the rug, see page 102. (DPC and FHC.)

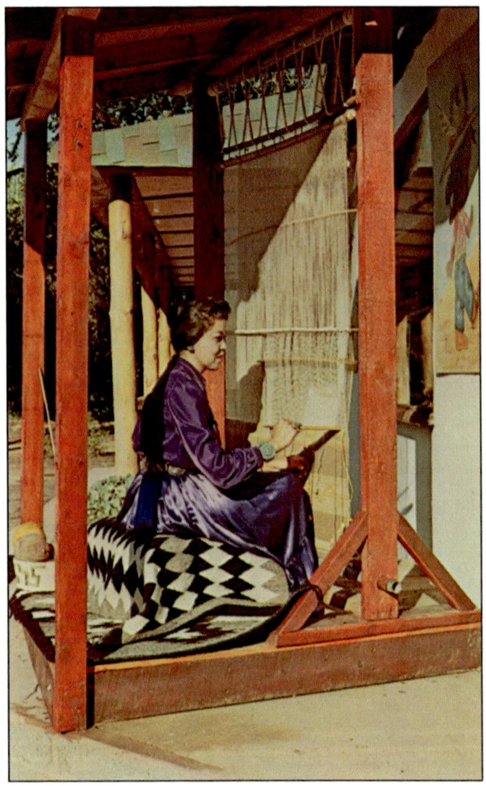

Elle and her relatives were not the first nor last Diné women to showcase their craft in public places. Navajo weavers, like jar-bearing Pueblo women, became cultural icons. Here, a weaver is "on stage" at the Indian Village in Zion National Park, Utah. Weavers continue to work as hired demonstrators at Hubbell Trading Post National Historic Site, Ganado, and at other Southwestern visitor centers. (SC.)

Even diminutive pictures like this three-and-a-quarter-inch-square print are packed with information. Seated under a portal (Spanish for porch) like that of the Palace of the Governors in Santa Fe, a Navajo family demonstrates weaving and silversmithing. A cradleboard-bound baby lies between the parents, and a little girl with a silver coin–adorned necklace sits curbside, observing the photographer. The rug on the loom, with its finely serrated diamonds, is likely a "Germantown Eye Dazzler." (US.)

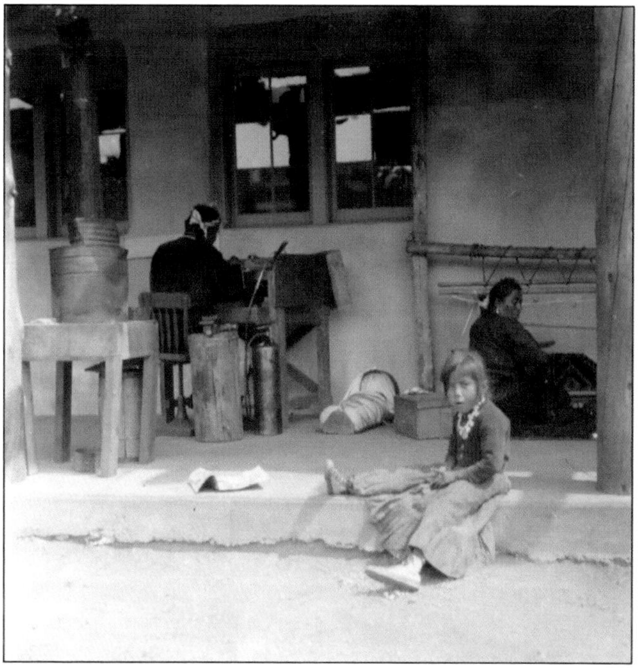

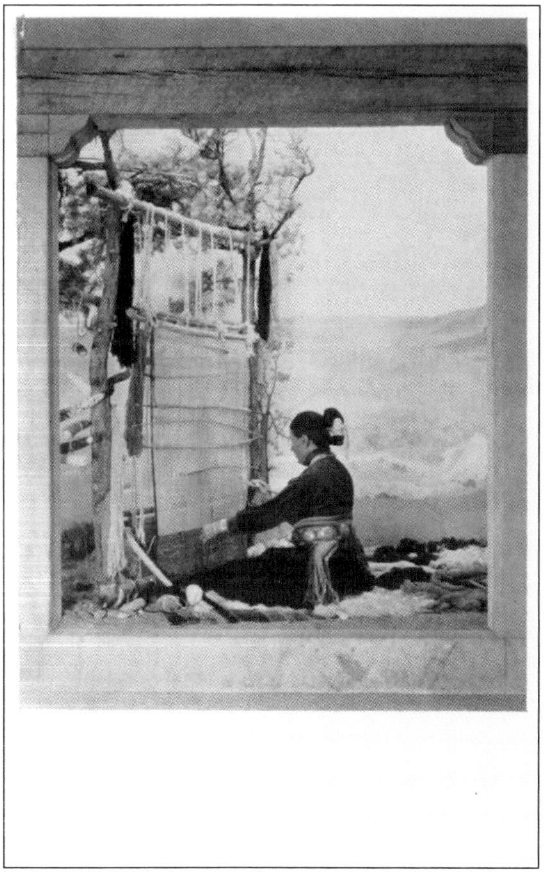

From 1933 until 1975, the American Indian Room at the William Rockhill Nelson Gallery of Art in Kansas City, Missouri, featured this diorama with a mannequin in Navajo attire. Mrs. Leo Danson, a Navajo weaver also known by her first name, Bah-Mary, modeled for John G. Prasuhn, the sculptor who created the mannequin. The museum acquired her tools, garments, and jewelry from the Fred Harvey Company.

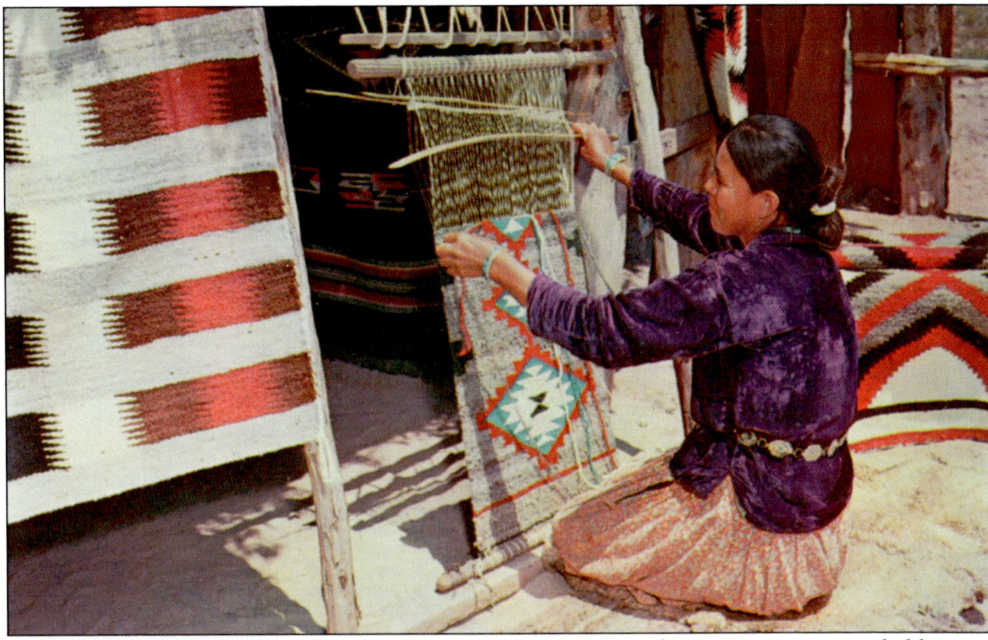

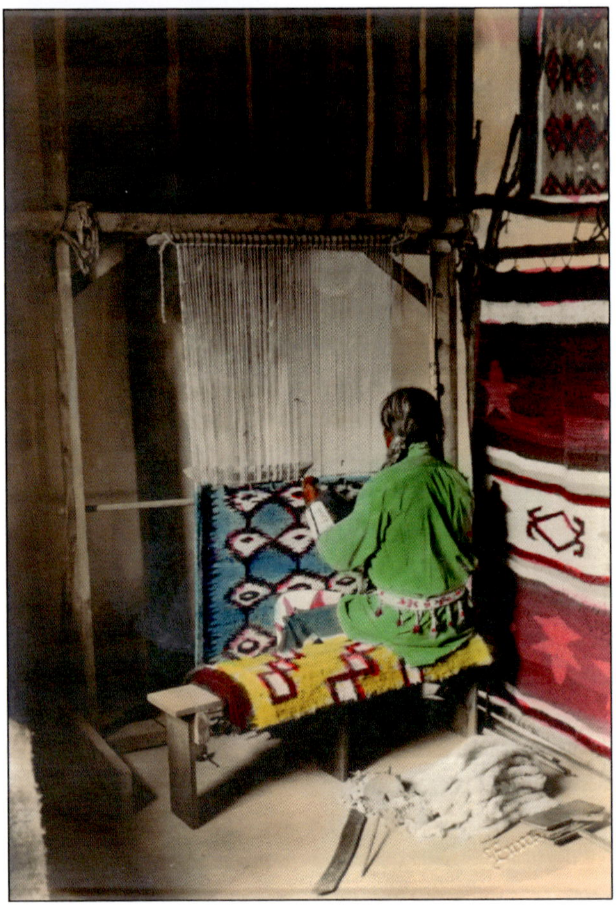

This weaver is surrounded by Navajo and Spanish American (Chimayo) textiles displayed in a sales area. She poses for the photographer in a position from which it would be difficult to weave comfortably or efficiently. Even today, such scenes abound in Southwestern shops and trading posts along Route 66. Weavers earn an hourly wage plus tips for photographs; their rugs are usually sold by their employers. (PS.)

The weaver's identity is not noted on this hand-tinted photograph, which measures six by four inches. Judging from his hairstyle and clothing, he is probably from one of the Rio Grande Pueblos, where Plains styles were adopted. Although surrounded by Navajo-style blankets, the loom is missing its heddle and shed rods. Is this really his loom and weaving? Perhaps the scene is set up, and the man is posing in a store's showroom. (US.)

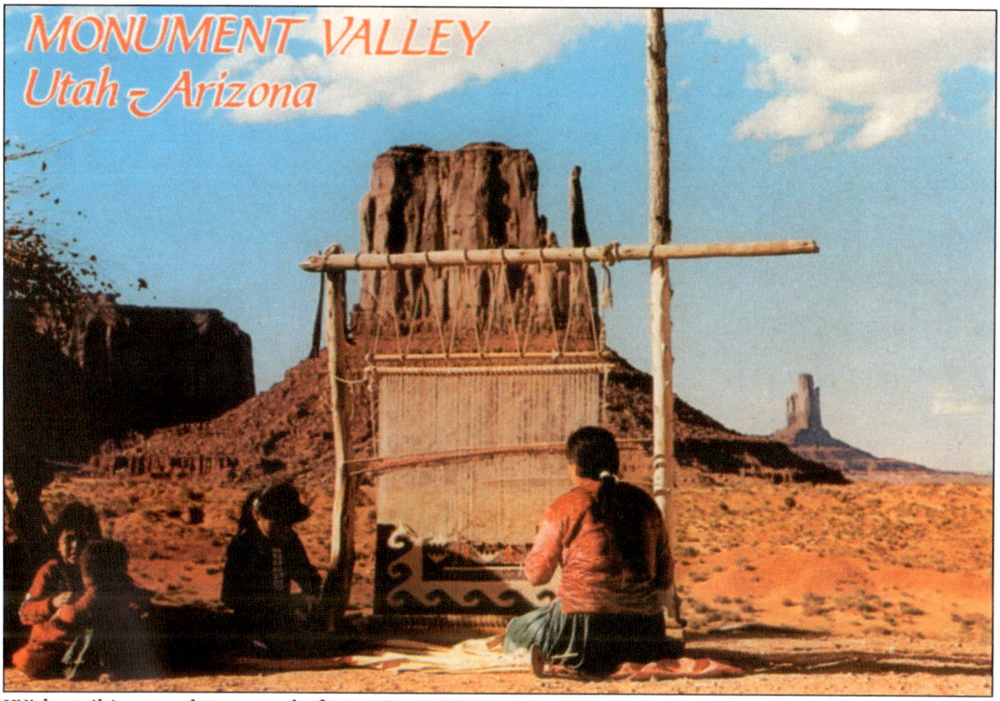

With striking sandstone rock formations, Monument Valley presented a compelling destination for early tourism and a dramatic backdrop for photographers. This northern region of the Navajo Nation, bordering Arizona and Utah, became emblematic of Navajo country in the early 1900s and has remained so ever since. Tour guides contracted with local Navajo families to pose for photo shoots, which continue today. (SC.)

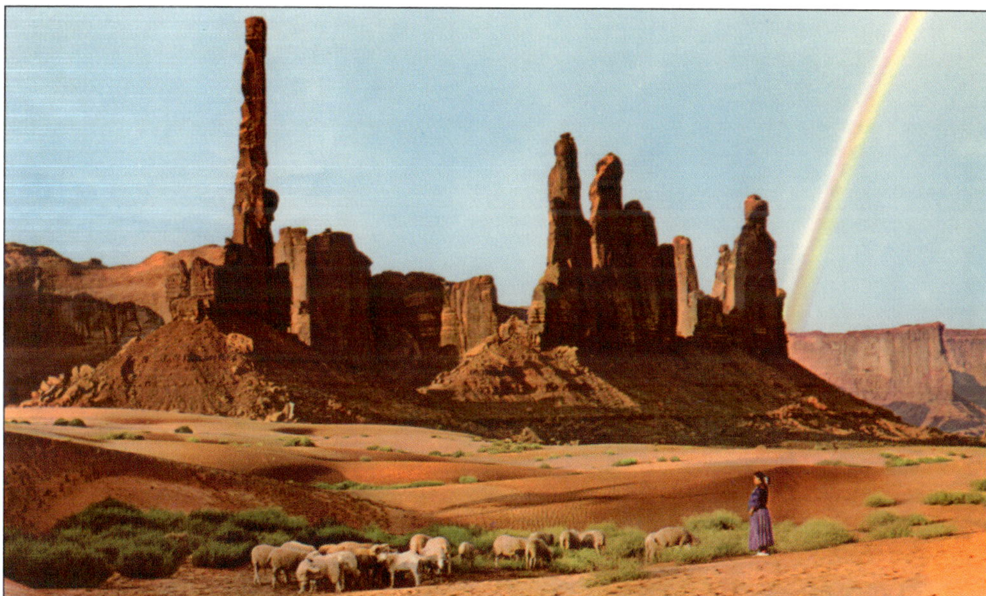

The fabulous rock formations of Monument Valley appear as backdrops to Navajo life in many postcards. With a 100-square-mile tribal park, the full area spans about 20-by-30 miles. Navajos call the valley *Tsé Bii' Ndzisgaii* (stretches of treeless areas or clearings among the rocks). An unlikely rainbow has been added here, although the landscape hardly needs enhancement. (PS.)

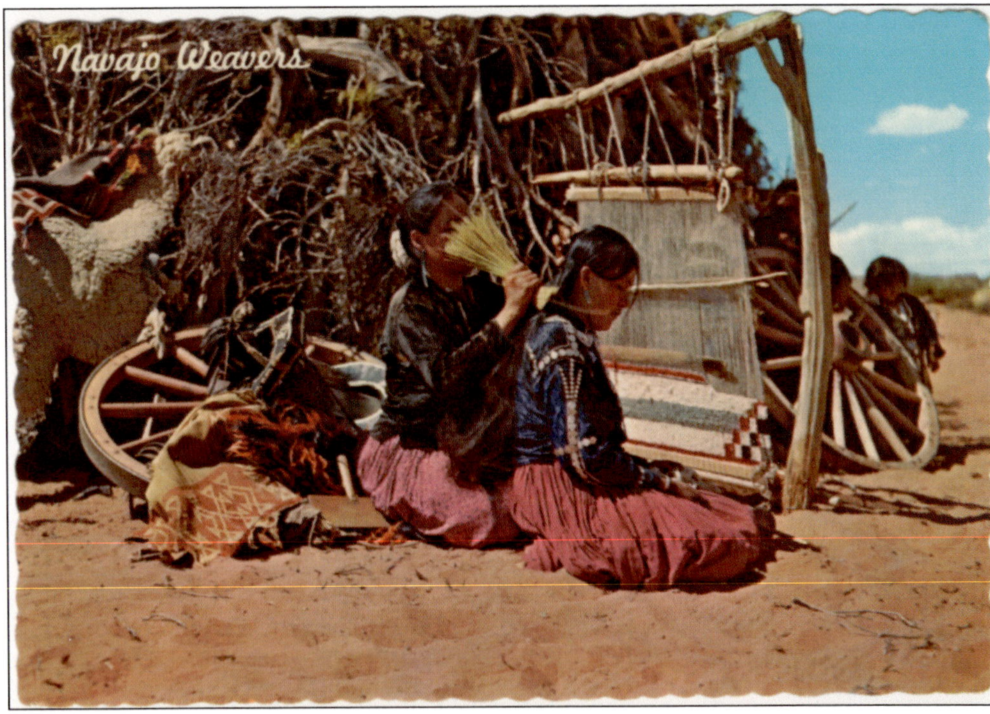

Two women prepare for a photo shoot by demonstrating how a traditional hair knot (*tsiiyéél*) is made using a brush (*bé'ézhóó'*) of dried wild wheat grass. The Diné hairstyle, worn by both Navajo men and women, expresses their identity, symbolizes caring relationships between people, and holds spiritual significance. Some say their long, uncut hair represents their memory. Modeling the hairdo, the younger woman demonstrates her skill in weaving a single saddle blanket. (Above, PS; below, HSC.)

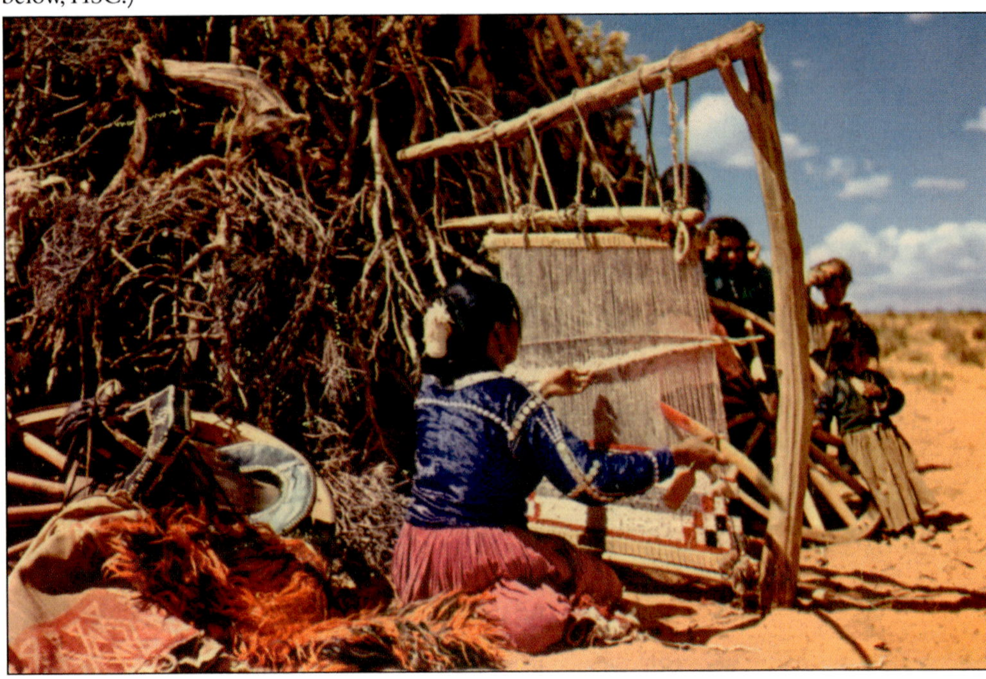

Although "Happy" Cly and her family appear in many Monument Valley postcards throughout several decades, this is the only one in this collection where she is identified by name. The caption also notes she is weaving "the traditional corn rug," which is a misnomer. Although corn is a traditional food plant, its presence in rugs is an individual artistic choice and a 20th-century trend. (Durand Studio.)

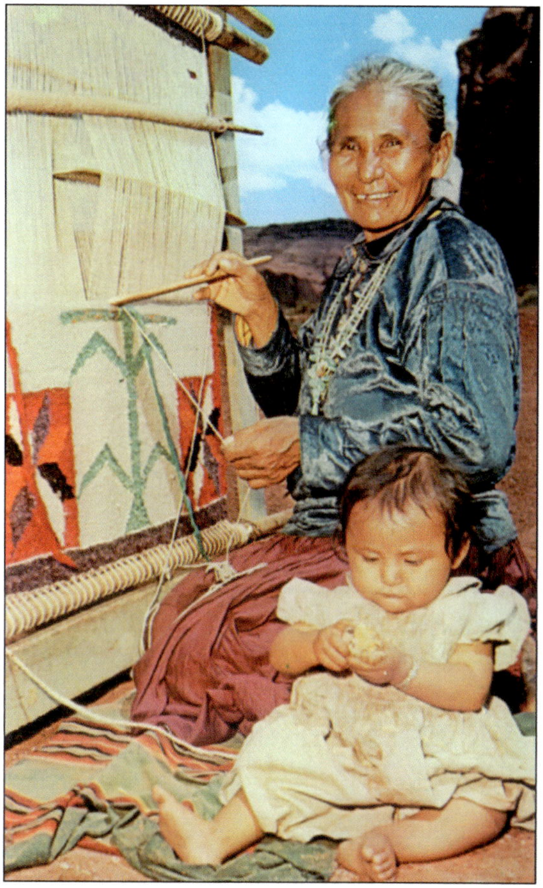

In this relatively early view of Happy Cly, she is surrounded by extended family members and emblems of the West like the Diné saddle with its tall horn. During the early 1950s, the Cly family became the "stars" of *Navaho Boy: The Monument Valley Story*, a silent film produced by Chicago filmmaker Robert Kennedy that portrayed a Diné family's healing rituals. (PS.)

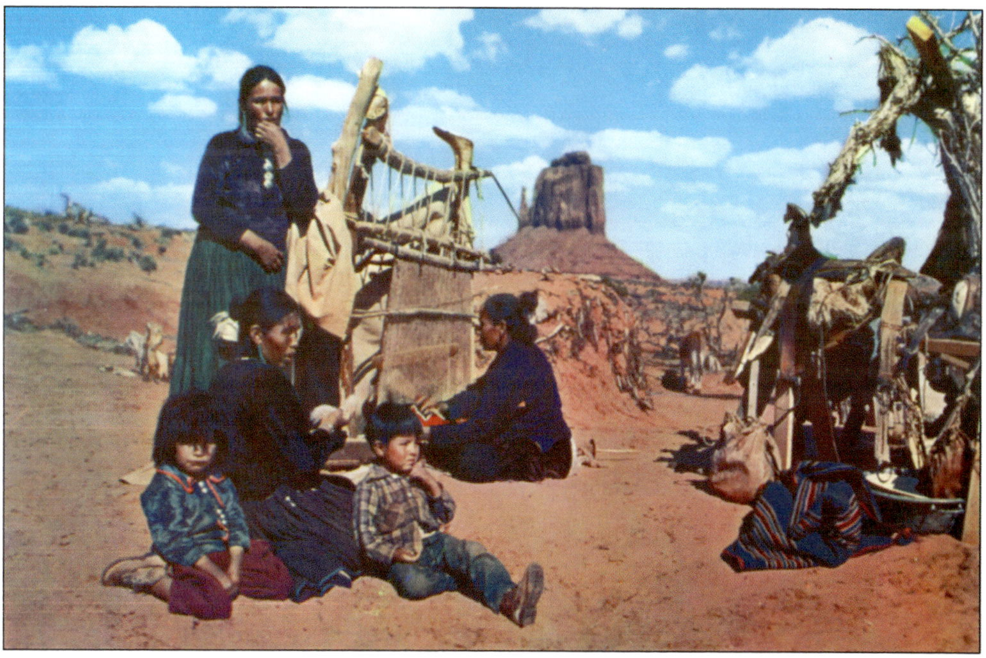

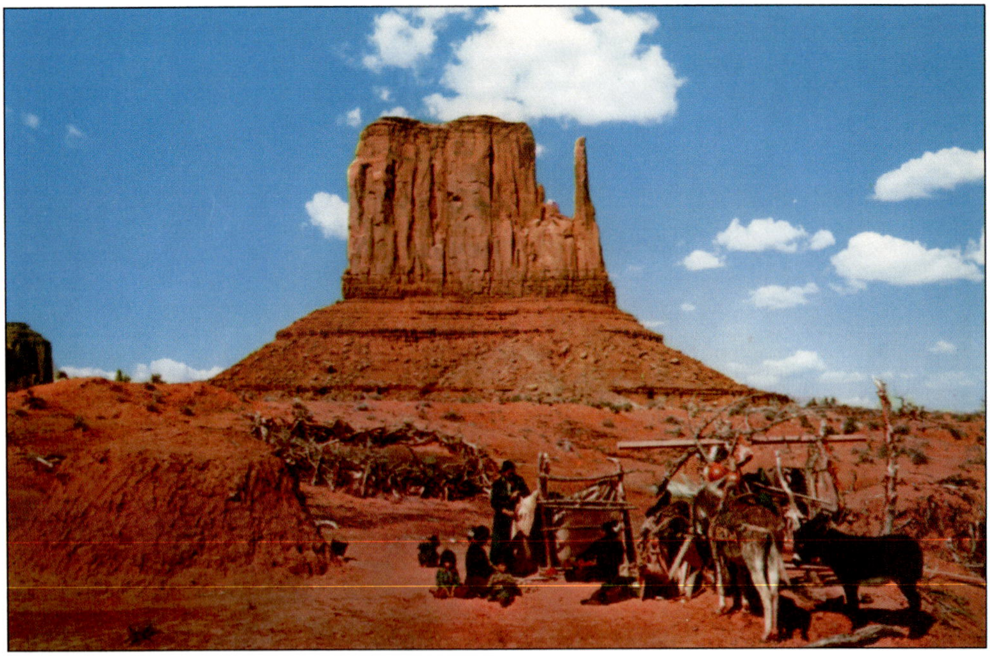

On these two pages are four views of the Cly family in Monument Valley, where the contrast of romantic settings meets the realities of rural life. In each scene, Happy Cly weaves a small rug or double saddle blanket. A burro, donkey, and horse serve as props but were useful for sheepherding and transport, too. The family earned income from photographers' fees and the sale of Happy's handwoven rugs. Men in the family also worked in the area's uranium mines, which left their homes and surroundings contaminated with dangerous radioactivity. Sadly, she and her husband, Willie (fondly known to locals as "Old Man Sagebrush"), and others died from lung cancer and related conditions. The image below was photographed by Ray Manley. (Both, PS.)

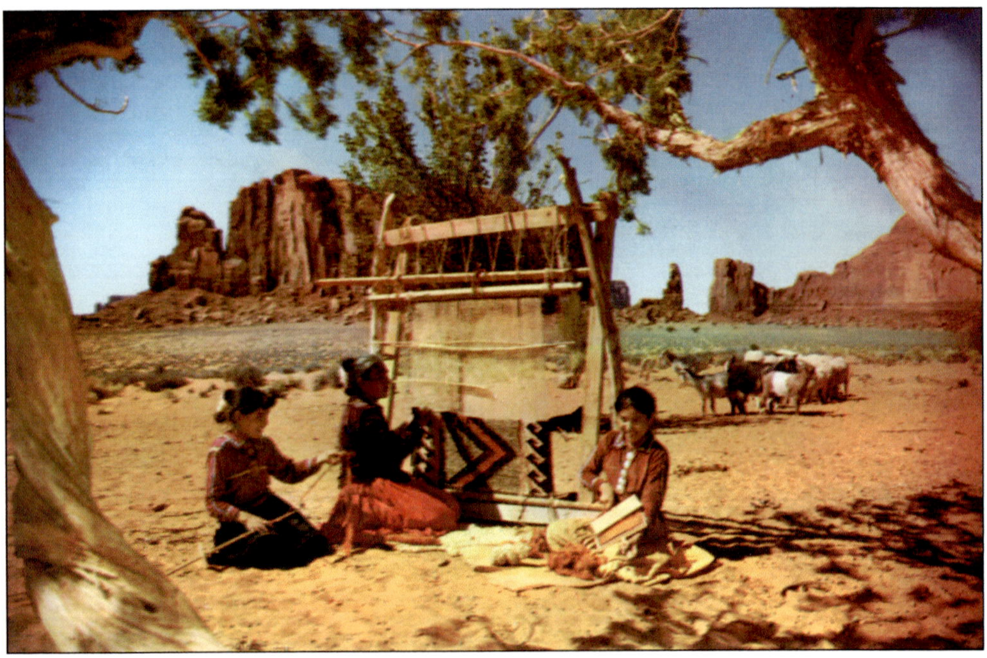

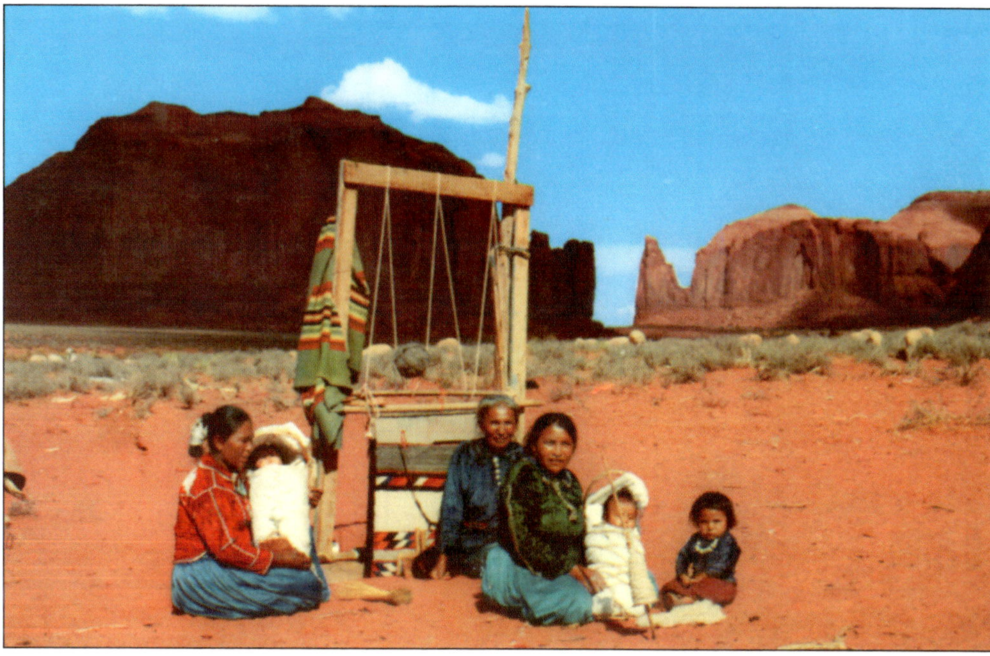

Three generations of women and girls in the Cly family pose for one picture (above), while Mrs. Happy Cly weaves alone in the other (below). Long after Mrs. Cly's death in 1960, a second film, *The Return of the Navajo Boy*, was made in 2000 by Robert Kennedy's son Bill, Jeff Spitz, and Bennie Klain in close collaboration with members of the Cly extended family. The acclaimed PBS documentary has been hailed as a champion of environmental justice and contrasts the idyllic 1950s of the picture-postcard world with the disastrous consequences of uranium mining that began in the area during the 1940s. (Both, PS.)

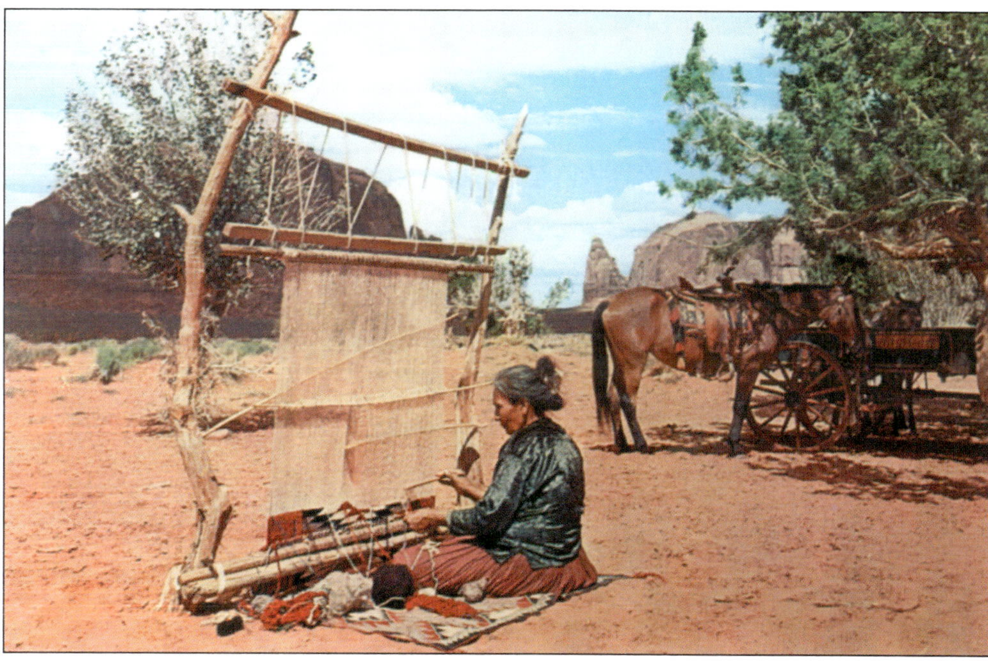

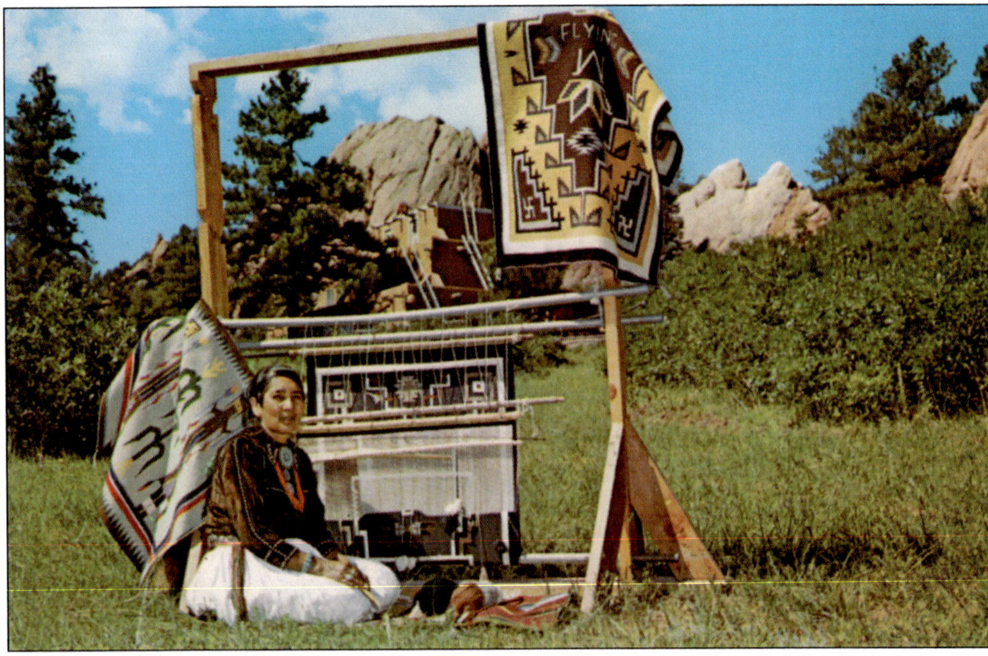

Today, Navajo weavers live in Denver, Los Angeles, and other places beyond the Navajo Nation. Even far from home, Navajo weaving sells! This postcard produced by the Flying W dude ranch in Colorado Springs advertises "one of our Navajo weavers who weave beautiful natural wool rugs for your inspection prior to supper each evening." Three styles of rugs are displayed, including the "Flying W" woven into the upper rug's design. (FWR.)

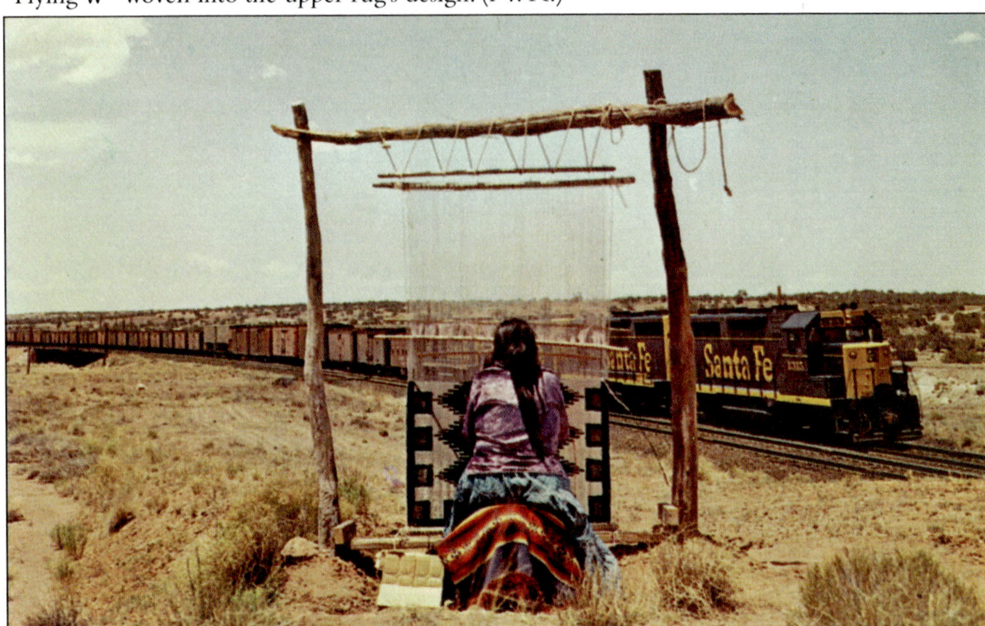

Despite a caption that reads, "Santa Fe Freight rolls east as an Indian weaver finishes her rug near Gallup, N.M.," this weaver is not quite halfway done with the rug on her loom. Sitting in an exposed and unlikely spot overlooking the tracks, she herself provides a vehicle for promoting Southwest tourism and stereotypes. (SFR and AVD.)

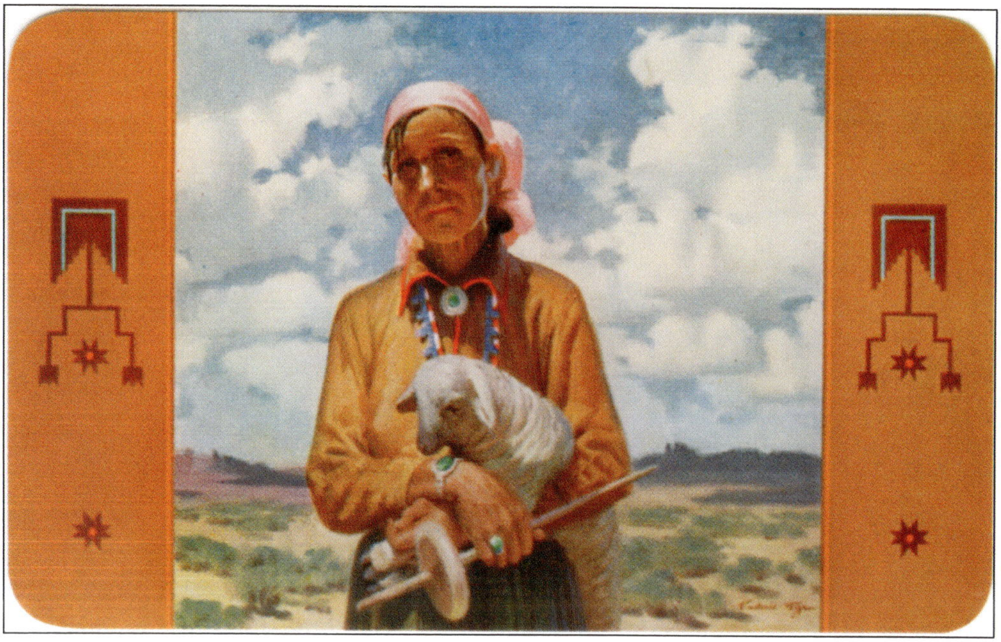

At right, a 1954 calendar and handy ruler sized for a wallet reminds consumers about the Santa Fe Railway—"Fast, dependable, passenger and freight service." On the reverse (above), a painting of an elder Navajo woman, probably based on a photograph, promotes a peaceful, pastoral image of the Southwest. For her, the lamb and spindle symbolize traditional wealth and her work ethic. (Both, SFR.)

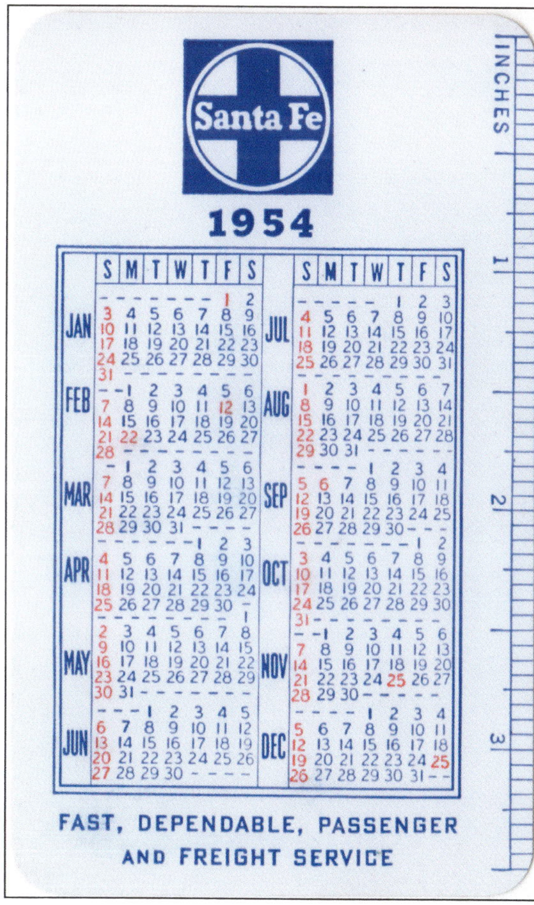

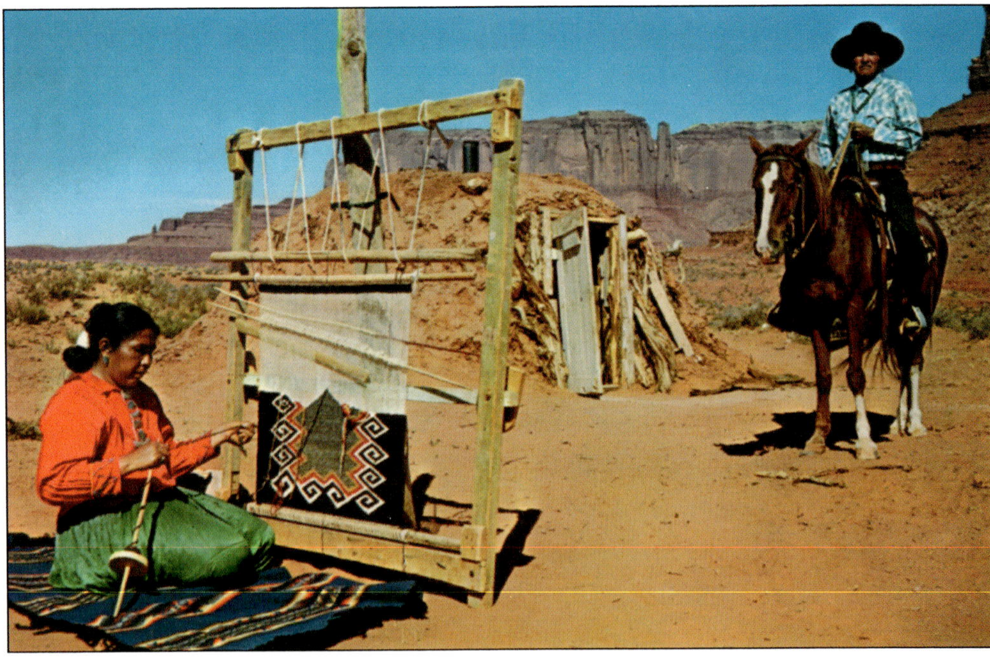

These scenes, photographed by Bob Bradshaw in the mid-1960s, reflect both the nostalgia and reality of Navajo life during this period. Horses held a special place in Diné culture; they were accorded special Diné songs and ceremonies. They were used not only for herding livestock but for rodeos and other competitions. While a man and a girl pose on horseback, one weaver makes a single saddle blanket (above) and the other works on a two-in-one rug where geometric motifs contrast with a row of supernatural beings (*yé'ii*). (Both, BCS.)

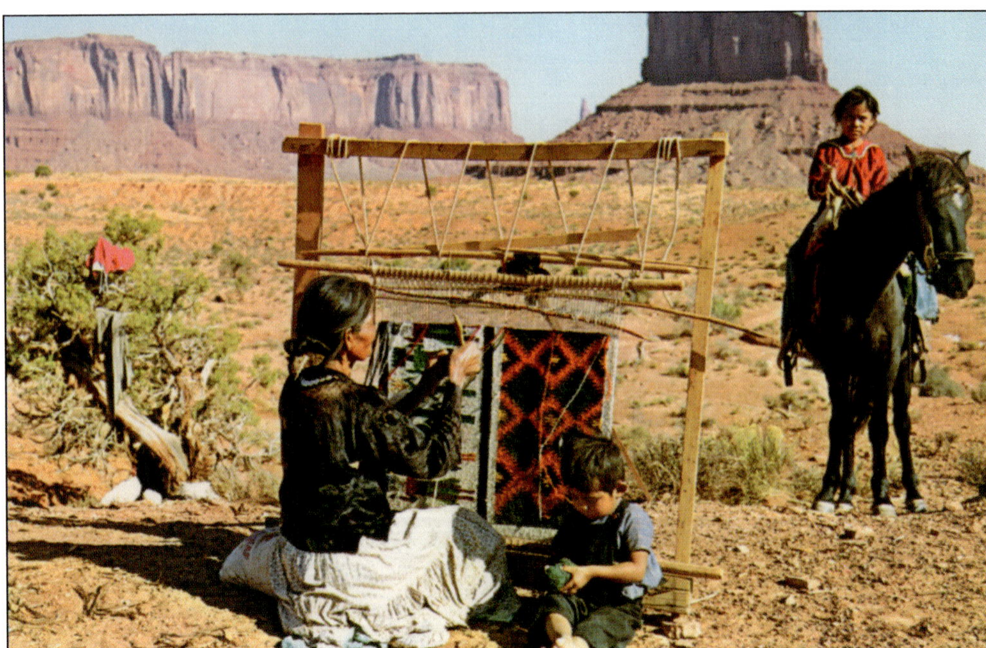

Three

Shepherding and Working the Wool

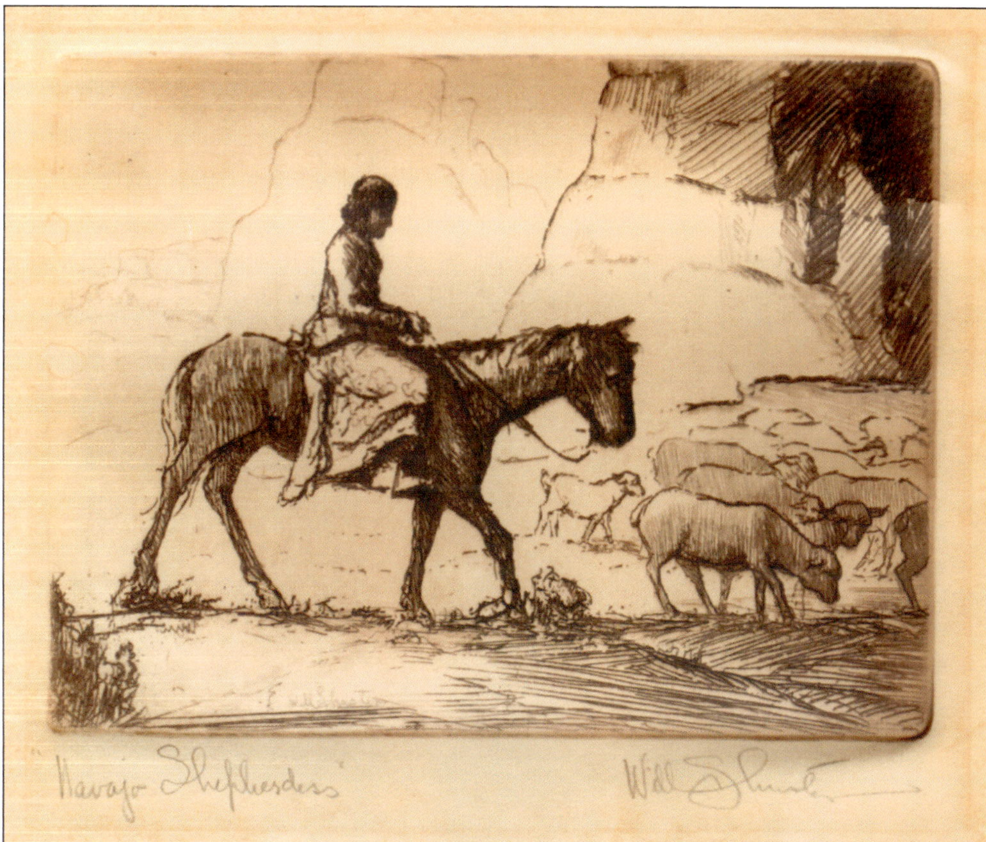

Sheep (*dibé*) are the mainstay of Diné life in practical, philosophical, and spiritual ways. "Navajo Shepherdess" depicts an iconic emblem of Diné culture and a familiar everyday scene to Navajos. The small etching, which measures three by four inches, was made around 1927 by Will Shuster, a renowned member of the artist collective Los Cinco Pintores in Santa Fe. (Courtesy of the Ocotillo Trust; gift of John and Dorothy Rohner.)

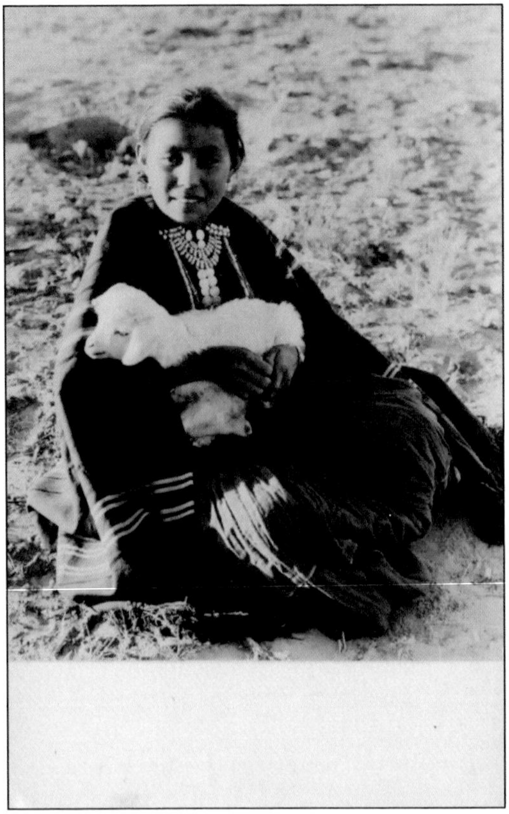

Sheep first entered the Southwest with the Spanish *conquistadores* in the late 1500s. Providing mutton, wool, and barter-on-the-hoof while requiring a family's care, they rapidly became integrated into Navajo economy and culture. Glossy, long-staple wool from the Iberian churra breed, known as *churro* (*dibé dits'ozí*), absorbed dyes well and replaced cotton in Navajo handwoven blankets. Later, other breeds—the greasier, curly merino and rambouillet (*dibé doolk'oolí*)—were introduced to increase meat production, but their crimpy wool took more labor and often produced lumpy yarns. By the end of the 1800s, churro fleece was rarely used, and commercial wool yarns became common. Beginning in the 1970s, flocks of churro were reintroduced, and the use of their handspun wool was revived. In her portrait titled "Navaho Girl" (left), Laura Gilpin captured the attachment between a girl and her lamb. The photograph at left is reproduced with permission from Amon Carter Museum of American Art, Fort Worth, Texas, © 1979. (Below, FFS.)

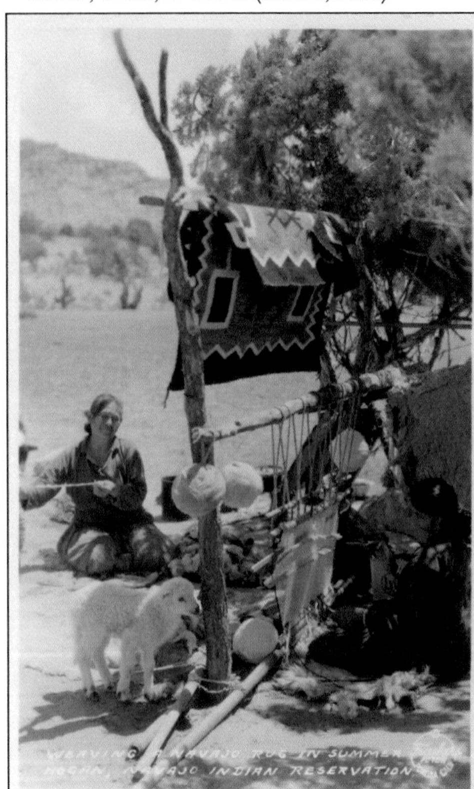

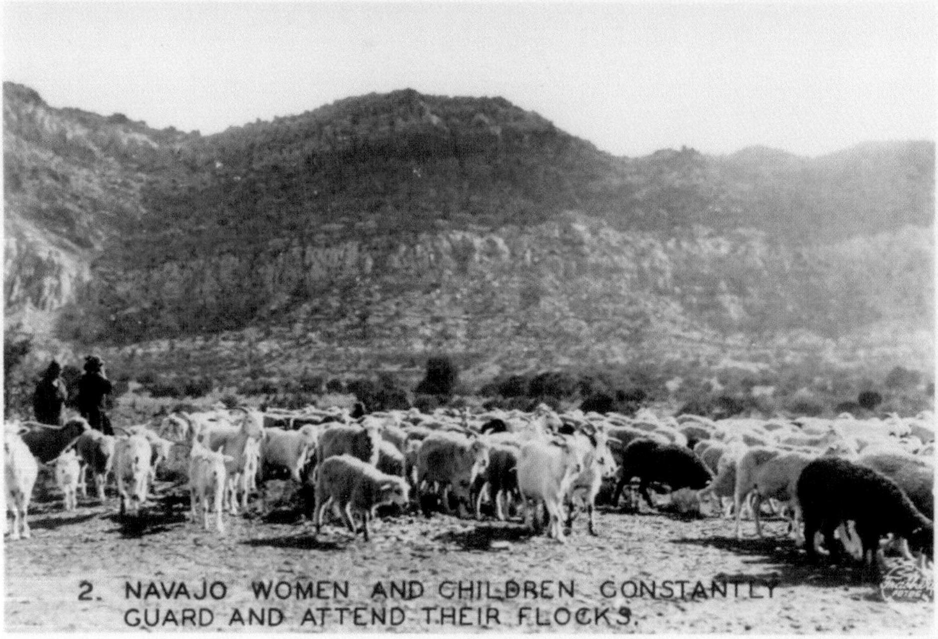

Throughout much of the 20th century, Navajo sheep derived from a mixture of breeds without a singular set of traits. Some would call them "mongrels." Weavers' herds often included some animals with gray and dark brown coats. Sometimes historic churro traits such as four horns still appear on an individual; otherwise, most sheep are hornless. On the other hand, most goats grow two horns. Angora goats that produce mohair and others used for their meat and milk have grown increasingly common in Navajo flocks. (Both, FFS.)

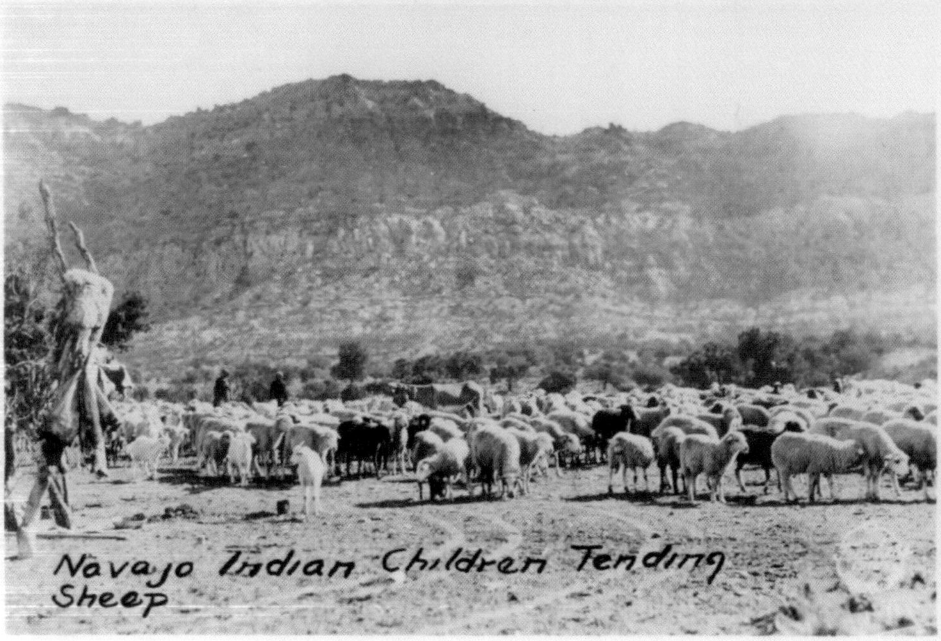

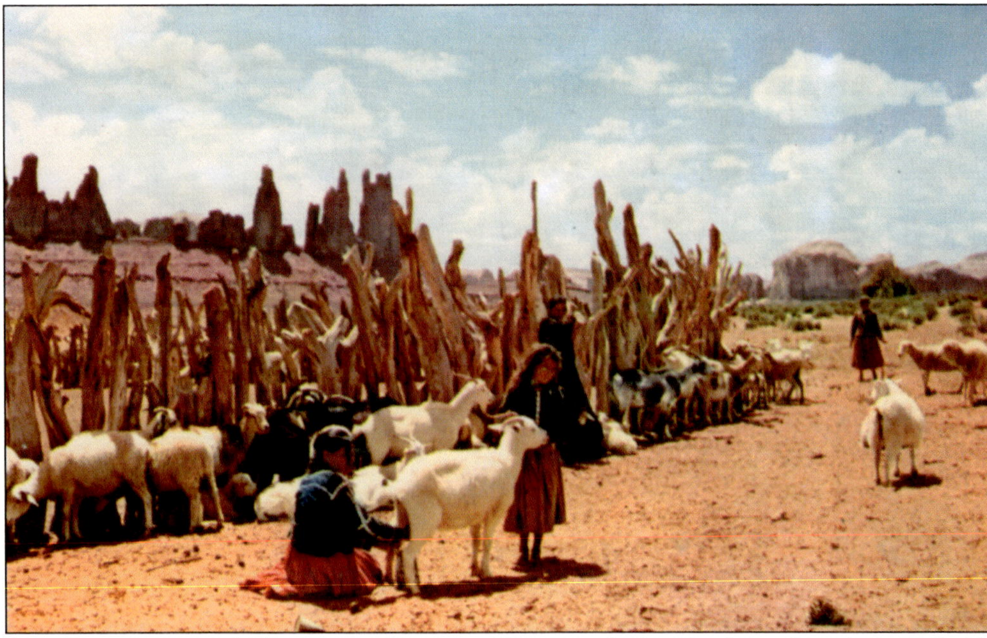

In spring, summer, and fall, sheep and goats usually graze during the day and are brought inside a corral at night. This sculpture-like enclosure is made of large juniper timbers. During winter, a shed or other shelter is sometimes provided. When grass is scarce, feed must be traded for or bought. Lambs are usually born around February, when cold weather demands extra care. (HSC.)

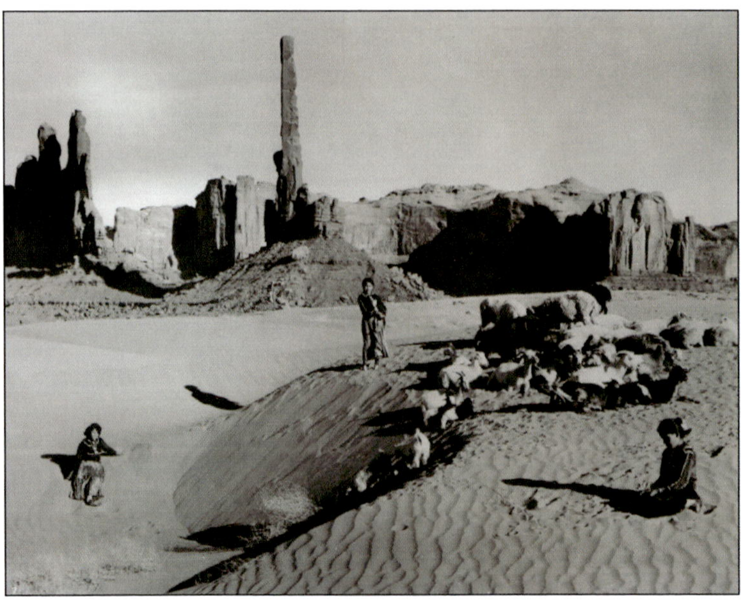

Sheep herders must cover many miles on foot or horseback to find good grazing sites in this arid country. Even young Navajo children have been entrusted with caring for sheep and other livestock. Many Navajo adults recall long childhood days of following their family's flock, occasionally getting distracted or sleepy, then losing a sheep or lamb to a marauding coyote. (US.)

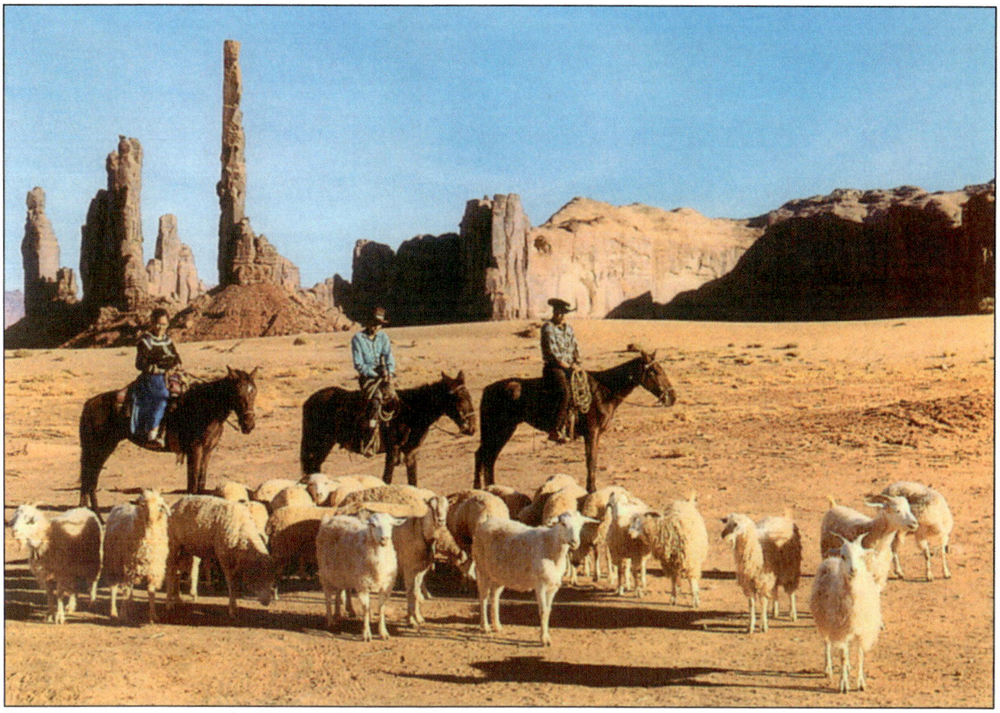

Navajos are not nomads; their traditional lifestyle, at least in some locales, involved moving between a summer and a winter residence, usually separated by no more than a day of travel with a horse and wagon. They followed this pattern for the seasonal well-being of their sheep and for children to attend day schools. In these scenes by Eric J. Seaich (above) and Josef Muench (below), Navajos pose in Monument Valley. Today, herders also use bicycles, motorbikes, and ATVs. People and their guard dogs are sometimes aided by trained guard llamas from South America. (Above, SC; below, NAU-CL, Josef Muench Collection.)

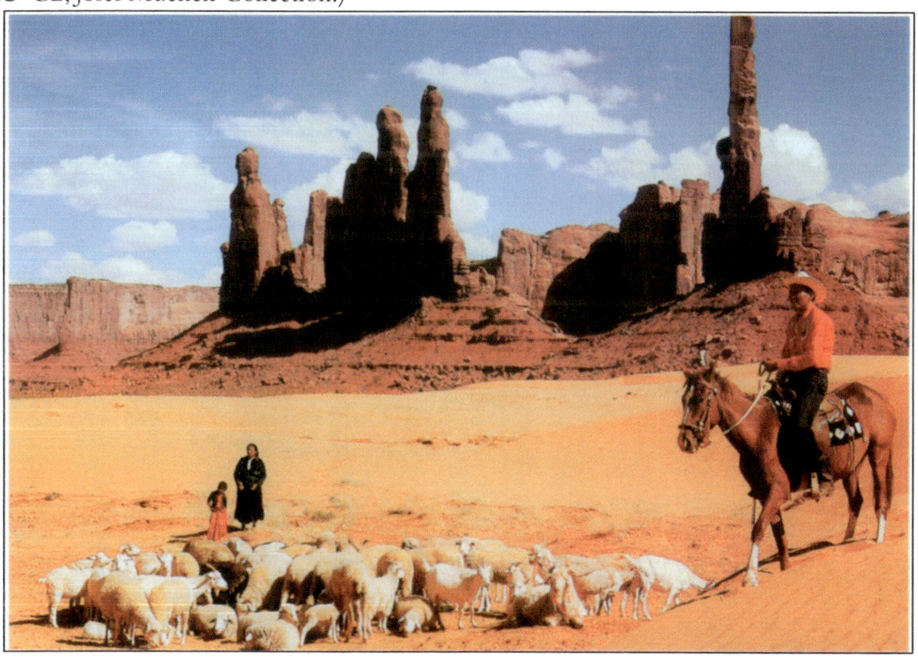

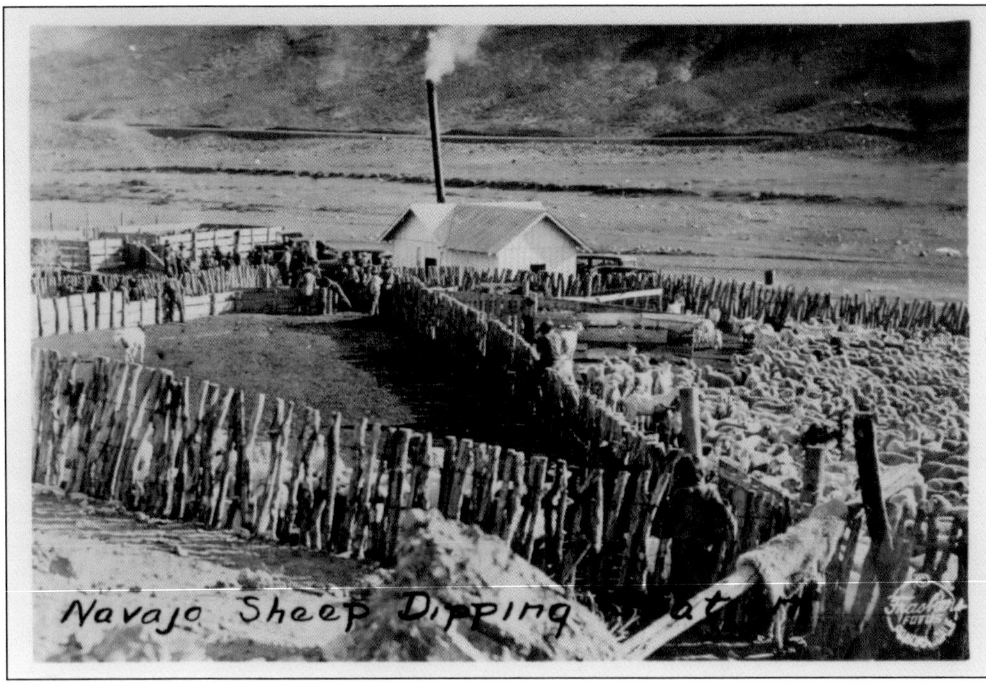

Throughout most of the 20th century, herders drove their flocks to an annual sheep dip, as shown in these 1932 scenes near Ganado, Arizona. The animals were pushed through a trough of chemical-infused water to control deadly parasites. Tribal chapter houses and local trading posts provided the sites for these community gatherings, where socializing, trading, and gaming also took place. Within a year after these photographs were taken, the federal government initiated a campaign to reduce the size of Navajo herds to combat overgrazing and large-scale erosion. Called the Second Long Walk by some, the brutal and insensitive program devastated Navajo families, destroyed their livelihoods, and once again broke Diné faith in Washington's leaders. (Both, FFS.)

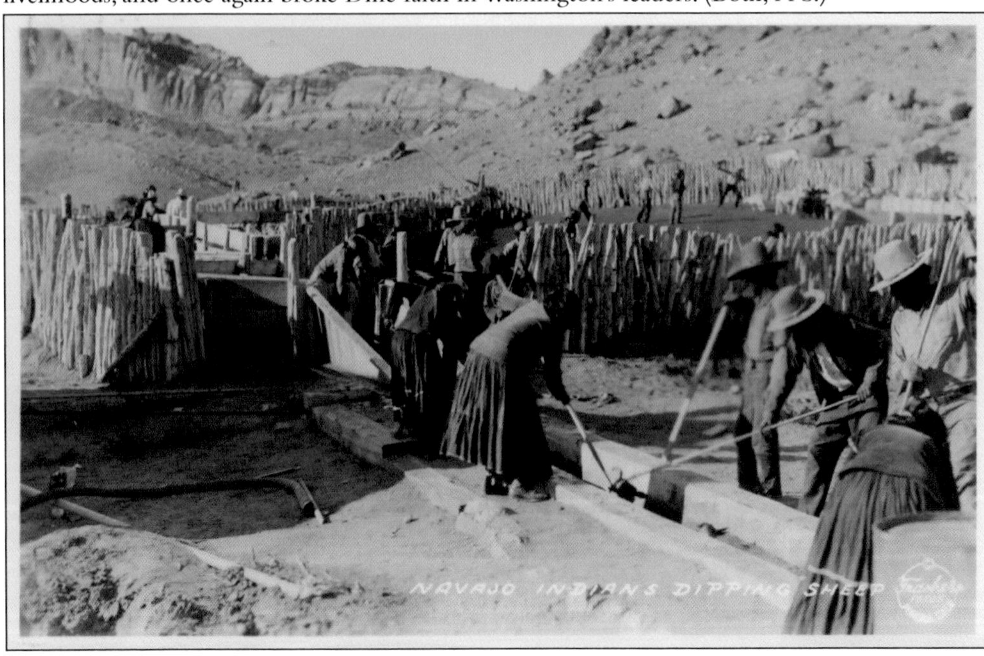

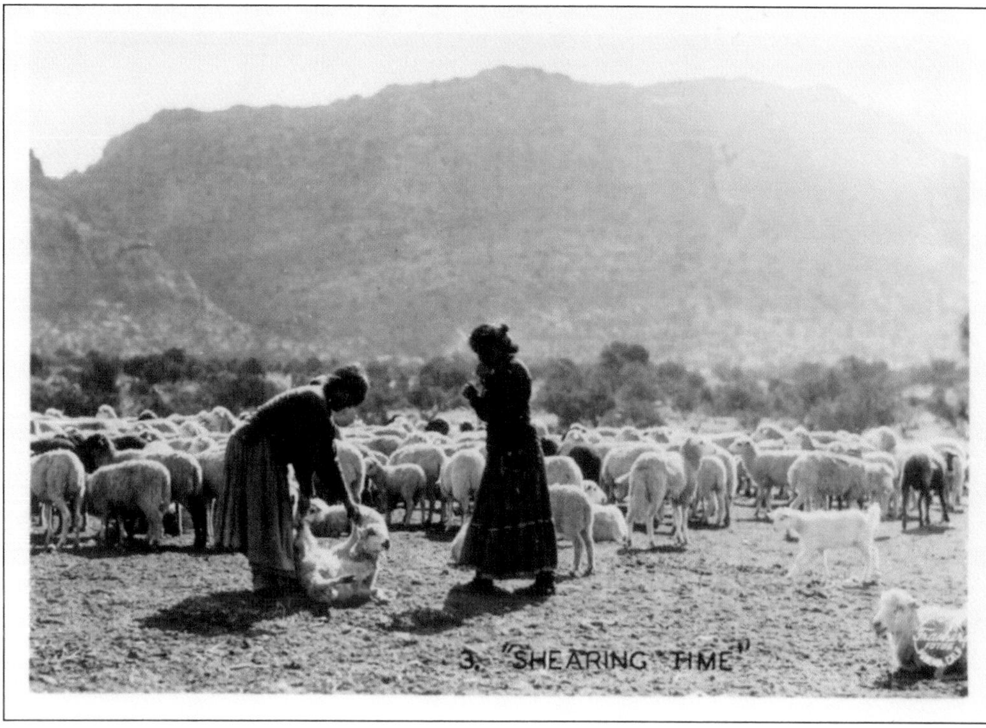

Sheep-shearing usually occurs in late spring, after lambing and before the onset of hot weather. Here, two girls select a sheep to be shorn and flip it onto its back; then, they choose a second animal. They tie the animal's feet together before starting to shear, cutting from the underbelly toward the sides and back. (Both, FFS.)

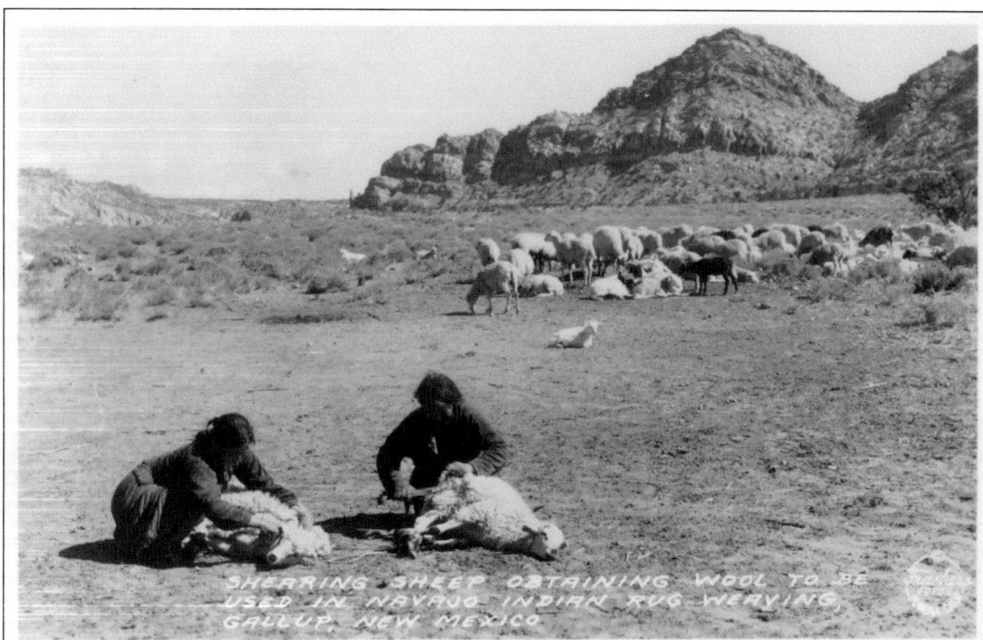

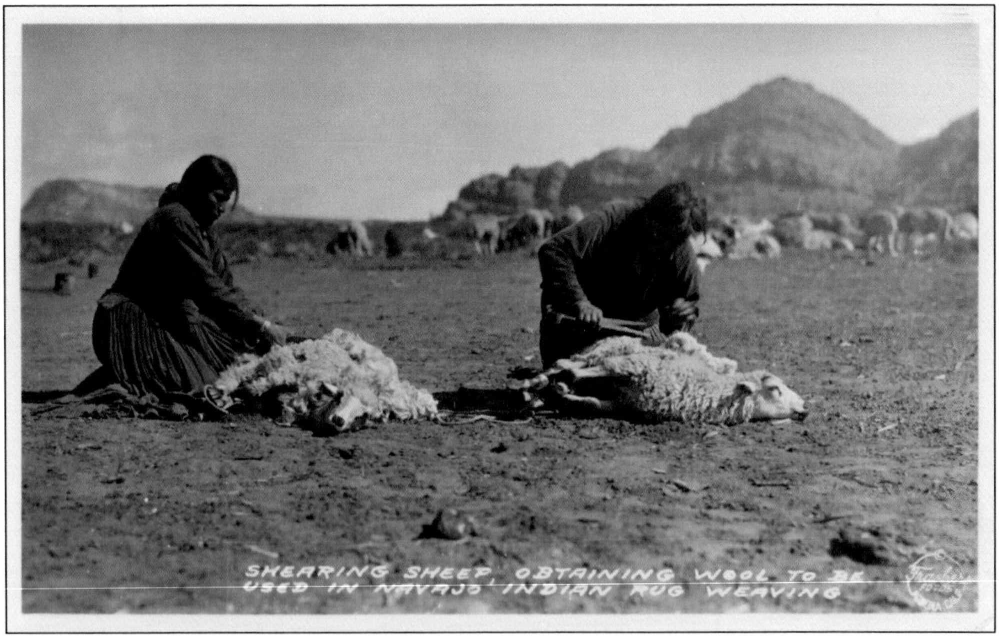

Store-bought steel hand shears (*bee tá'dígéshí*), now available online and still used by some families, have a spring-loaded handle for quick scissoring. Their long blades must be sharpened often to make a crisp cut. Before these were available, shearers used a large butcher knife or the sharp edge of steel cans to shear sheep, albeit not smoothly. Nowadays, when electricity or a generator is available, electric shears are sometimes employed. No matter what tools are used, care is taken so that the sheep's skin is not nicked and the wool is not stained. (Both, FFS.)

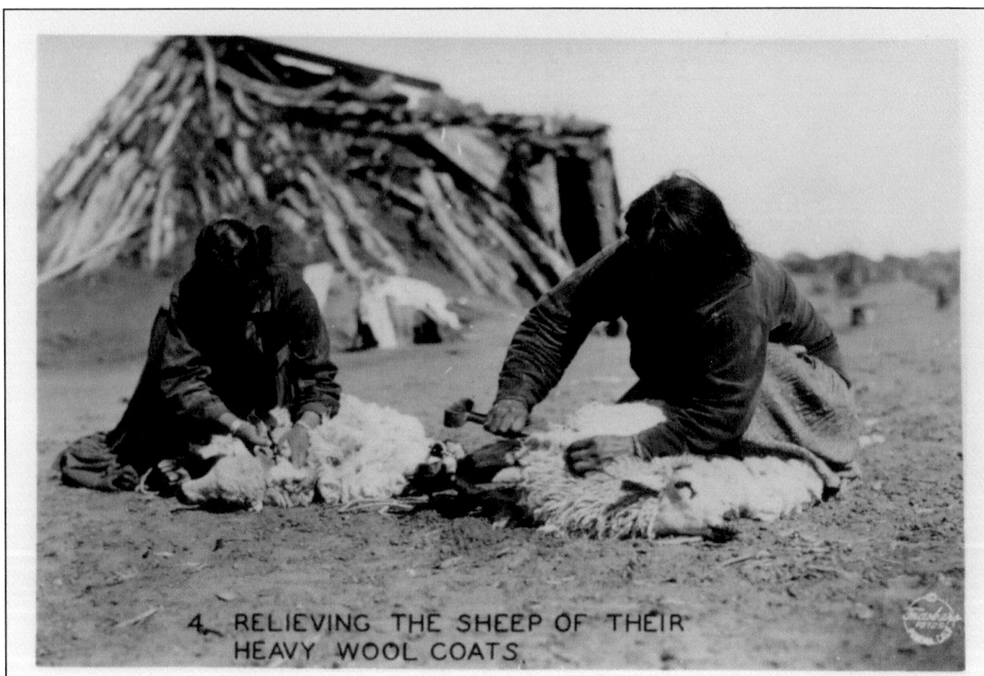

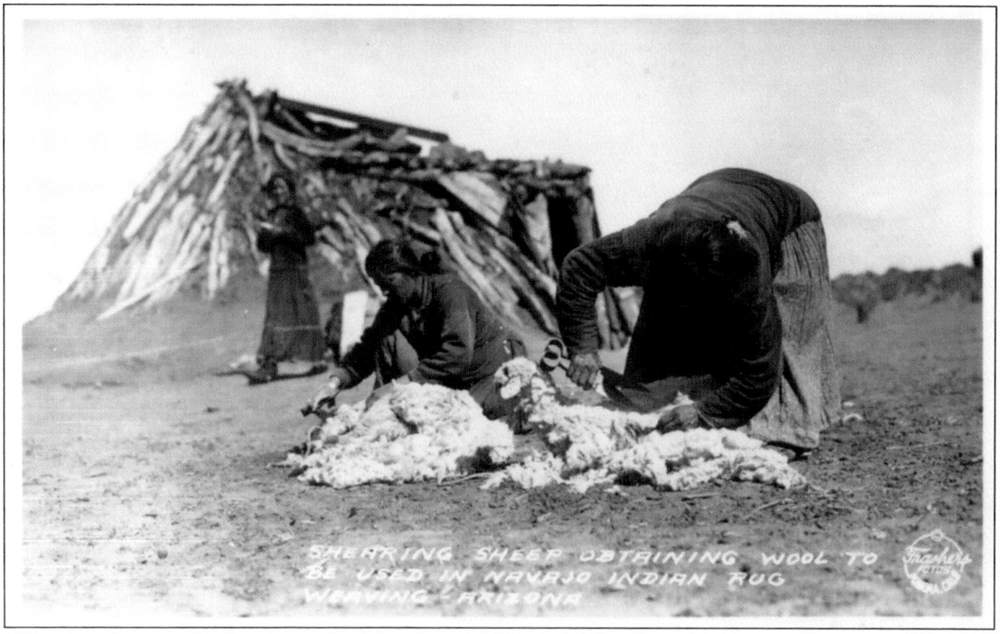

Who is winning the race between these two shearers? The fleece is generally removed in one piece, like unzipping an animal from a hooded coat. This keeps the fleece clean and makes it easier to sort the wool. Once the sheep are shorn, they often frolic and gambol in celebration of their new haircuts. Instead of being washed in water, the fresh-cut fleece (*agha' daníjool*), which is full of oily lanolin, is spread on the ground to dry out. Sometimes rubbing it with white gypsum clay (*łeesh łigaai*) absorbs oil and grease. Once aired out, the wool is hand-sorted by quality—belly wool is finest; back hair is coarser and sunburned; head, leg, and tail wool fibers are shorter. (Above, FFS; below, US.)

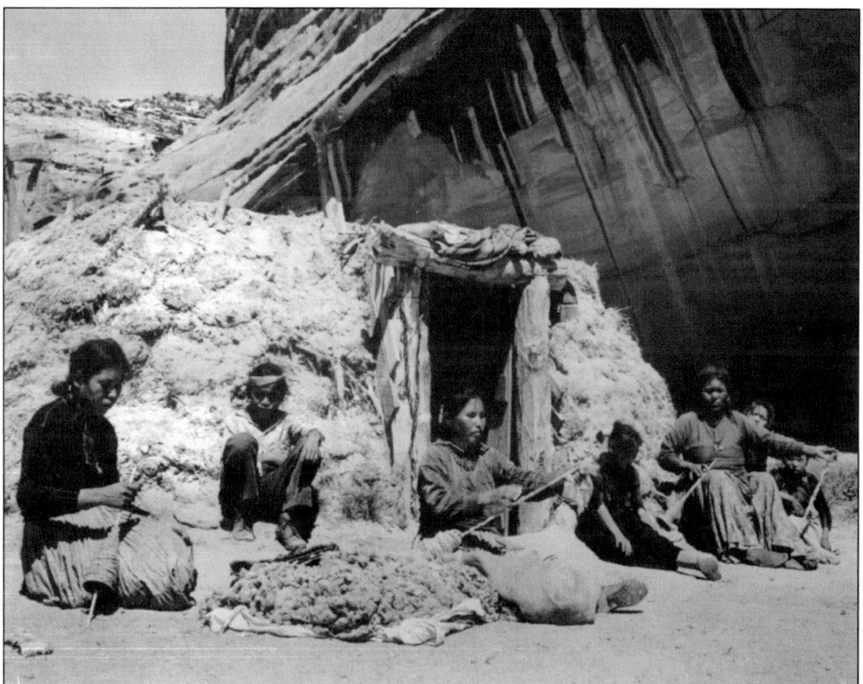

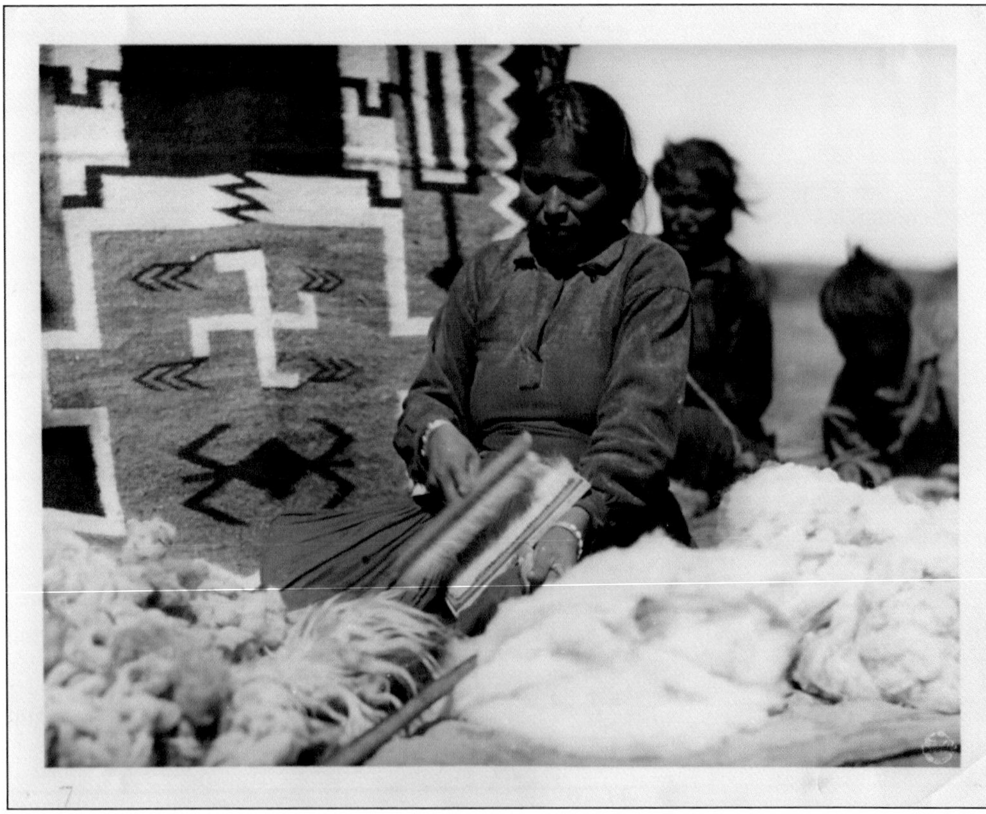

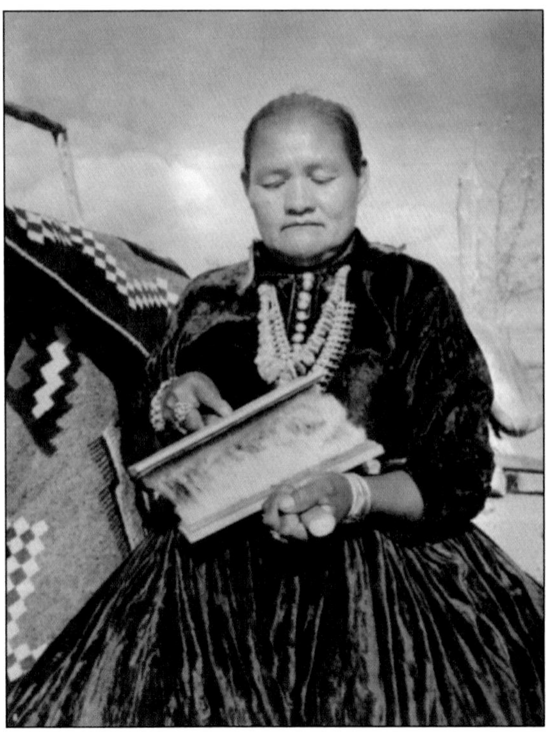

To create handspun yarn that is smooth and even, sheep's wool is carefully sorted, picked apart by hand, and laid onto a pair of handheld commercial carders—flat wooden tools with sharp metal teeth and stiff handles, also sometimes called "cards" (*bee ha'nilchaadí*). The wool batt is repeatedly stroked until most loose debris falls out and the combed wool fibers are aligned in one direction. (Above, FFS; left, US.)

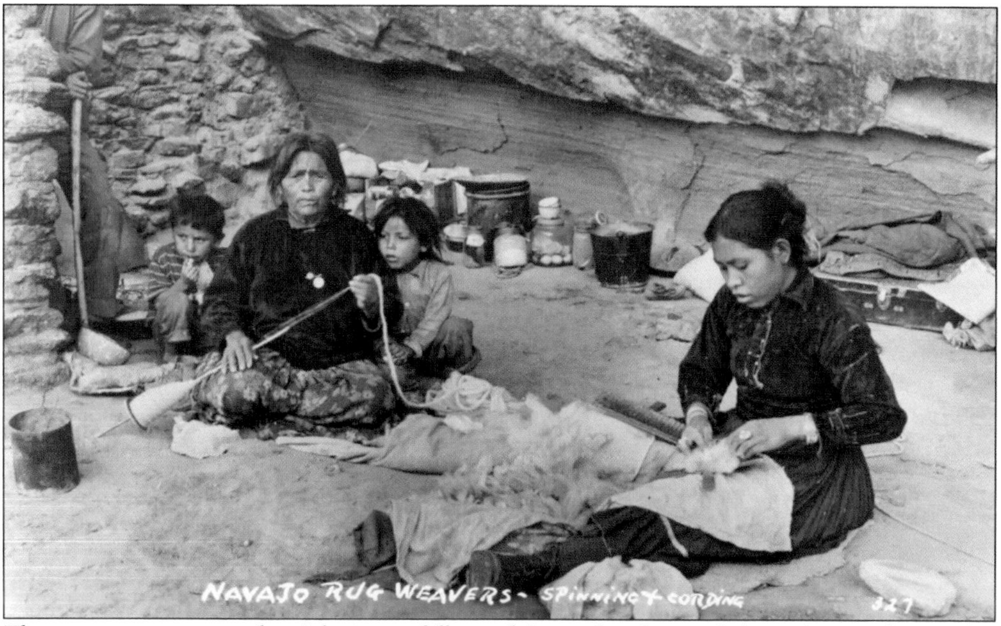

The young woman on the right is carefully applying tufts of uncarded wool across her carder. Spinners say that the amount of hand-sorting and picking of the raw wool determines the fineness of yarn they spin. The elder woman on left is spinning a fine, thin yarn from a pencil-thin strand of wool already loosely spun at least once. (CSNM.)

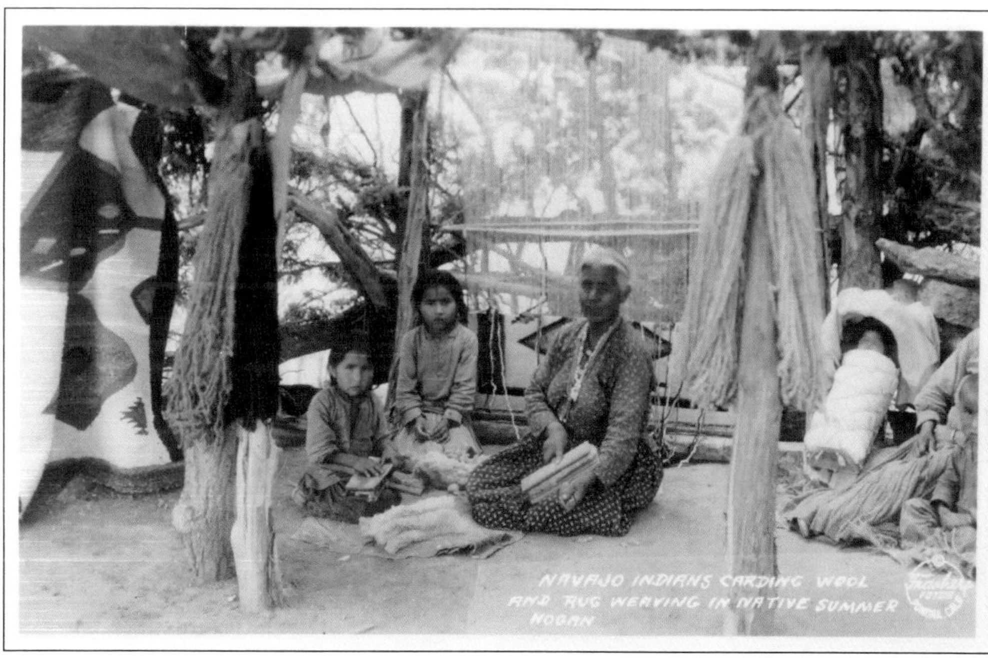

Although these little girls, pictured near Cedar Ridge Trading Post in 1932, appear stage-struck, Navajo children often eagerly engaged in sorting and carding wool for their families. Many Navajo adults fondly recall helping their mothers, aunts, and grandmothers with these tasks. Carded wool was also used as batting inside handmade quilts. Handspun wool, dyed in several colors, hangs in skeins from the shade house supports. (FFS.)

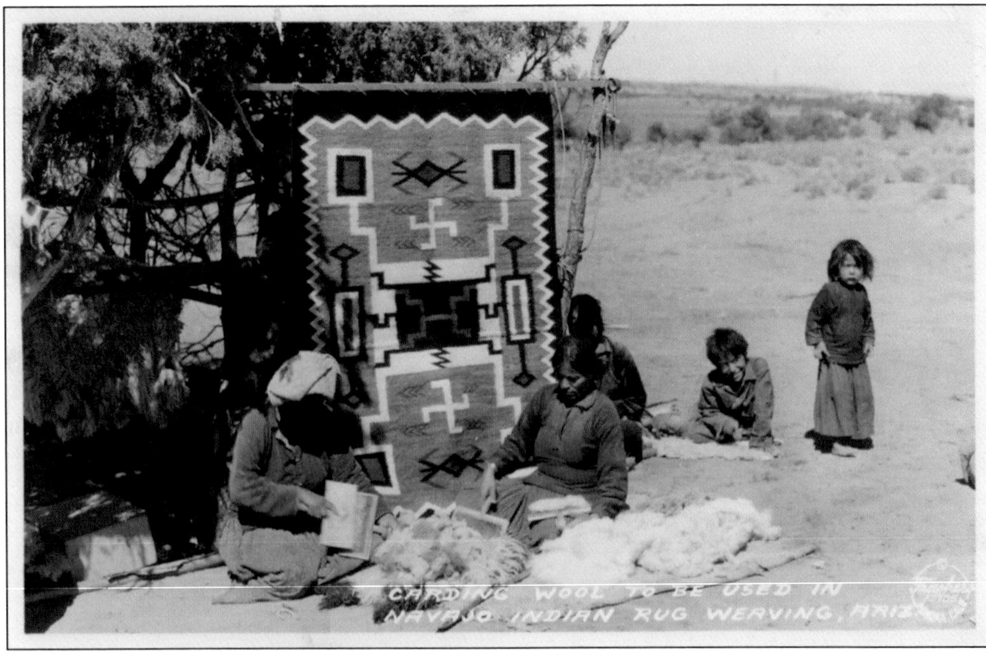

These women are carding pure white wool, but one postcard also states, "The black and white wool is 'combed' together to obtain the grey yarn." In addition, there are sheep with natural gray-brown coats (*'aghaa' łibáí*) that do not need blending and are highly valued by weavers. The background color of this rug shows rich shades of such natural gray. Natural "black" sheep's wool is rarely a deep tone but rather a dark brown that gets sun-faded on the sheep's back. Natural black is often overdyed with a natural or synthetic black colorant to get a darker color. (Both, FFS.)

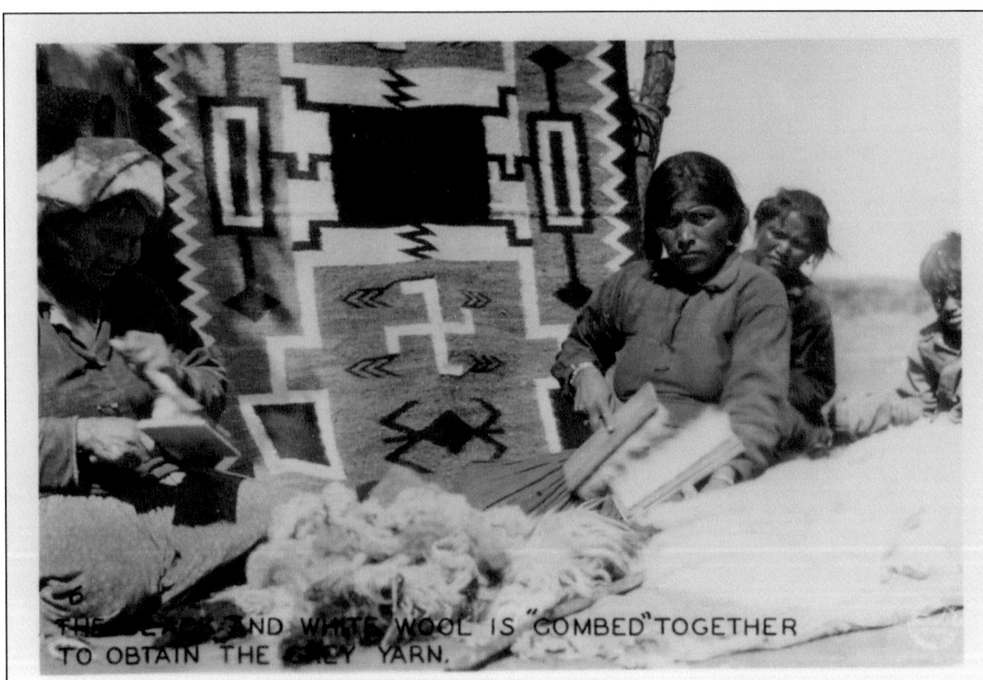

Once sheep's wool is sufficiently carded, the smoothed woolen batt is rolled off the cards to form a cylinder in which the fibers are spirally aligned. After the weaver lifts this "rolag" (a Scottish Gaelic term) from the card, the clean and fluffy wool (*'aghaa' hanoolchaad*) is ready to spin. Later in the 20th century, commercially cleaned, carded, and dyed "processed wool" cut short this laborious process. (FFS.)

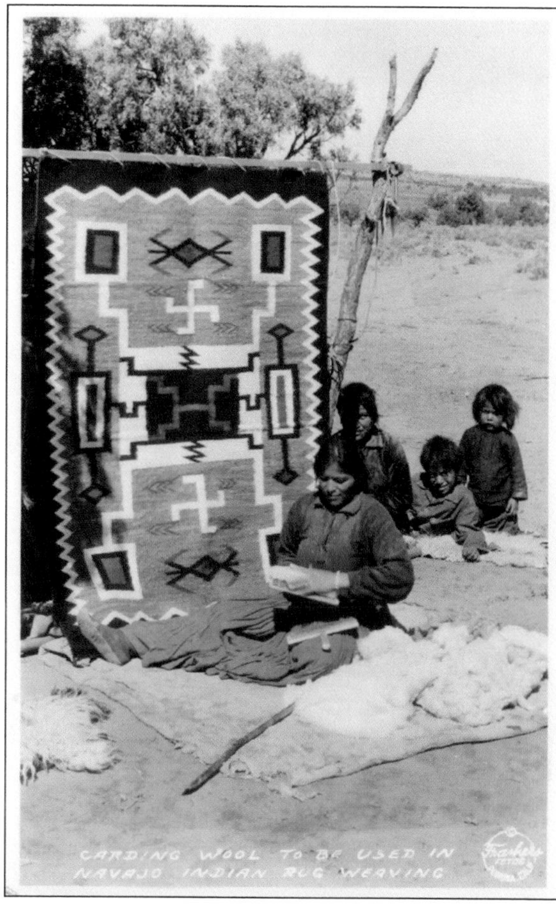

Weaver Happy Cly is carding natural black wool (or possibly wool dyed red—see following pages). The rug on her loom shows off the speckled "combed gray" along with a dark color (likely black not red) and natural white. Although labeled "N.M." (for New Mexico), this scene took place near the Cly home in Monument Valley, which spans Arizona and Utah. (CSNM.)

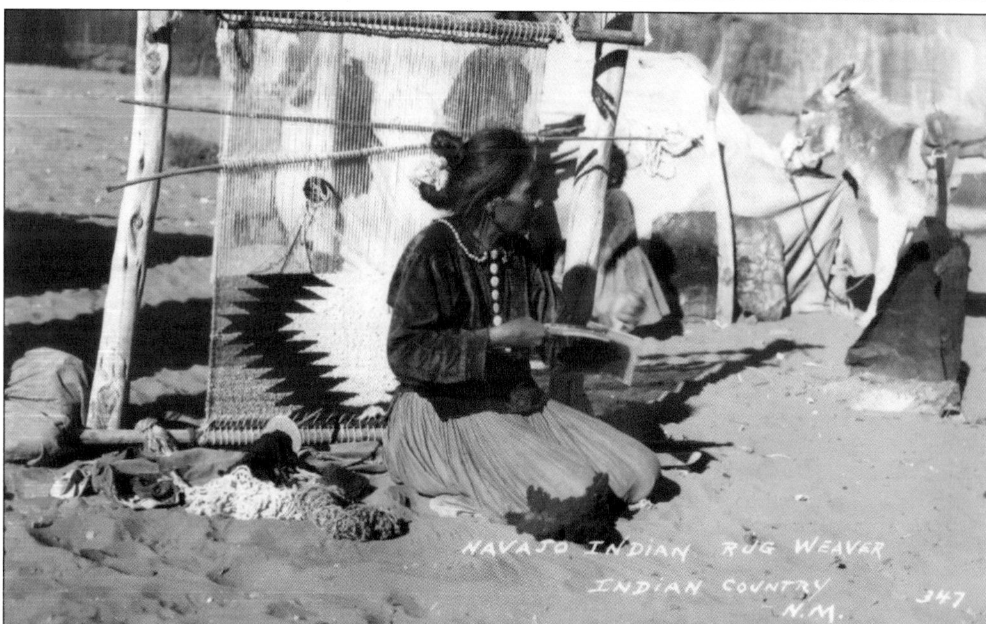

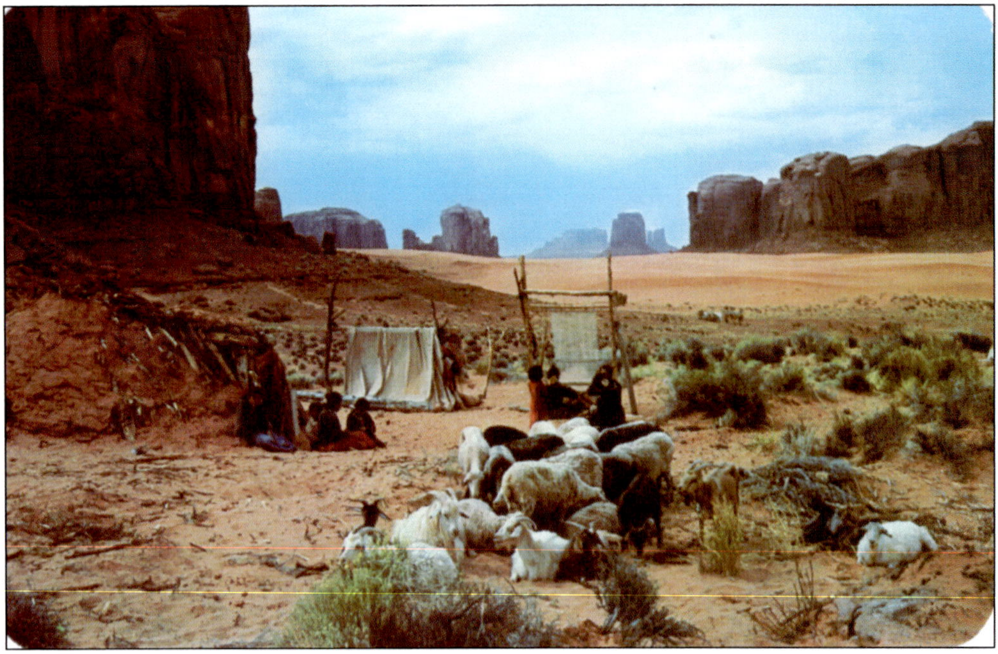

This idyllic Diné scene in Monument Valley underscores the romantic beauty of the American Southwest. Meanwhile, the practical Navajo herd includes white, gray-brown, and dark brown-black sheep, plus several goats with horns. Colored wool is prized by weavers who use it as-is and overdye it for darker shades. Commercial wool buyers avoid it, as dark fibers would contaminate their marketable white stock. (Roach; Sanborn Souvenir.)

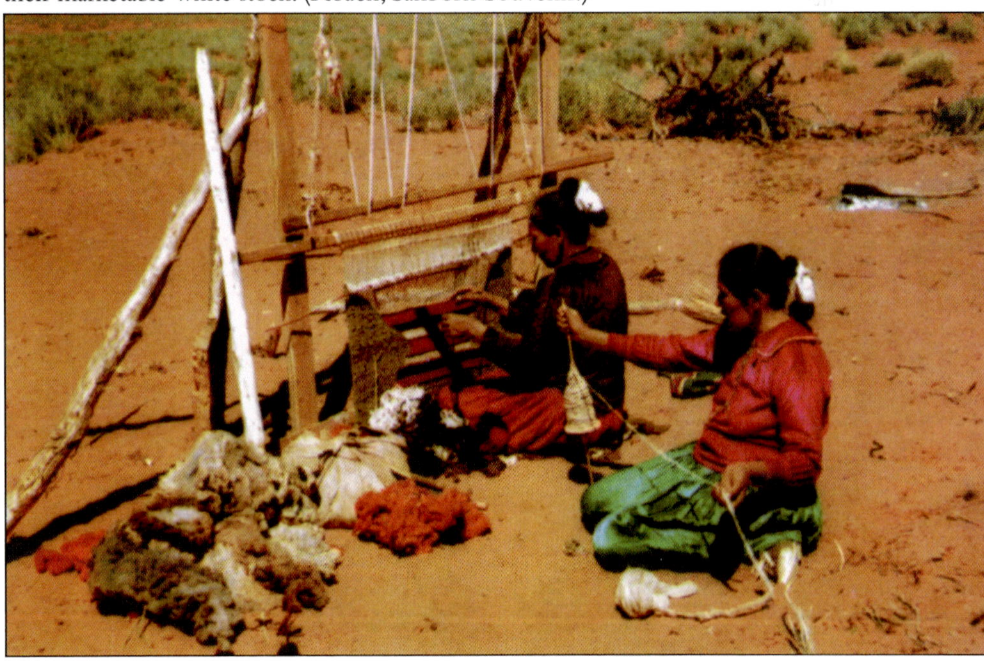

A "Jacob sheep" fleece in variegated grays and browns is laid in the foreground. On Happy Cly's loom, the gray triangles are evenly carded examples of this wool. Although the spinner is twisting pure white wool, a clump of unspun red-dyed wool awaits her efforts. Most Diné dyeing takes place after spinning, but raw wool was sometimes dyed beforehand. (LHL.)

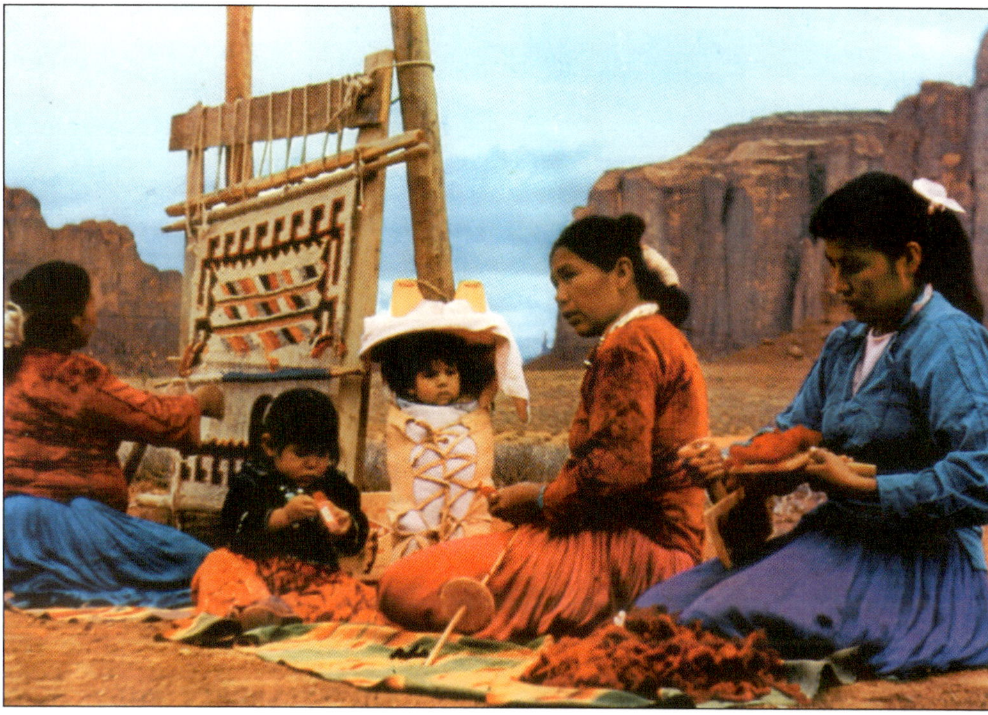

Apparently, red fibers dyed in the wool are being sorted, carded, and handspun in these staged scenes photographed by Eric J. Seaich (above) and Ray Manley (right). This red may actually be a rich natural brown distorted by the color printing of the time. But since it appears in several postcards from different sites and sources, the photographs may attest to the practice of spinning pre-dyed fleece. Dyeing fleece gives weavers the opportunity to blend colors. Weaver Happy Cly, at right, is using the same red color in her rug on the loom. Penciled on the reverse of the postcard at right is "'52" (Above, SC; right, PS.)

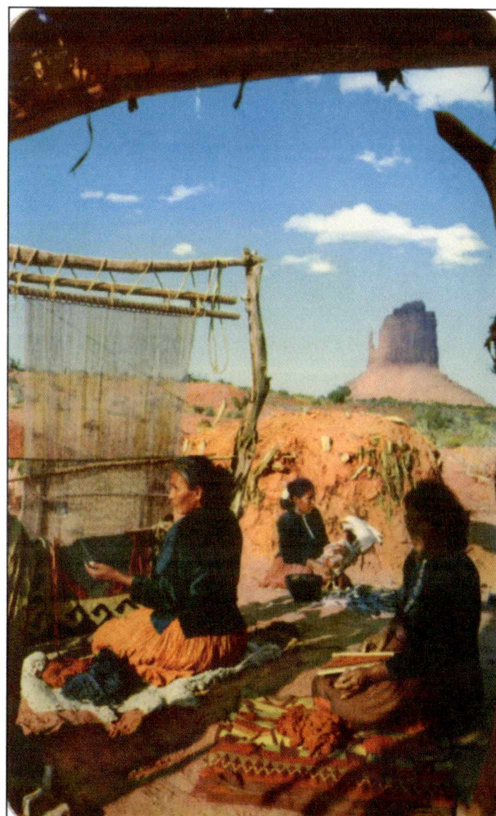

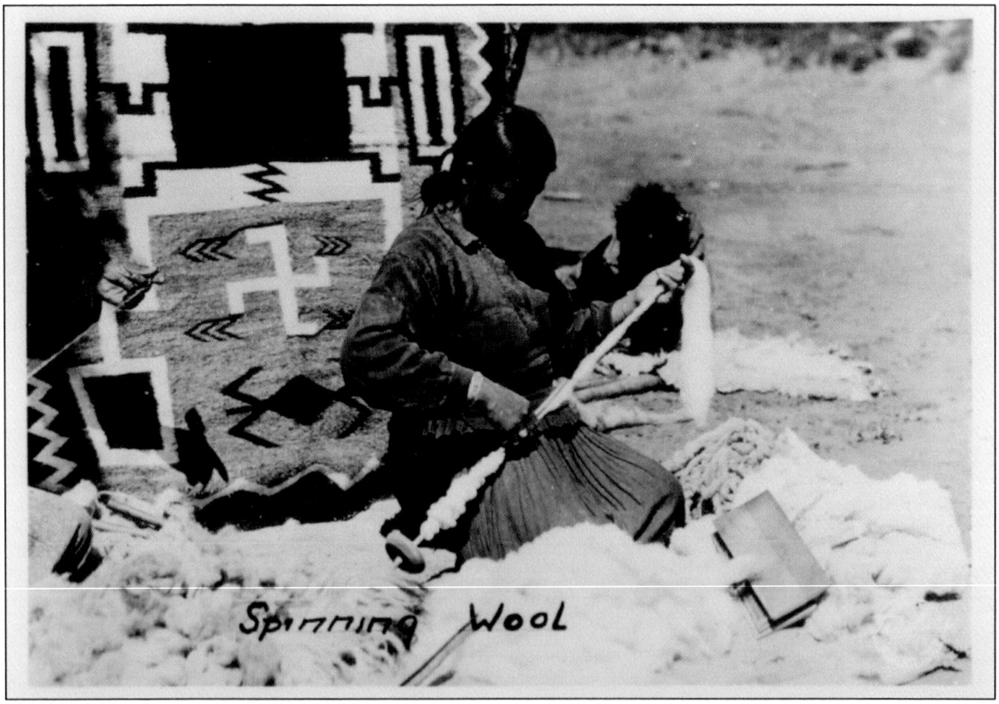

The Navajo handspindle (*bee 'adizí*), also called a thigh or lap spindle, is composed of a long straight stick (spindle) with a flat round disk (whorl or flywheel) attached to the lower end. With a wooly rolag held in her left hand and attached to the spindle's tip, the spinner rolls the spindle up her thigh with her right hand, giving the wool a slight twist (above). She then holds the spindle upright and wraps the first-spun wool around the spindle (below). These actions are repeated many times to create a continuous length of rough-spun wool. While the wooden tools aid with momentum and yarn storage, the spinner's fingers and hands do most of the work, manipulating the wool and smoothing out the resultant yarn. (Both, FFS.)

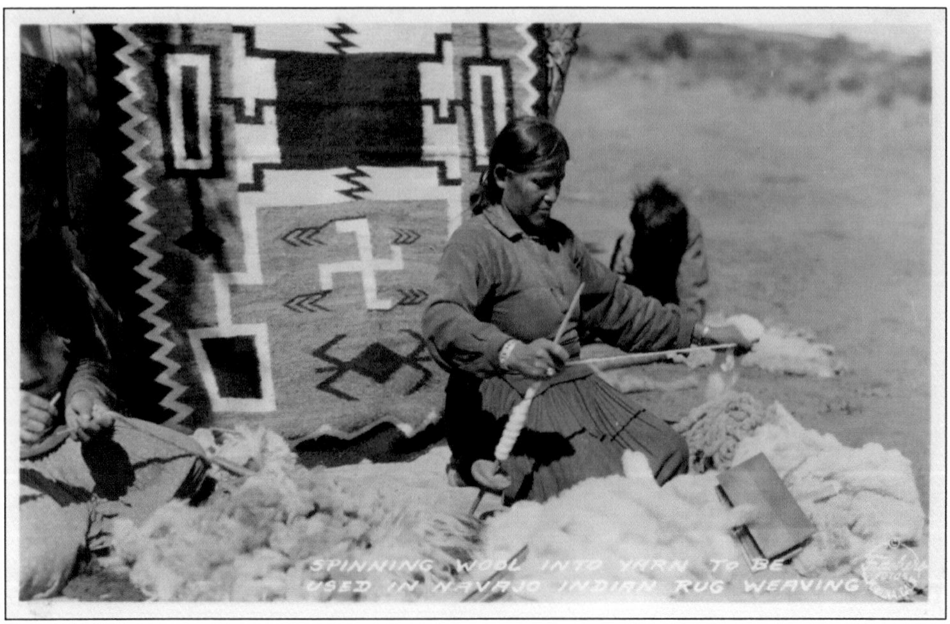

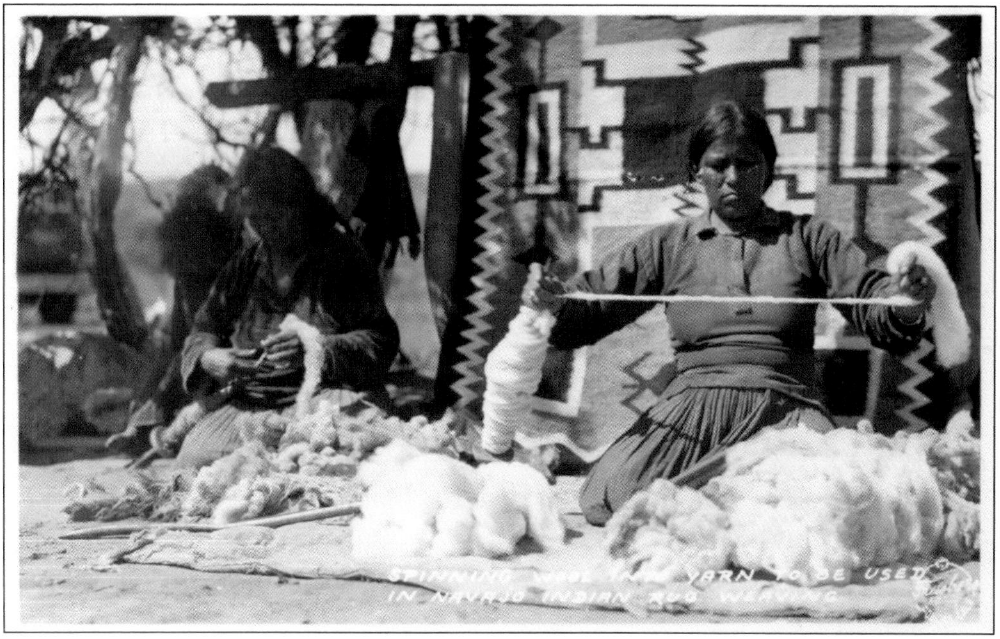

Navajo hand-spinning involves several phases in which the wool may be twisted and re-spun once or twice for the weft (pattern) yarns or as many as six or seven times to make stronger, smoother warp (foundation) yarns. Here, the women are doing the first spin of their carded rolags, giving a little twist and stretching out the aligned fibers. With subsequent spinnings, the yarn will become thinner and tighter. As more yarn wraps around the spindle, the added weight makes it easier to continue the twisting action. When a spindle stick is fully loaded with first-spun wool, the soft strands are removed and form a loose pile or large ball of semi-spun wool. (Both, FFS.)

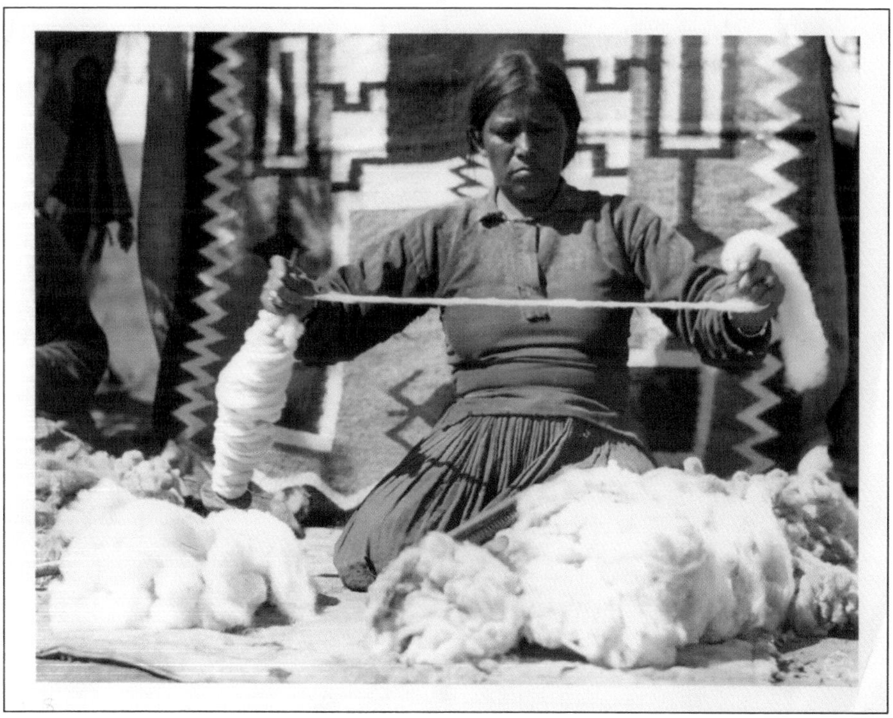

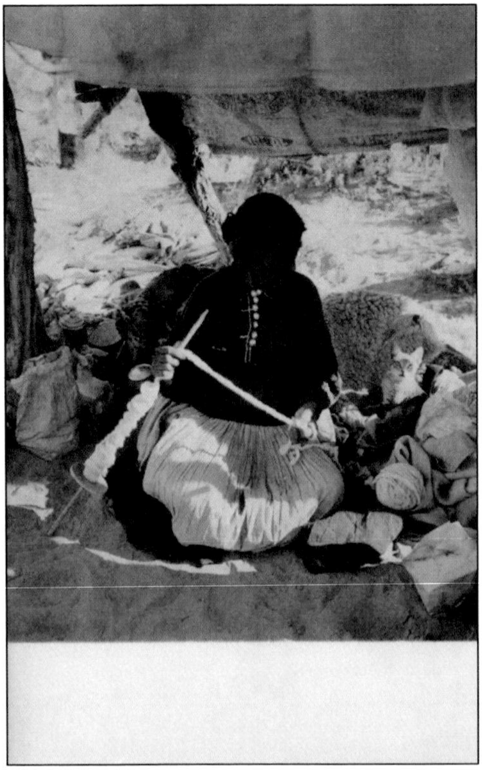

A Diné woman is "helped" by a cat in this sentimental 1940s photograph titled "Navaho Woman Spinning," by Laura Gilpin. Navajo spinners spin in a clockwise ("sunwise") fashion, drawing the spindle toward themselves and imparting a Z-twist to their yarns. When strands are plied together for strength and weight, they are twisted in the opposite direction, resulting in an S-twist. This photograph is reproduced with permission from Amon Carter Museum of American Art, Fort Worth, Texas, © 1979.

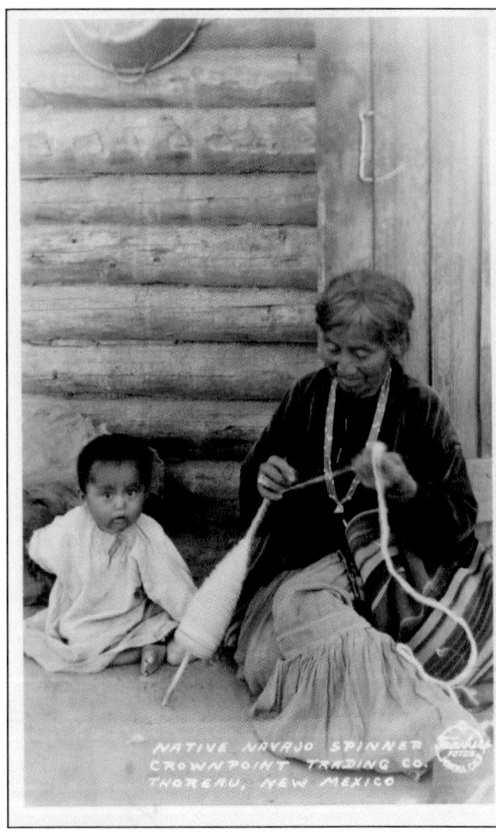

Using her fingers adeptly, this elder spinner smooths and stretches fibers into a fine, tightly twisted yarn. She will repeat this until she is satisfied with her yarn's size and texture. Older Navajo women often spin for younger weavers in their family. Their useful roles continue, even when poor eyesight and reduced coordination prevent them from weaving. (FFS.)

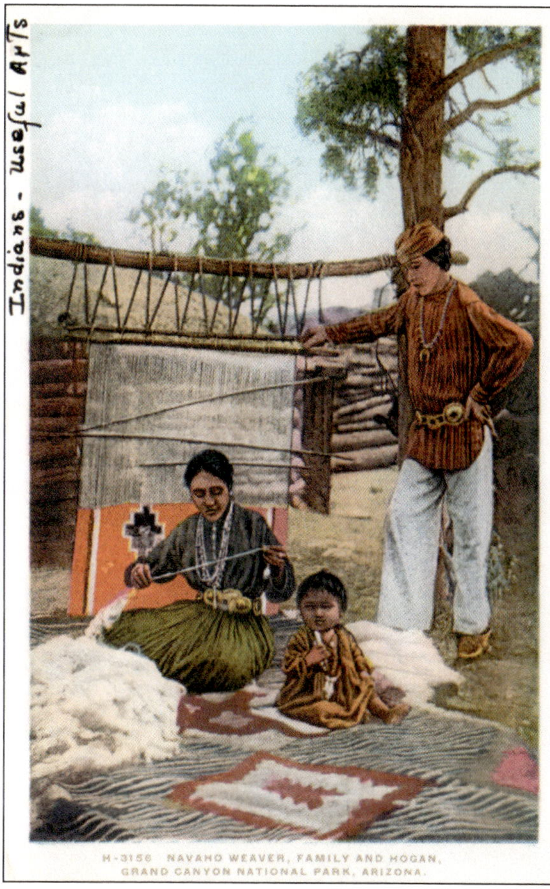

In the early 1900s, Navajo families were hired to demonstrate all aspects of Diné weaving and silversmithing on the South Rim of the Grand Canyon, where a Navajo-style home and the Hopi House salesroom designed by Mary Jane Colter were built. Wool carding and spinning fascinated the public as much as weaving. Yarn-making was also essential to keep the weavers supplied with working materials. The woman wearing a green skirt is spinning freshly carded wool rolags. The woman in a pink skirt is re-spinning dark brown wool from continuous strands of first-spun wool. The man and boy are dressed alike in clothing, jewelry, and concho belts that were not worn every day. (Both, FHC.)

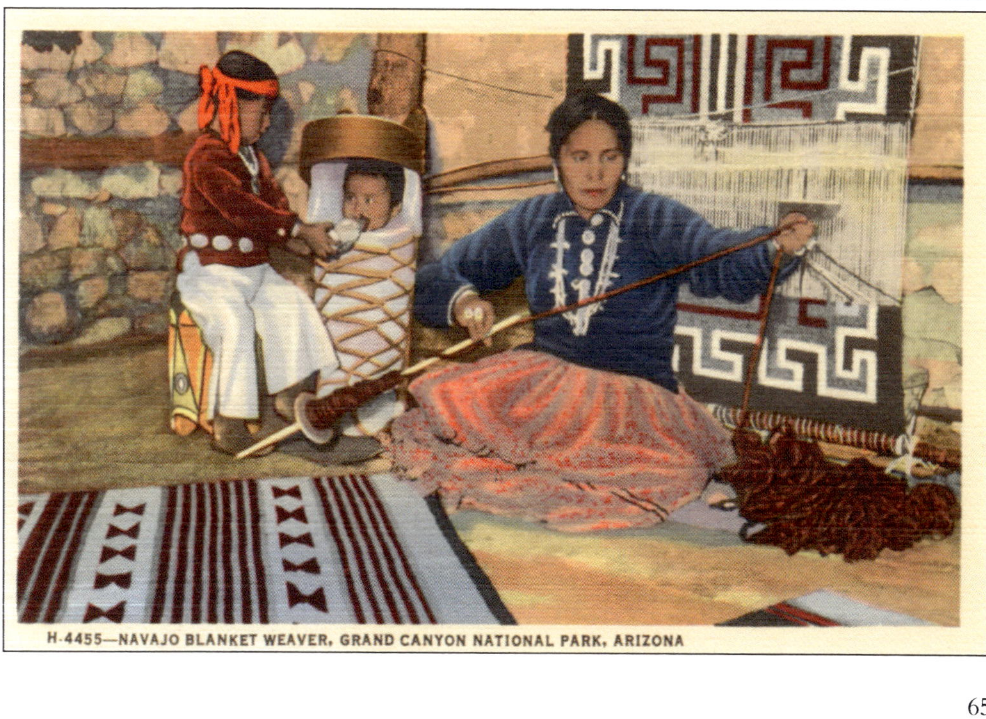

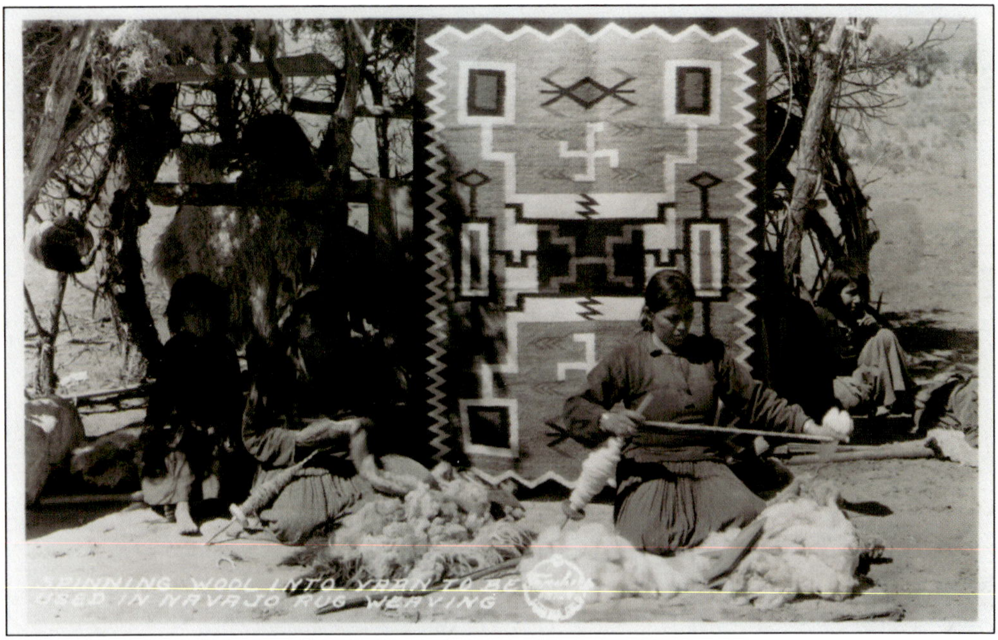

The spinning scene repeated in these postcards brings back nostalgic memories for many Navajos. For an additional picturesque touch, the baby wrapped in its cradleboard was added to the hand-tinted postcard! The classic "Storm Pattern" rug, popular since the early 1900s, serves as a backdrop throughout this postcard series. Stories about its symbolism vary—the central rectangle represents a fire, hogan, lake, or "storm house"; the stepped radiating lines are zigzag lightning; the four corner boxes are the sacred mountains, winds, or cardinal directions. Motifs of a "water bug" (red and black) and "whirling log" (white and red *náhookǫs*, or swastika) sit at each end. Another Storm Pattern rug appears on pages 108–109. Penciled on the reverse of the card shown below is "1933." (Both, FFS.)

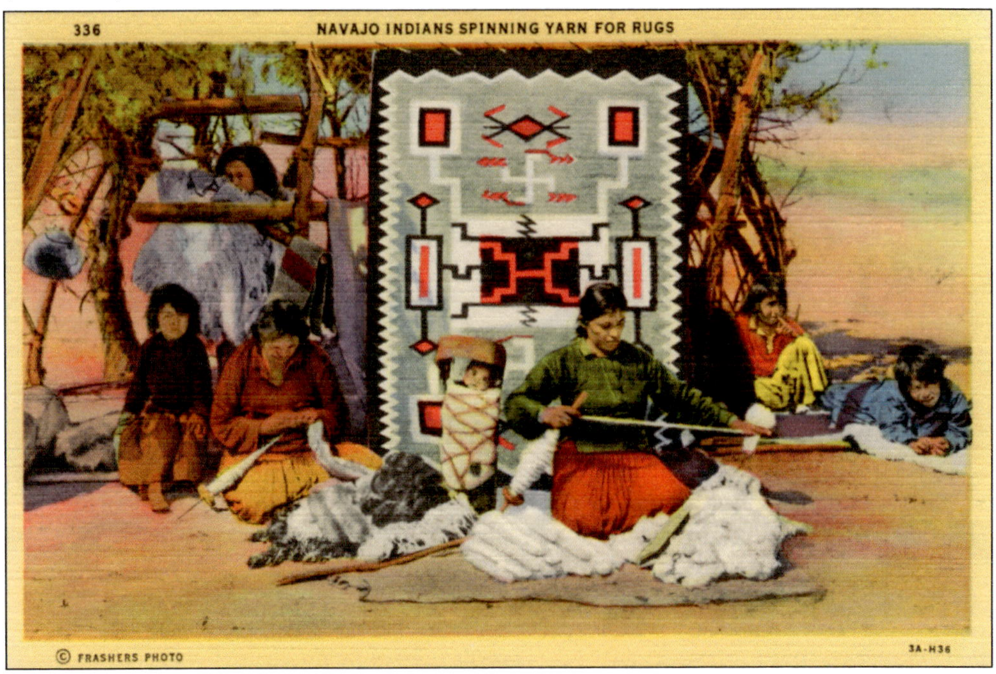

This Navajo woman may be using her handspindle to re-spin wool from the ball of rough-spun wool. Alternately, she may be transferring rough-spun wool from her handspindle to the large ball. Either way, she is midway through a series of time-consuming processes resulting in finely handspun wool, ready to use in its natural color or to be dyed with vegetal or synthetic color sources. (US.)

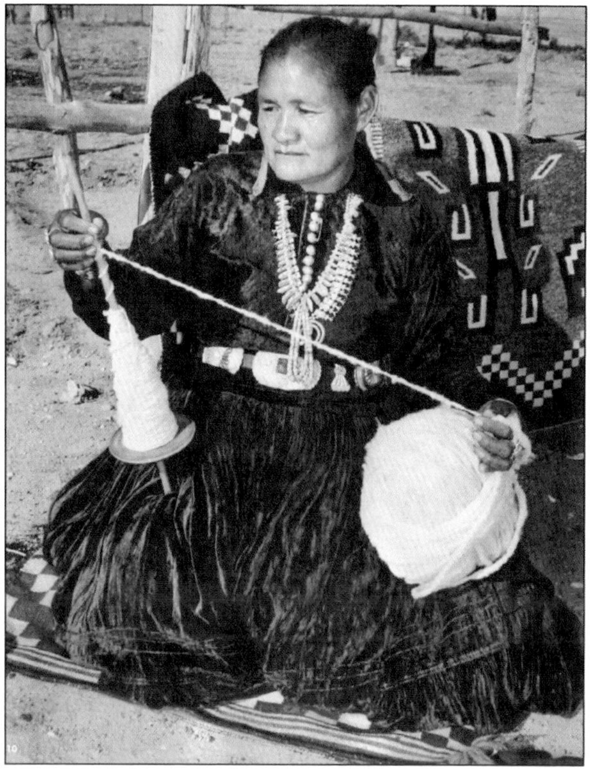

Large balls of thickly spun wool await re-spinning into yarns like those in this weaver's handsome rug-in-progress. In this photograph, titled "Navajo Weaver, Canyon de Chelly, Ariz. 1964," by Richard Erdoes and originally measuring 11 by 14 inches, an empty handspindle rests below, ready for the next project. This print is reproduced with permission from Eric Peter Erdoes.

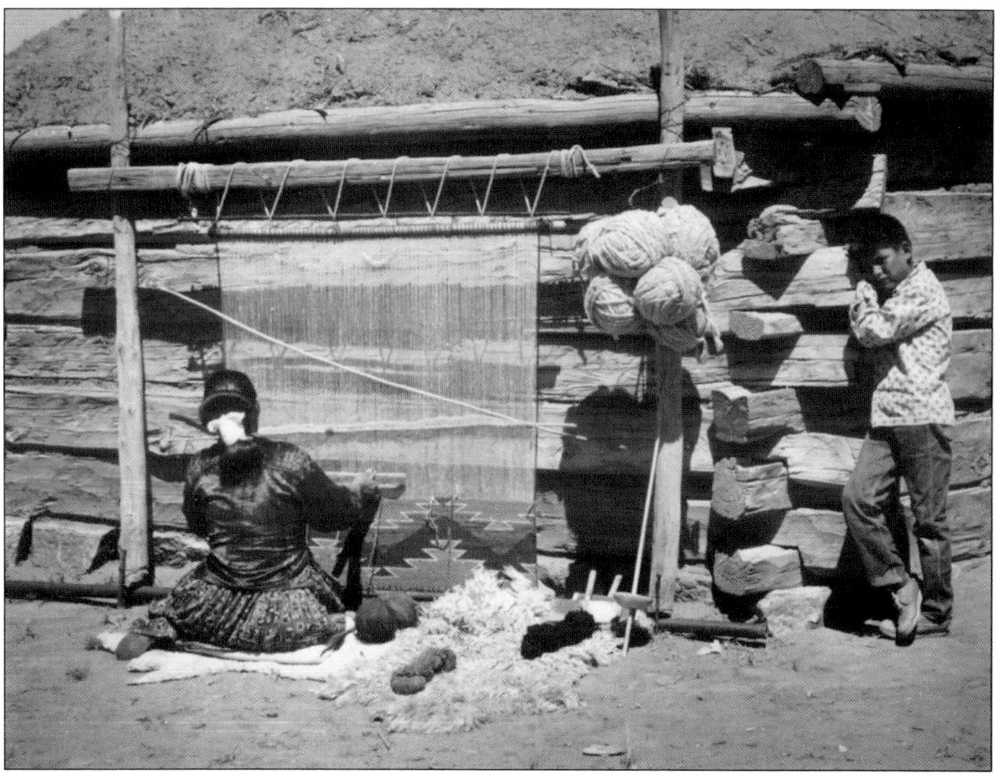

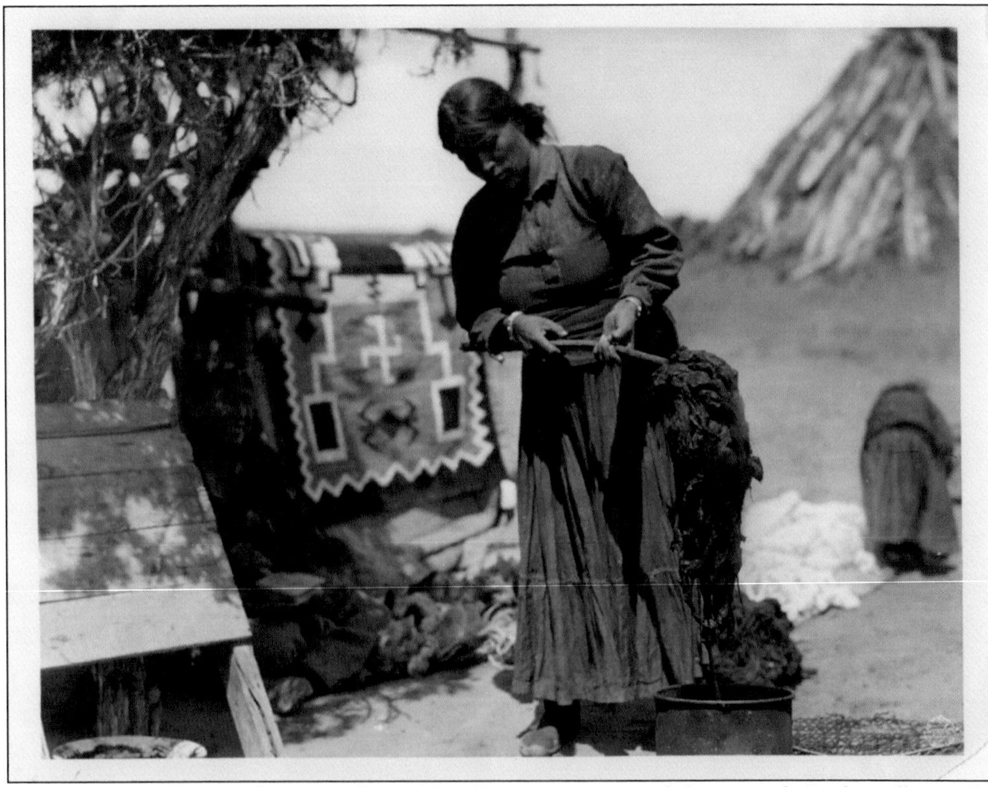

Native plants and minerals were collected locally to create natural dyes, mostly in the yellow, gold, orange, green, and brown range. Since the 1880s, other colors were obtained via store-bought packets of synthetic dyes. Either way, dyeing commonly involved cooking the dyestuff in a pot of water, then simmering skeins of yarn in the concoction. Nearby bushes provided a convenient drying rack. (Both, FFS.)

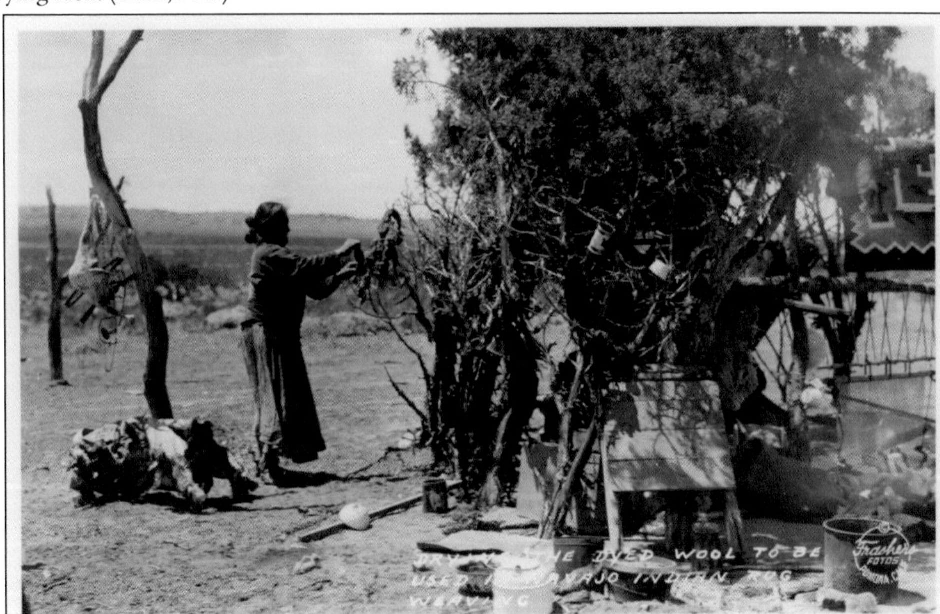

Four

Weaving at Home

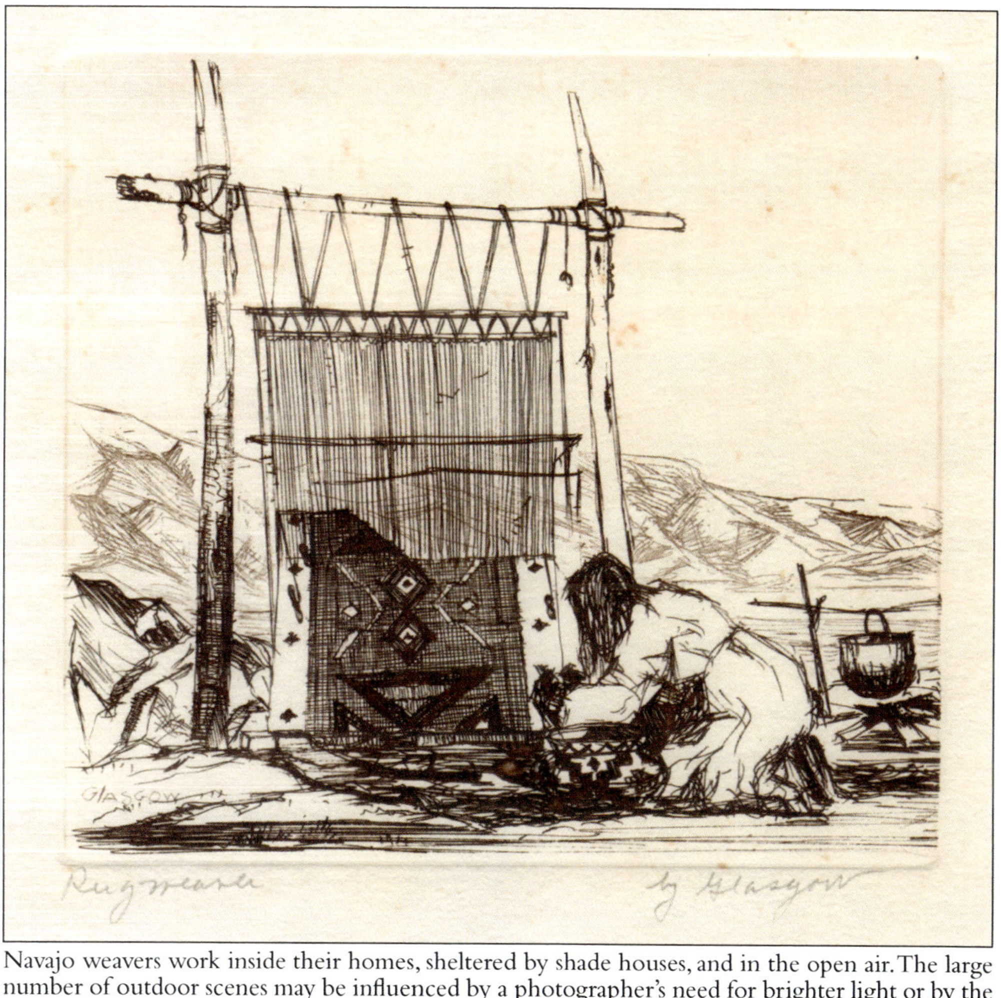

Navajo weavers work inside their homes, sheltered by shade houses, and in the open air. The large number of outdoor scenes may be influenced by a photographer's need for brighter light or by the summer seasons, when visitors travelled to Navajo country. In "Rug Weaver," an etching created by Bernard Glasgow around 1940 and measuring four by four inches, a Navajo woman works near her outdoor kitchen. This print is reproduced with permission from Liz Glasgow.

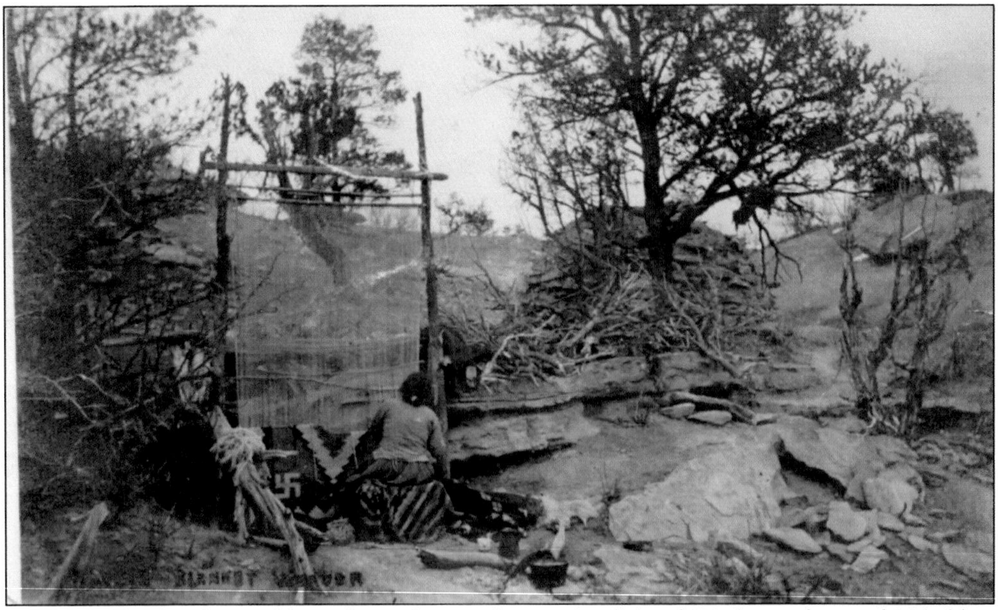

A loom of this height would not fit inside most hogans (traditional Diné round or multisided log, stone, or mud homes like that in the background), nor could it be easily photographed inside the windowless structure. This weaver is working on a large rug with elements popular during the 1890s and 1900s—a central serrated diamond, "whirling log" (*náhookǫs* or swastika) corner motifs, and a terraced border. (US.)

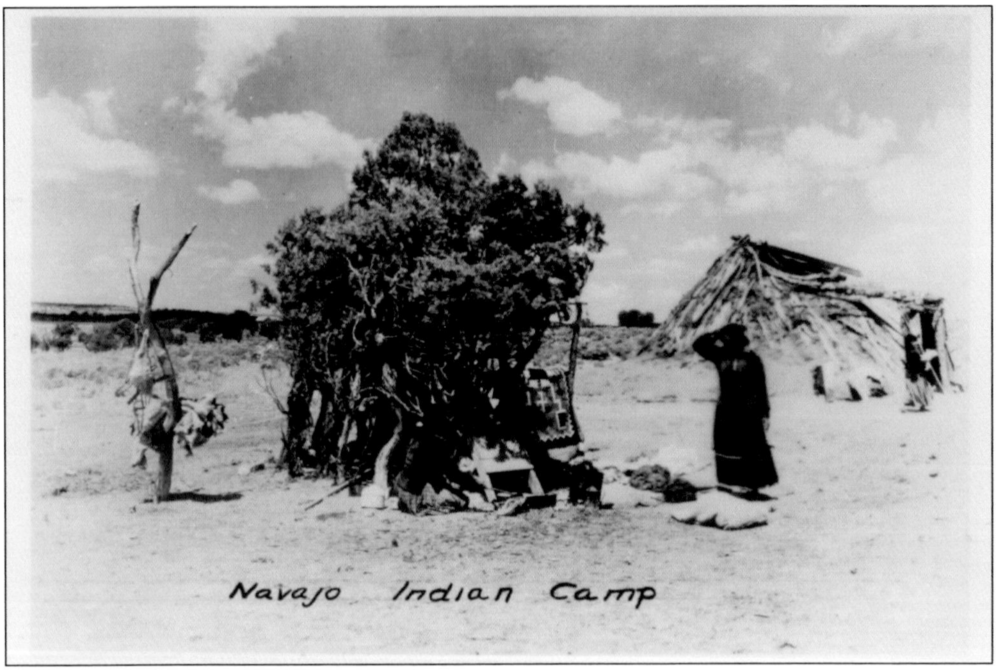

Although they were commonly called "camps" by outsiders, Navajo homesteads were permanent residences occupied seasonally and based on outdoor living. In this windswept scene from the 1930s, a weaver seeks shelter alongside a clump of juniper trees as she cooks on an open fire. A nearby dead tree serves as an outdoor "food safe" to stash bundles that contain dried meat and other foodstuffs. (FFS.)

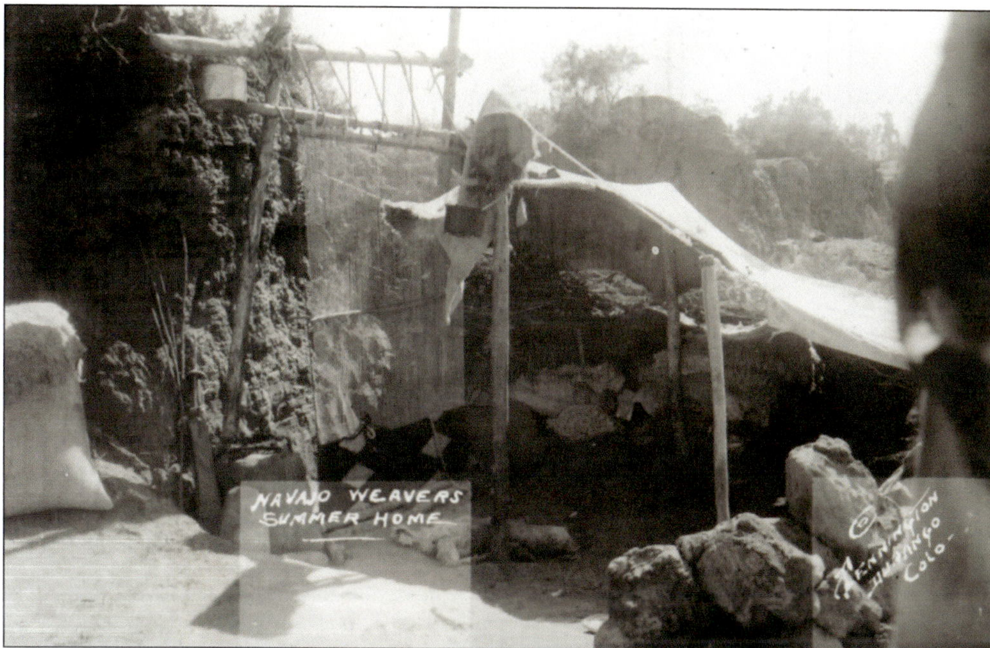

During hot desert weather or rainy mountain conditions, a summer home might simply consist of poles and tarps. This tall loom shares support with the structure. A cookpot and bucket hang on high to preserve their contents from curious animals or children. Extra weaving sticks, a handspindle, and a tool bag sit next to the loom. The tent houses sheepskin bedding and a pile of carded wool. (WPS.)

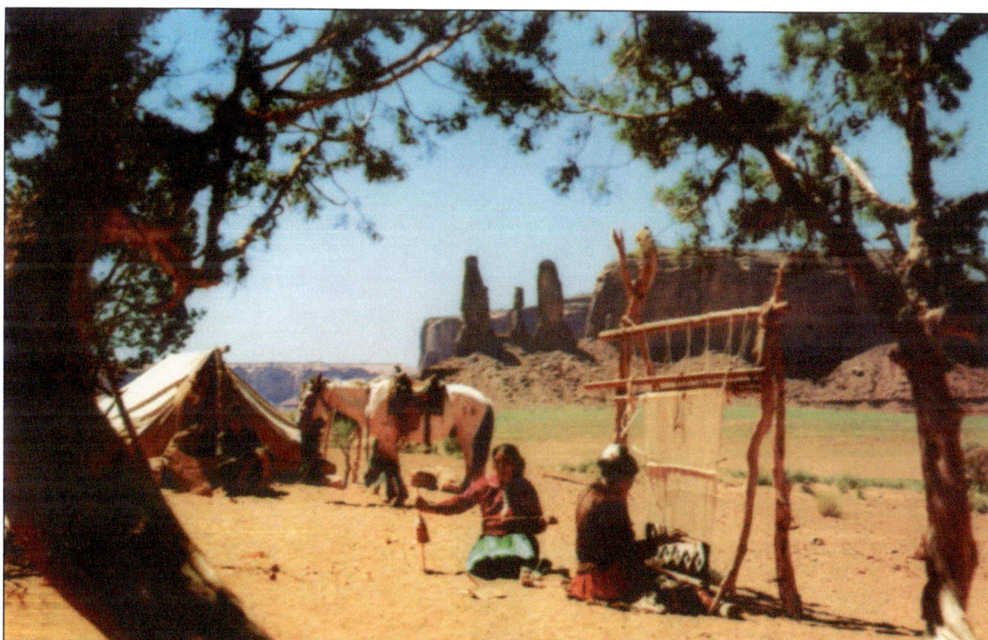

A canvas tent pitched in Monument Valley provides temporary shade while the weaver and spinner pose in the full sun for a visitor's camera. The Cly family, shown here, became famous for hosting many professional and amateur photographers and moviemakers at their homesite in southern Utah. Photography and tour fees supplied a portion of their income for several decades. (LHL.)

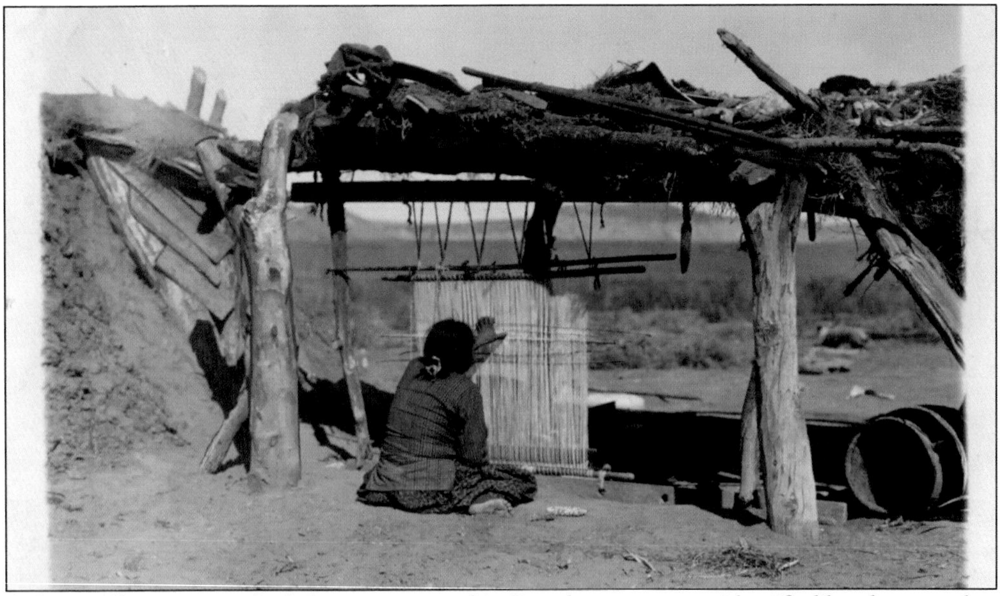

A freestanding summer shade house protects this Ganado-area weaver identified by photographer George H. Pepper in 1904 as the wife of Many Horses. The flat roof consists of timbers, sticks, and brush. Posed in the sun at the back of her loom, the weaver just prepared her loom for a twill-weave saddle blanket. This five-by-seven-inch print matches a glass plate [N02448] and a lantern slide [L01494] at the National Museum of the American Indian, Smithsonian Institution, Washington, DC.

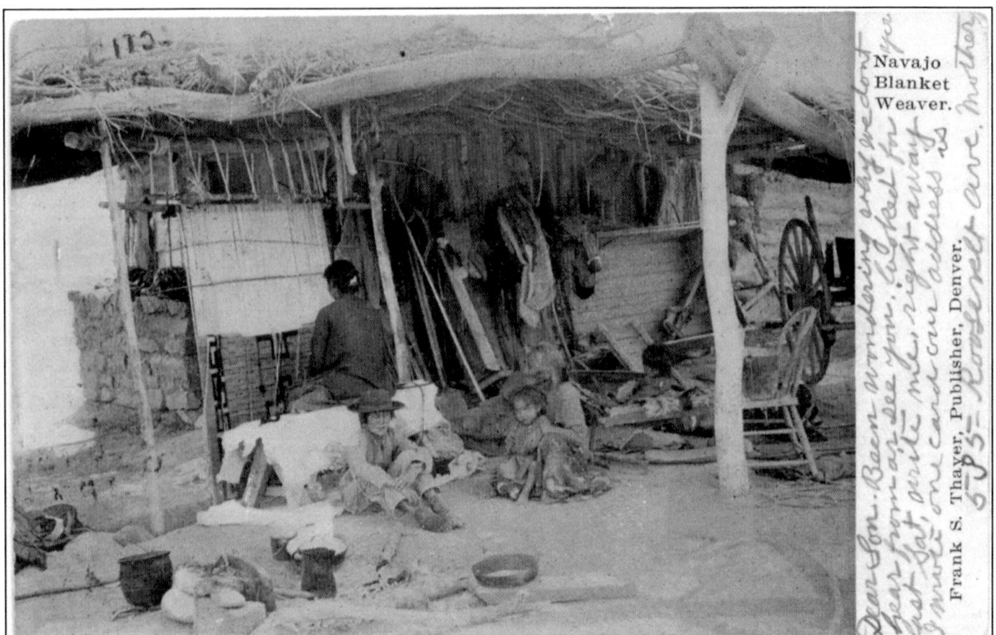

The all-purpose nature of a shade house, which served as kitchen, tack room, play area, and garage, is not unlike today's converted carports and adjoining patios. Roofs were used to store household items and to dry corn and other foodstuffs. With a "Greek key" border and background of dashed lines, the rug resembles many commissioned by trader J.B. Moore between 1897 and 1911. This card is postmarked 1908. (FST.)

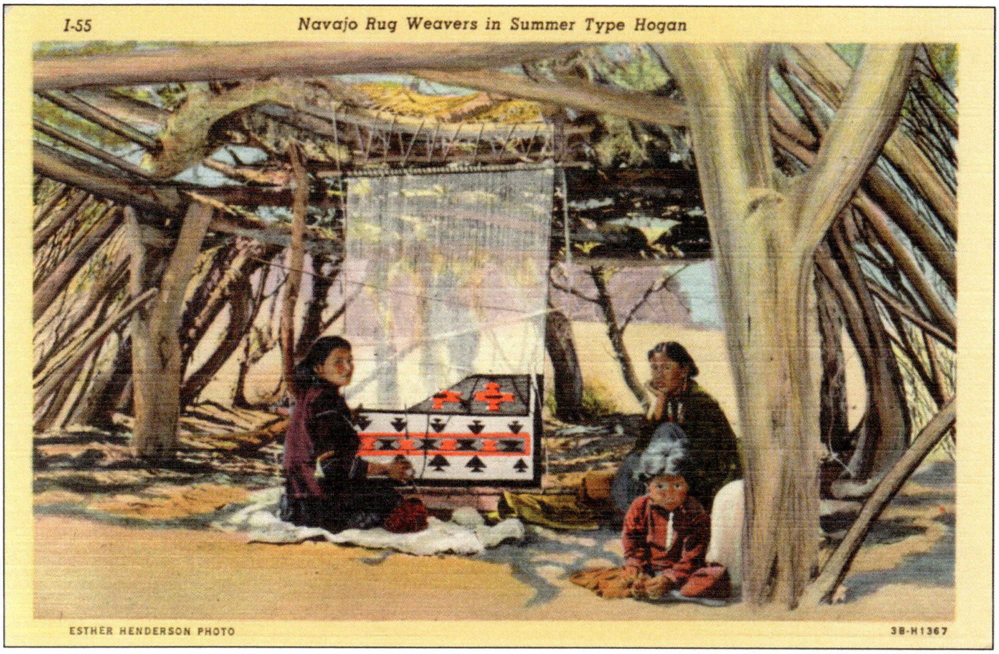

Upright logs and sticks adopt a "lean-to" form in many shade houses (*chaha'oh* in Diné or *ramada* in Spanish). This loom is built into the roof beams, and its right-side support is missing. The partially woven rug shows rows of geometric motifs surrounded by a solid border in a typical 1940s style. This image was photographed by Esther Henderson; "1943" is penciled on the reverse. (Lollesgard Specialty, Tucson.)

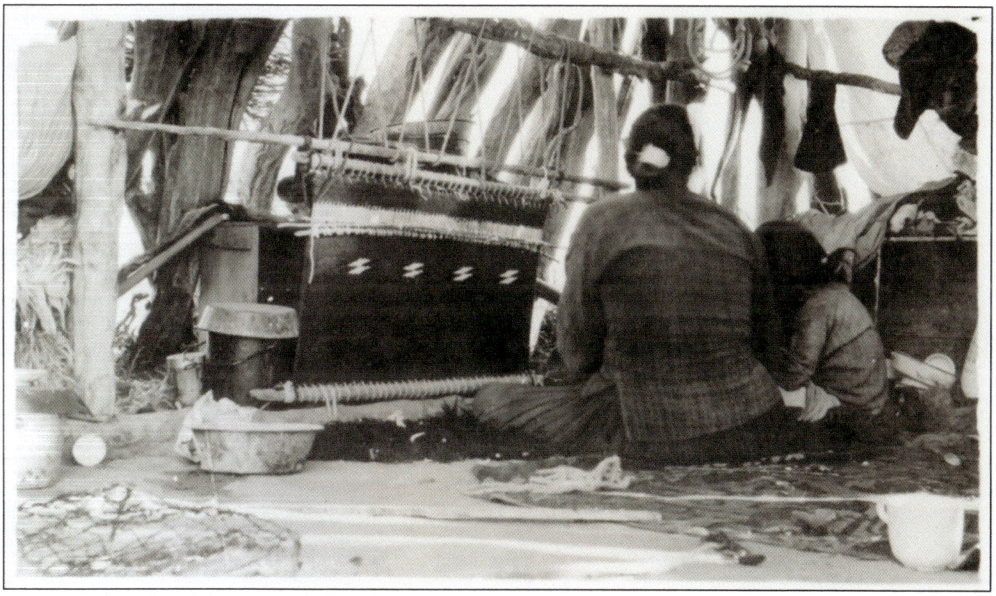

Sitting in her family's rustic chaha'oh, a weaver nears the end of painstaking work on a chevron-patterned blanket. The last few inches must be tightly packed using a long sailmaker's needle or threaded umbrella rib and could take a full day to complete. In this case, the blanket is larger than what is visible; its upper edge is doubled and lashed behind the loom. The original photograph, not a postcard, measures three by five inches. (US.)

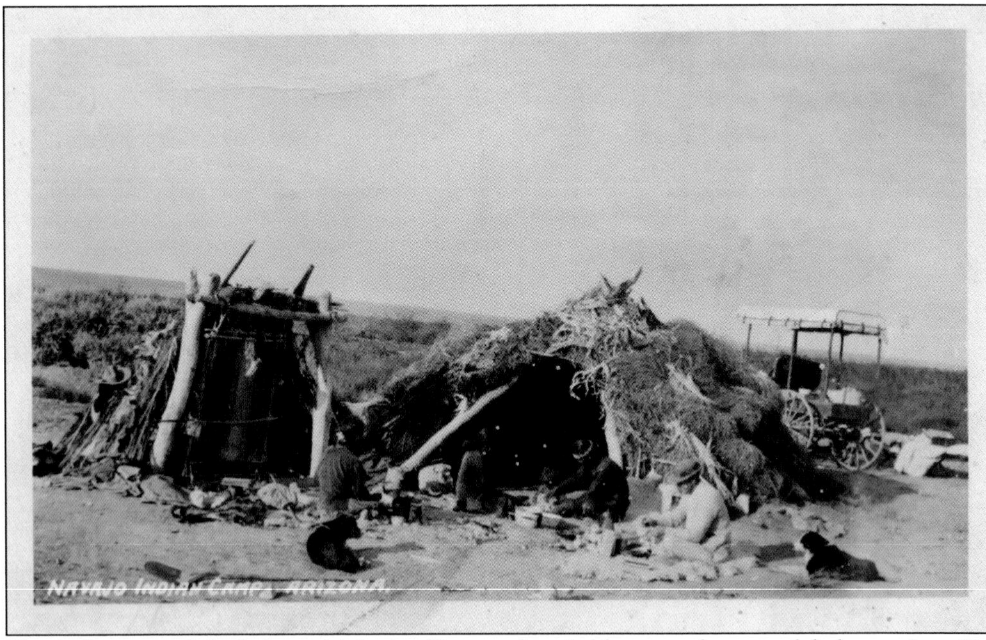

Navajo homesteads include multiple dwellings and varied house styles remodeled over time. On the left is a forked-stick shade with vertical poles. A loom built into its doorway forms a permanent part of the structure. A family dines in front of a rough forked-stick hogan, refurbished seasonally with brush and local plants. Dogs for herding sheep and a buckboard for transport complete the scene. (FFS.)

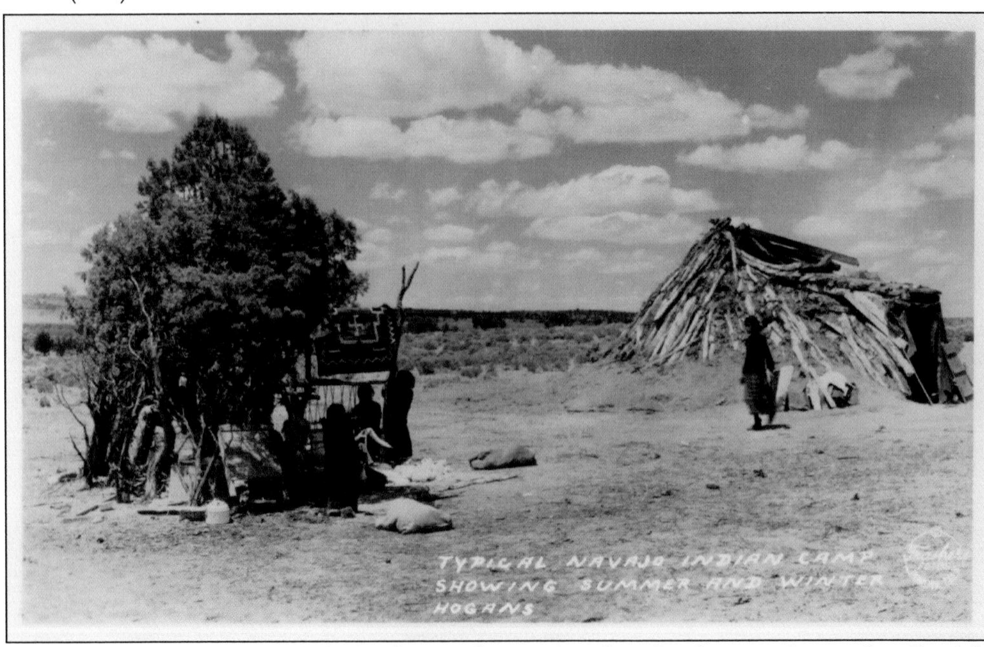

A loom stands in the juniper's shade (for comfort or the sake of a photographer, perhaps?) while a conical forked-pole hogan with extended entry sits in the background. Sometimes, this type of dwelling is plastered with mud for added insulation. Even today, many Navajo families spend as much time as possible outdoors, considering their entire property as "home" and making less distinction between a house and its yard. (FFS.)

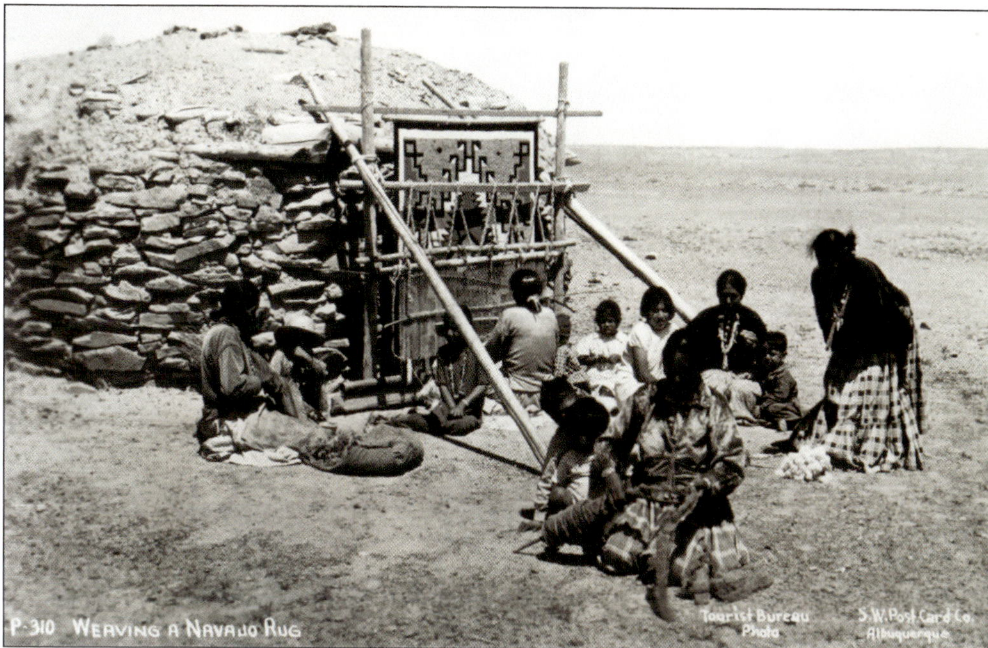

A round, stone-faced hogan with a mud-covered log roof serves to support a large loom, which entirely covers the east-facing doorway. The timber side-props almost seem to hold up the building. With not a tree in sight, the scene has the appearance of a festive picnic involving at least 13 women and children gathered for the photographer. (SWPC and NMST.)

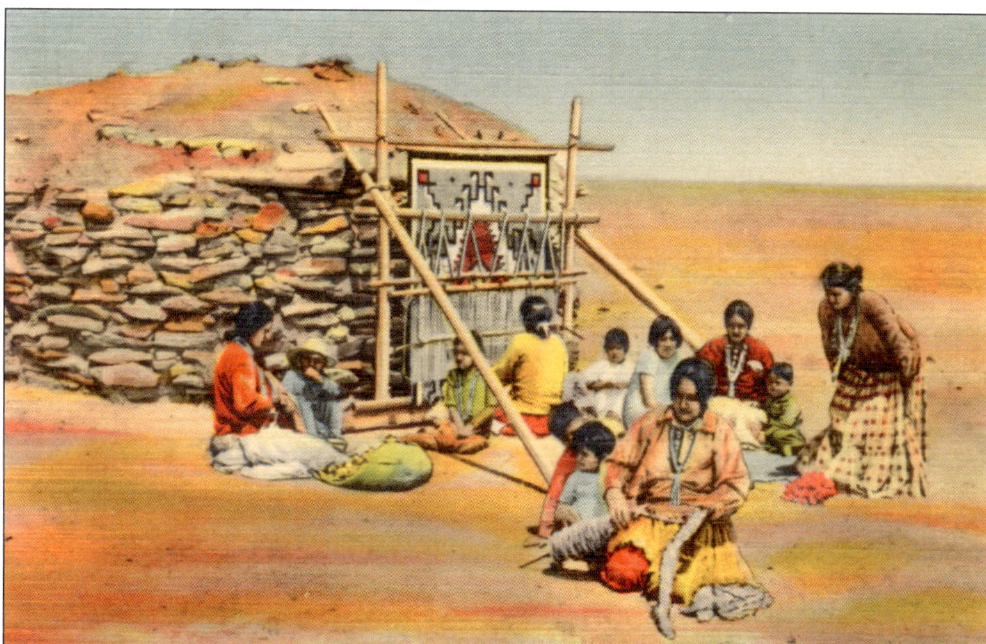

From the 1920s to the 1940s, Curt Teich & Company produced more postcards than any other publisher. In this 1947 hand-tinted version of the above image, the rug may or may not show its true colors. If accurate, the pattern would be called a Ganado or Klagetoh regional rug pattern; without red, it might be considered a Two Grey Hills style. (CTC and NMST.)

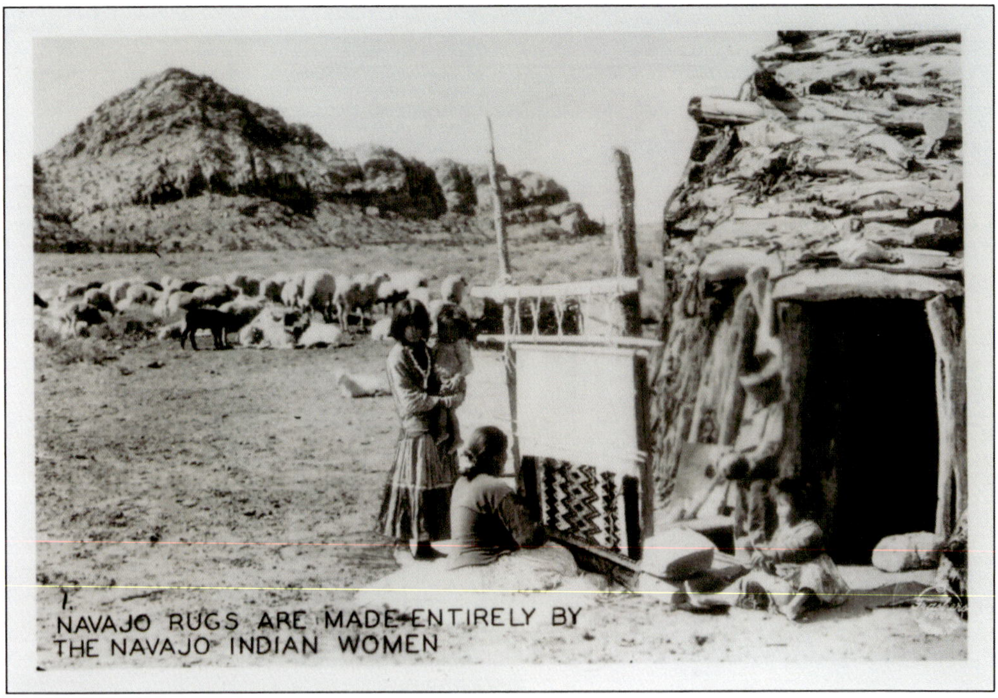

This composite image, which also appears on two different postcards shown on the back cover and page 2, is a patchwork of at least three original photographs taken by Burton Frasher. The flock and background are reversed from the image on the bottom of page 53. The children, weaver, loom, and hogan derive from a scene depicted in the upper image on page 77. And, finally, the rug on the loom has been "borrowed" from another woman's work shown on page 98. (FFS.)

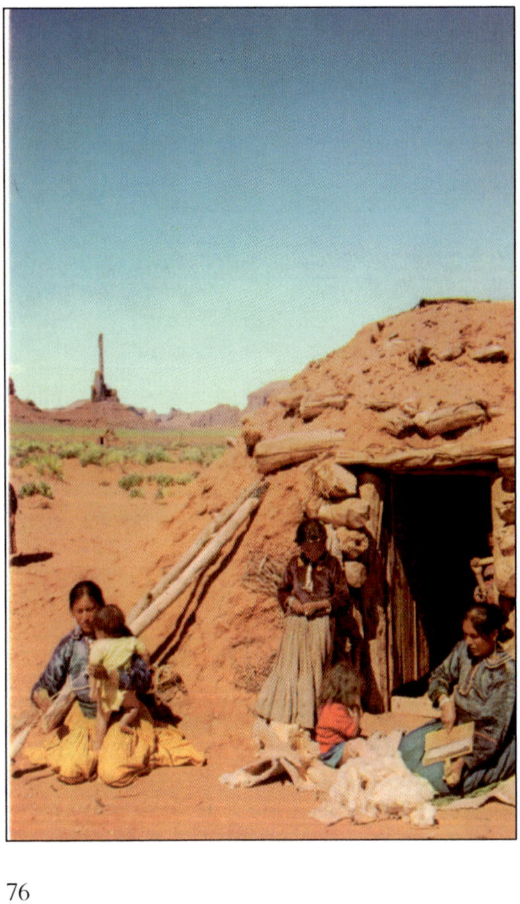

Navajo women and children pose by a mud-plastered log hogan. A forked-pole hogan sits in the background. Monument Valley's Totem Pole column rises in the far distance. All three elements provide a picturesque setting for touring photographers, who likely paid the family for such a photograph session. (RPPL.)

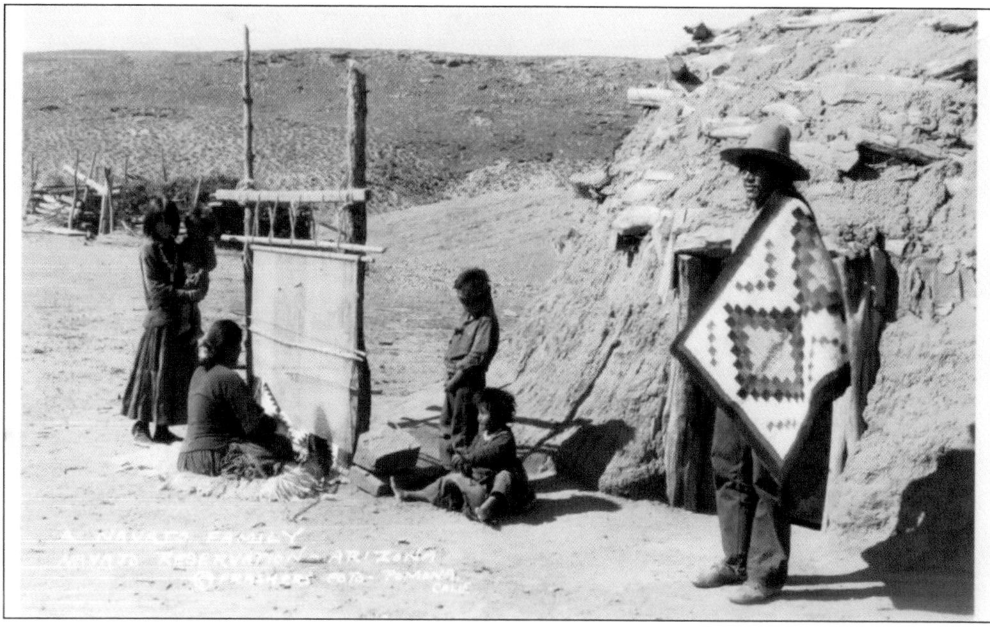

A mud-plastered cribbed-log hogan near Ganado, Arizona, provides a backdrop for this family's weaving demonstration with a log-and-brush corral in the background. The Navajo man displays a rug with two stepped diamonds and a solid border. Rug sales represented a significant part of many families' livelihoods. Some men assisted by building looms, making tools, and occasionally marketing their female relatives' woven goods. (FFS.)

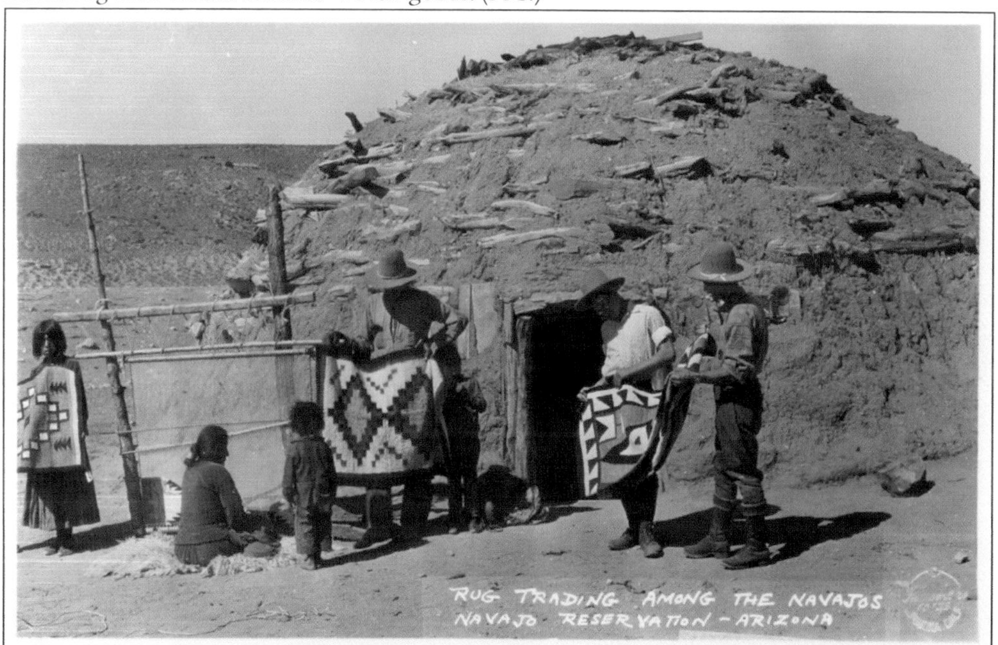

Local and itinerant traders occasionally brought favored clients to weavers' homes; more often, they relied on weavers coming into their stores. Two *bilagáana* (Anglo or "white") men in high boots examine a fancy-bordered rug in 1930. All four rugs show common geometric designs typical of the 1920s, but none match the "Ganado Red" regional style that gained fame in this area several decades later. (FFS.)

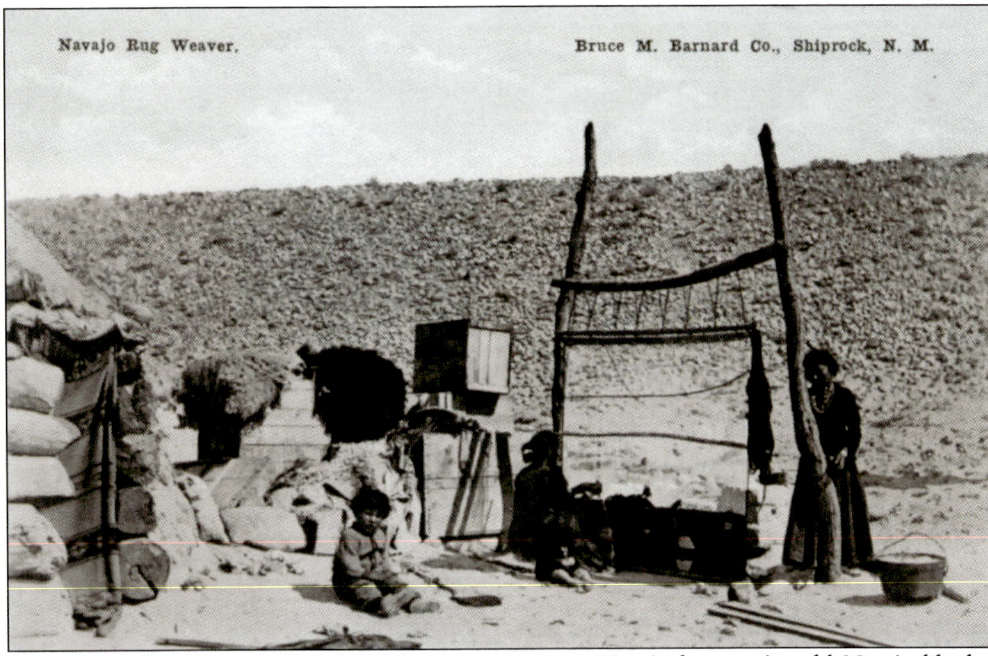

Front doors face east—toward the rising sun—on most Navajo homes. An old Navajo blanket hangs over the doorway of this stacked-log hogan—a common sight in early times. Packing crates await some future use, possibly as building materials and loom parts. The draped sheep fleeces are likely for bedding and seating. (ECK.)

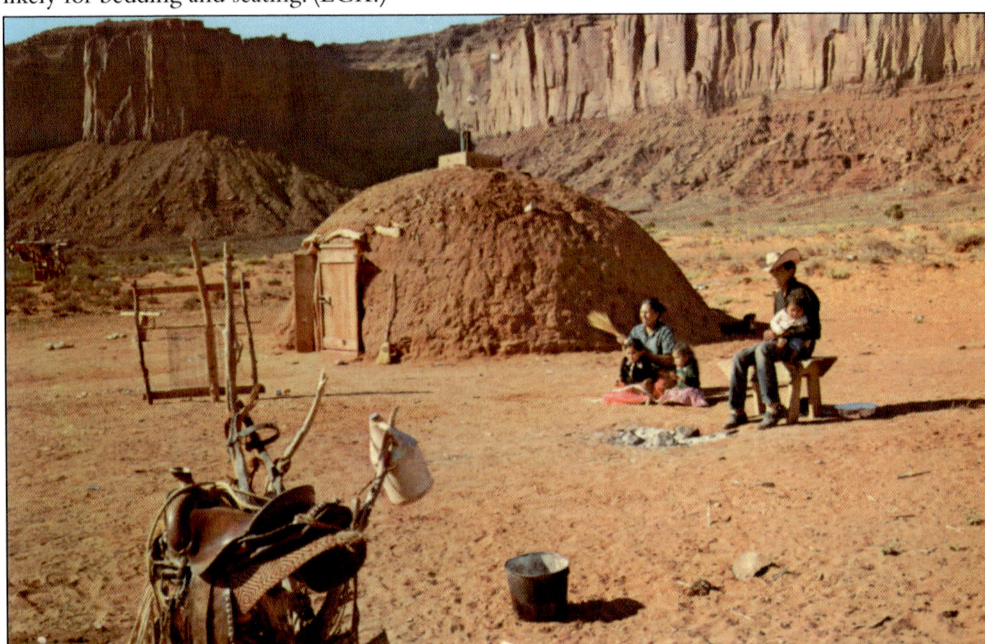

A wooden door provides a modern touch on the hogan shown in this photograph taken in northern Arizona by Hubert Lowman. A boxed-in stovepipe (instead of a basic smoke hole) is visible on the roof. In the foreground, the saddle with a twill saddle blanket may be a prop, but it also might reference a local Diné joke—if a woman puts her man's saddle outside, it means she intends to divorce him. (PS.)

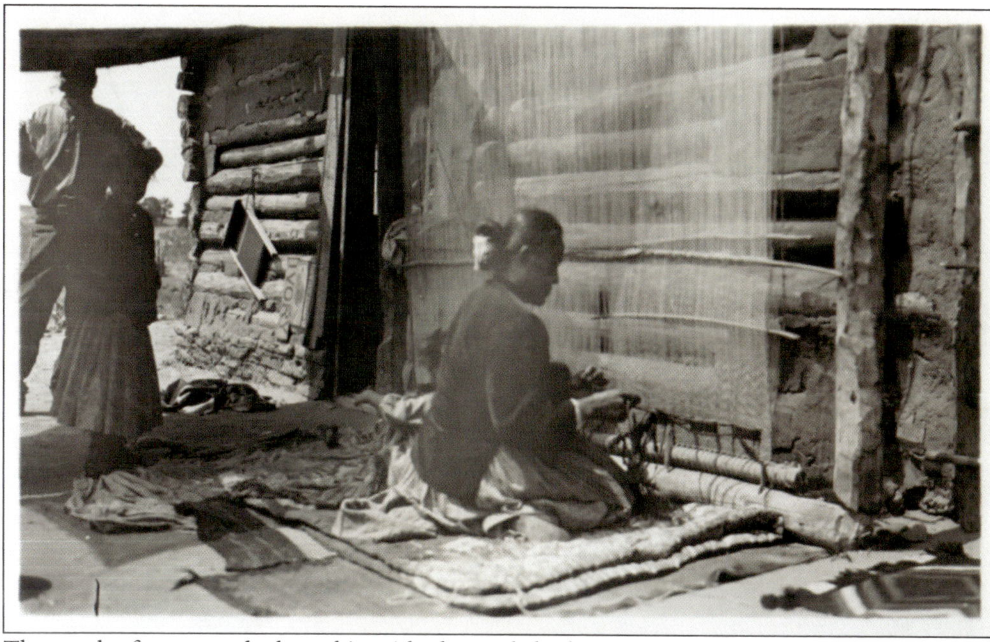

The porch of a rectangular log cabin with plastered chinking serves as this woman's "studio," where she weaves on a finely spun warp. To her right lies a Germantown "Eye Dazzler" saddle blanket with fringe; underneath her folded quilt are several old handwoven textiles. A washboard and Ivory soapbox to her left suggest other tools of her trade. (MPS.)

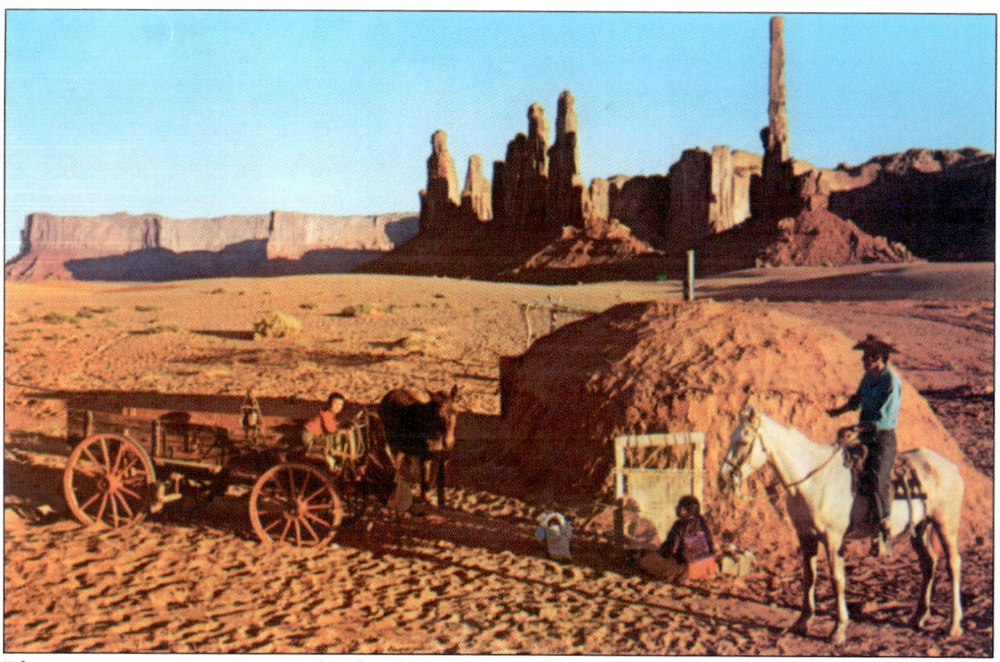

The western sun is setting on this family's tableau in Monument Valley. The dome-shaped hogan's door faces east, where a shade structure and second loom may stand. The weaver has just begun weaving a rug or saddle blanket on her lumber wood loom. Since the mid-20th century, men's traditional roles have shifted to raising cattle and horses—hence the emergence of Navajo cowboys. (PS.)

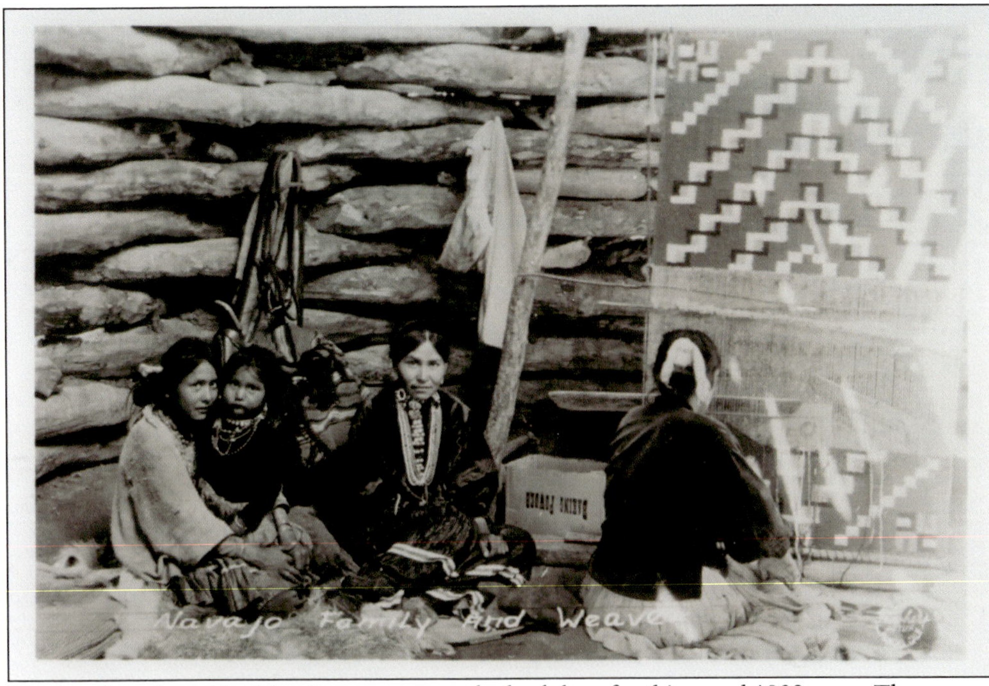

The interior of a cribbed-log hogan serves as the backdrop for this posed 1932 scene. The women and girls from the China Springs area, north of Gallup, have dressed for the cameraman in shiny velvet and cotton velveteen blouses, gathered skirts, jewelry, and other finery of the time. (FFS.)

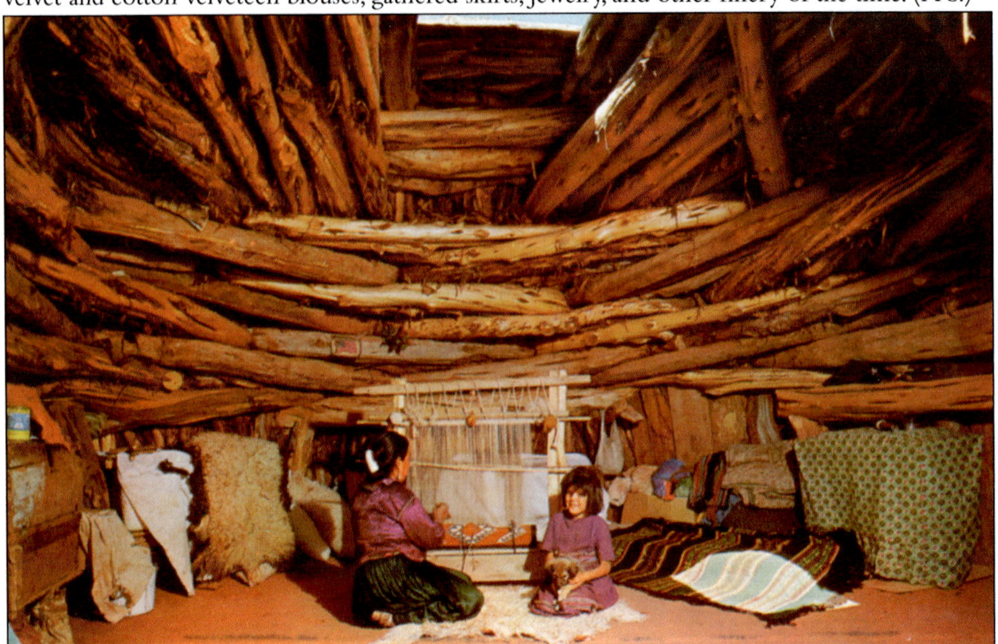

Labeled a "primitive circular hogan" in the original caption, this elegant cribbed-log building with a ceiling smoke hole represents an essential element of Diné heritage. Some Navajo families still maintain an old-style hogan with a dirt floor for healing ceremonies, peyote rituals, and other religious practices. Other symbols of this centuries-old legacy include the weaver's hairstyle, velvet clothing, Pendleton blanket, sheepskins, and loom. (PS.)

Five

At the Loom

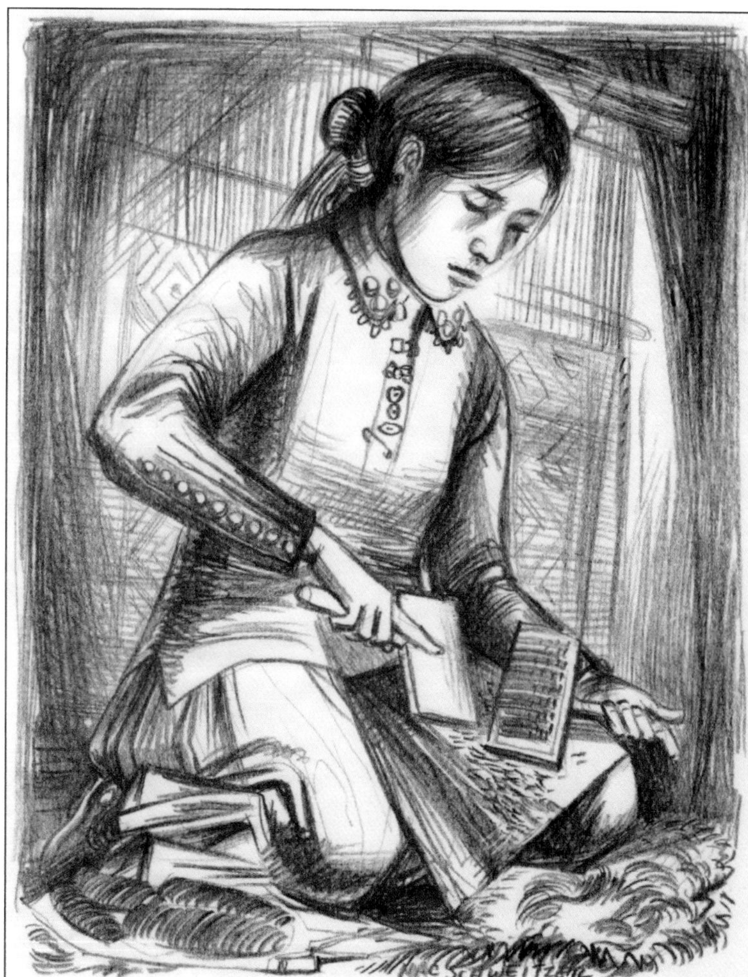

An iconic Navajo loom rises behind this Navajo girl in Mac Schweitzer's lithograph titled "Carding Wool," originally measuring nine by seven inches. A tool of great beauty and spiritual significance, the legendary first Diné loom was made of sky and earth cords, sunbeams, precious crystals, and sheet lightning. Subsequent loom materials range from live and dead trees to rough timbers and milled lumber to metal and PVC pipes. (Courtesy of the Ocotillo Trust.)

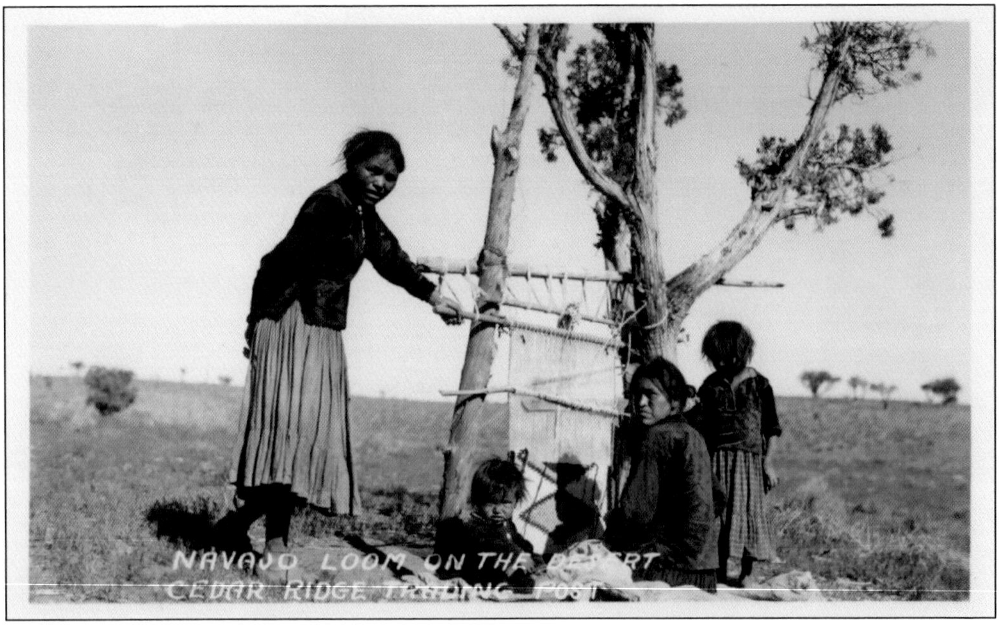

A juniper tree serves as loom support and provides a tiny bit of shade. Juniper wood makes for good tools because it is straight-grained and lacks the sticky sap of piñon trees. Despite the crooked look of upper loom bars, the rug and warp (foundation yarns) are aligned thanks to an effective rope tensioning system. A flour sack likely holds the women's yarn and weaving tools. (Both, US.)

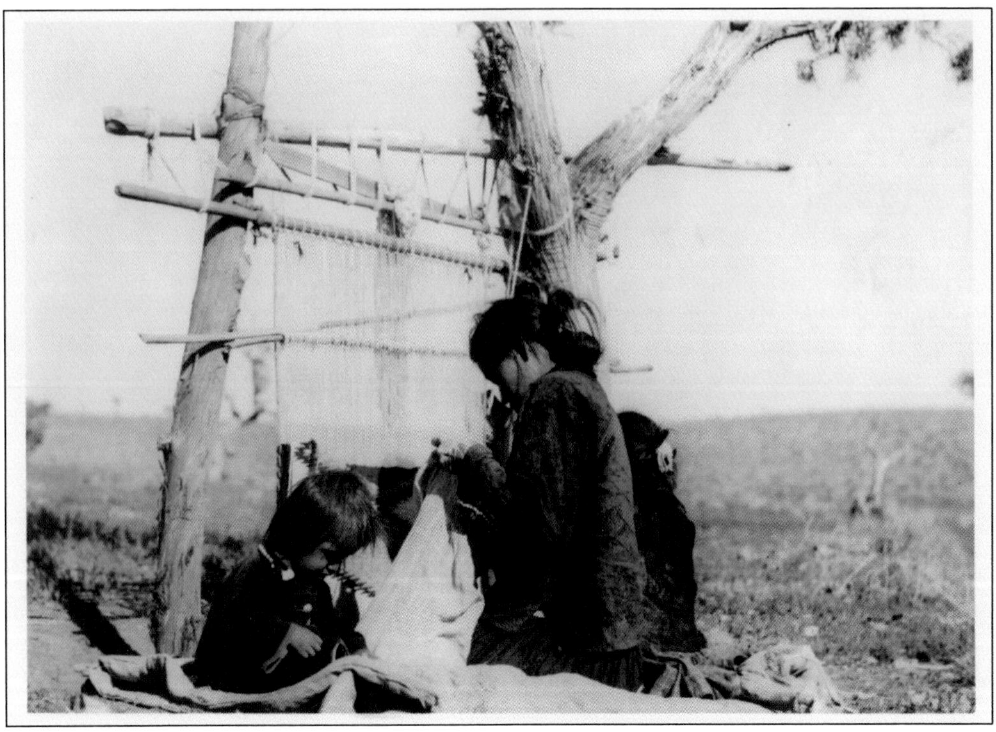

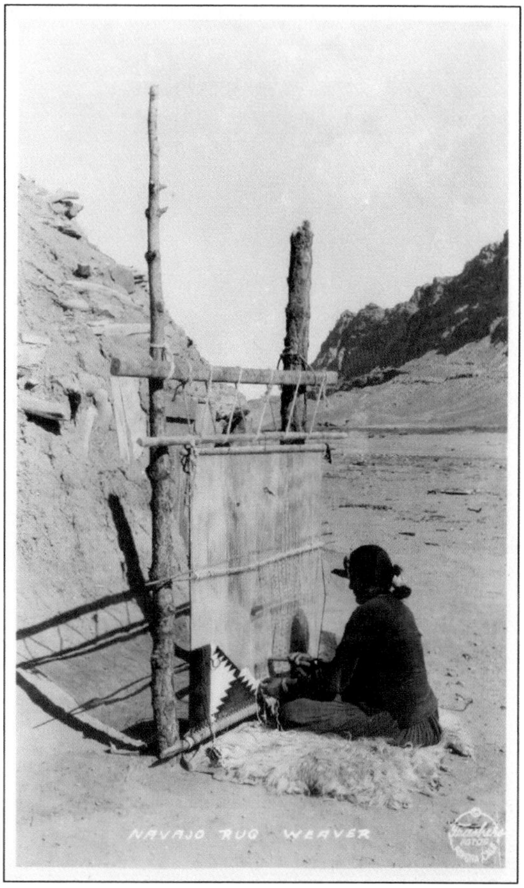

Two straight Ponderosa pine poles were used to make this sturdy loom photographed from several angles in 1930. The barren landscape around Ganado and other areas resulted from the local people harvesting trees for building materials and firewood over many decades, coupled with serious droughts. Overgrazing and erosion led to voluntary and then forced sheep reduction several years after these photographs were taken. Today, Navajo people still feel the psychological, social, and political impacts of the federal government's misguided decisions and inappropriate actions. (Both, FFS.)

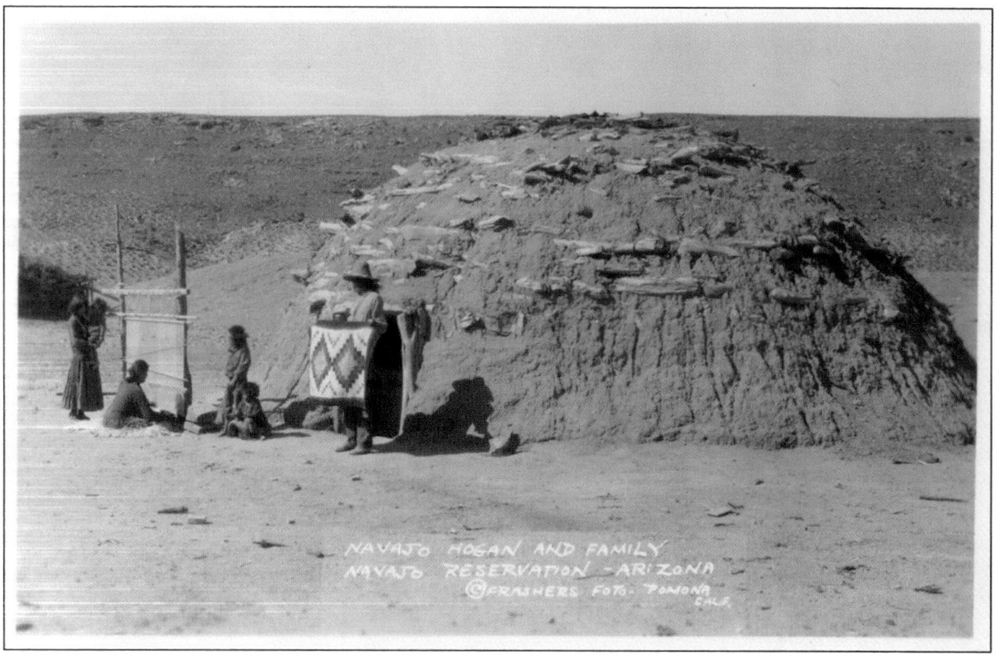

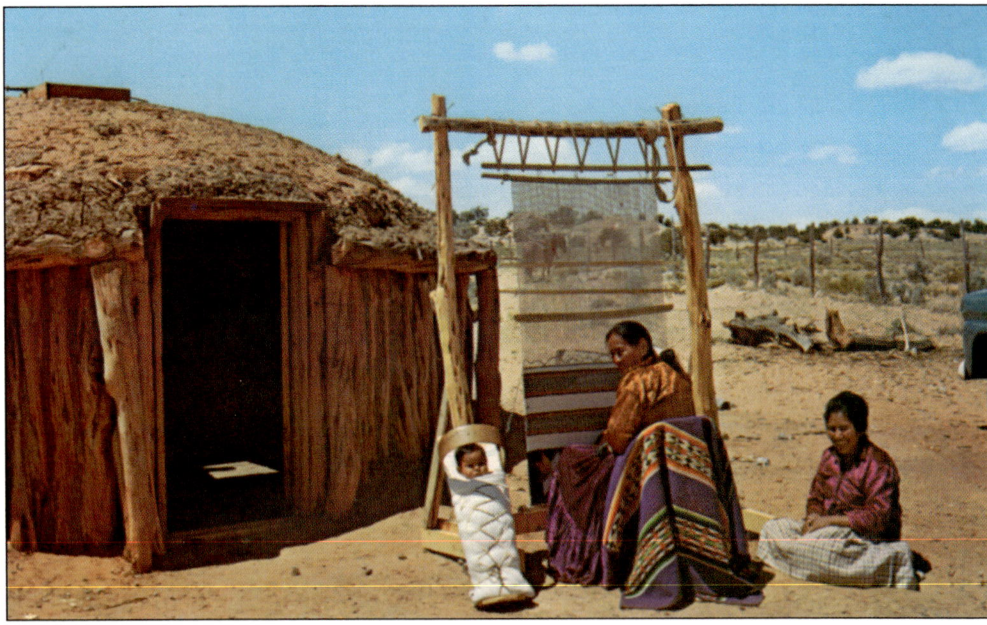

Changing times are reflected in the milled lumber of the doorway and loom base in contrast with the rough-hewn timbers of the hogan wall, loom side supports, and upper beam. A baby in cradleboard, horses beyond the warp threads, and glimpse of a blue truck attest to a mix of traditional and modern lifeways that continue today. The photographer of this image was Mel Davis. (SC.)

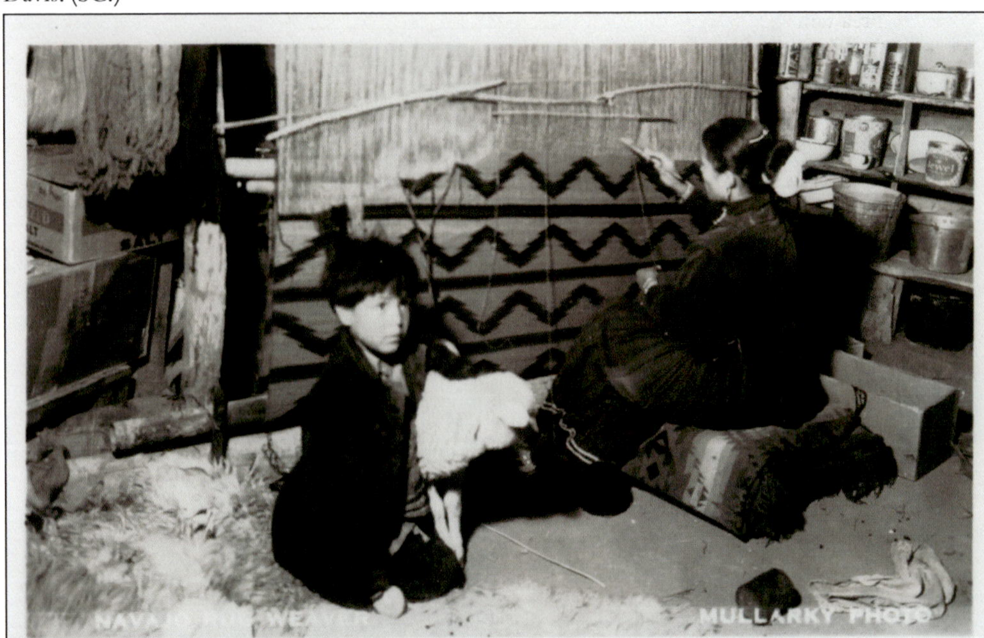

This photograph taken sometime between 1902 and 1907 documents an early use of a steel pipe for the loom's lower beam. Practical for large looms, where the warp threads' tension might bend lesser materials, metal loom parts are now common. The transitional blanket/rug's pattern dates from the 1880s to the early 1900s. The shelves hold tins of baking powder, Swift's Jewel shortening, and PET milk. (MS.)

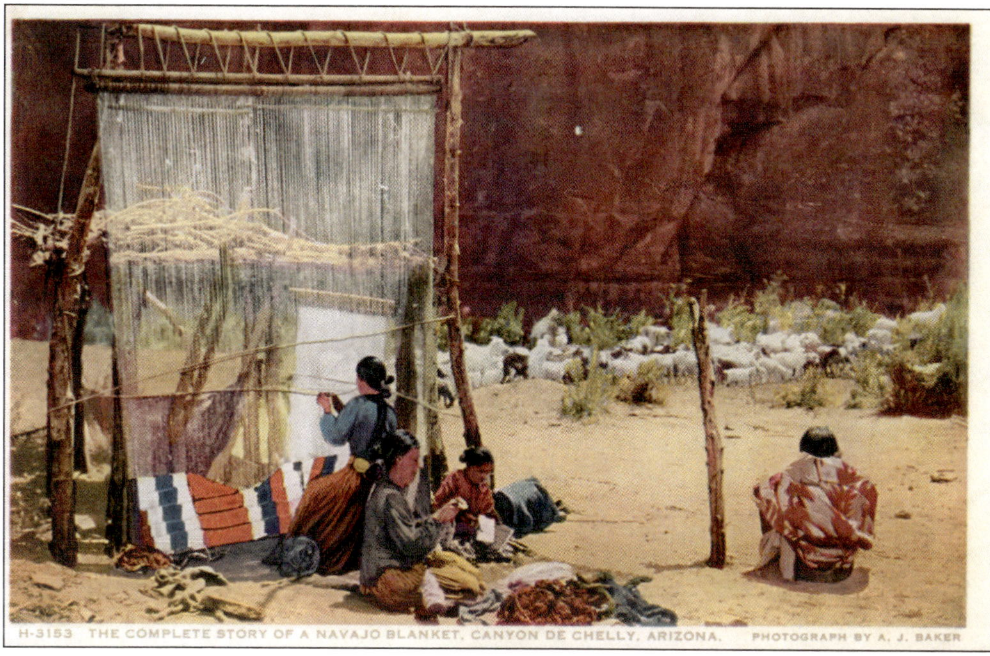

A tall loom (*dah 'iistł'ǫ́*), backed by a ramada and a second loom, rises in Canyon de Chelly. The weaver can still reach her work, but as she progresses, the woven area will move out of her reach. She will have to either elevate her seating or lower the unwoven web in the loom frame; both solutions are still used today. The photographer of this image was A.J. Baker. (FHC.)

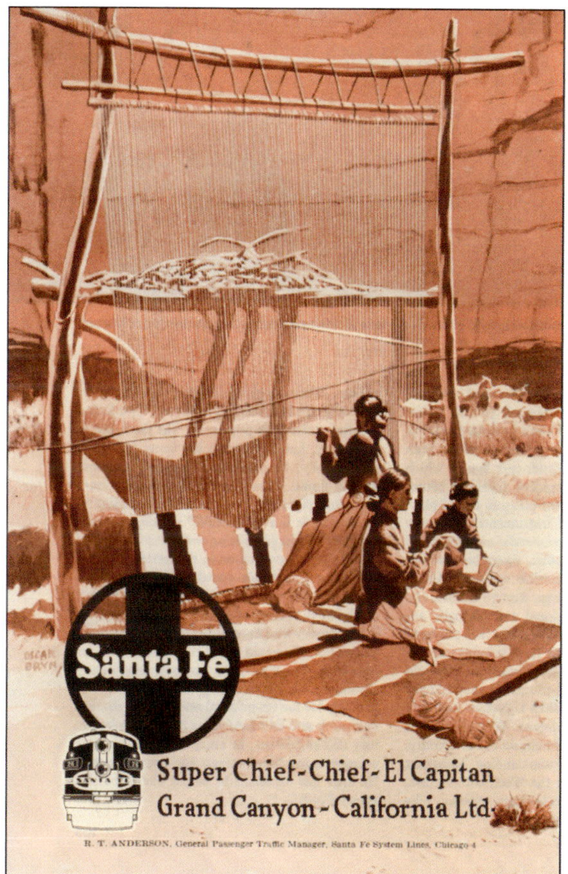

The full text of this 1953 *Holiday* magazine advertisement, capitalizing on a stylized view of A.J. Baker's idyllic weaving scene, says: "Wonderful way to see the wonders of the West—Every one of Santa Fe's five famous trains between Chicago and California is planned, equipped and staffed to make your trip through the colorful Southwest so much fun you'll hate to have it end." (SFR.)

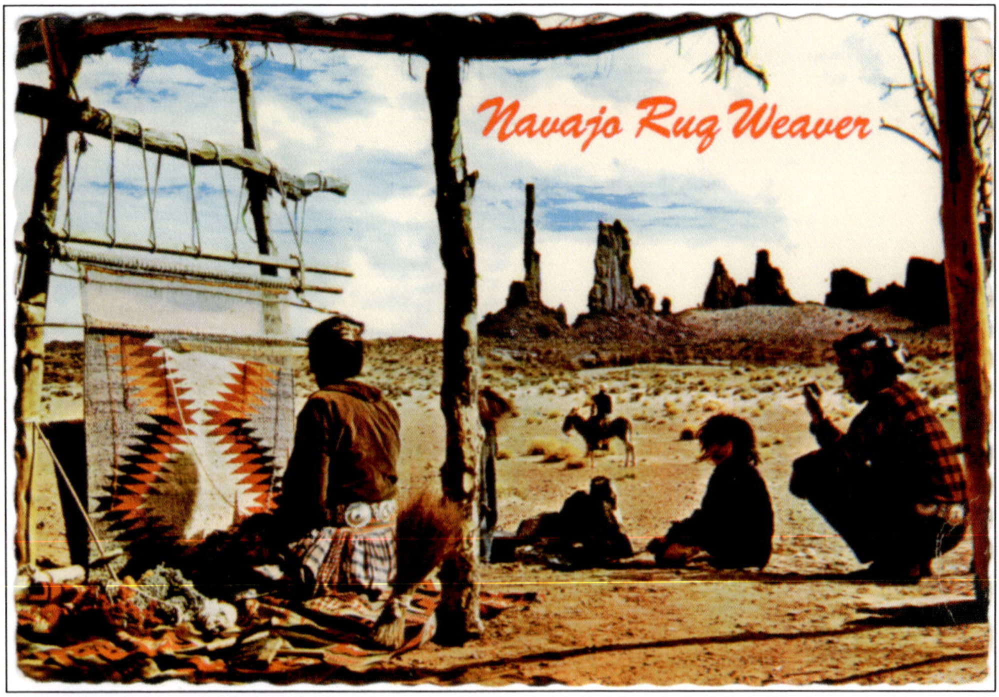

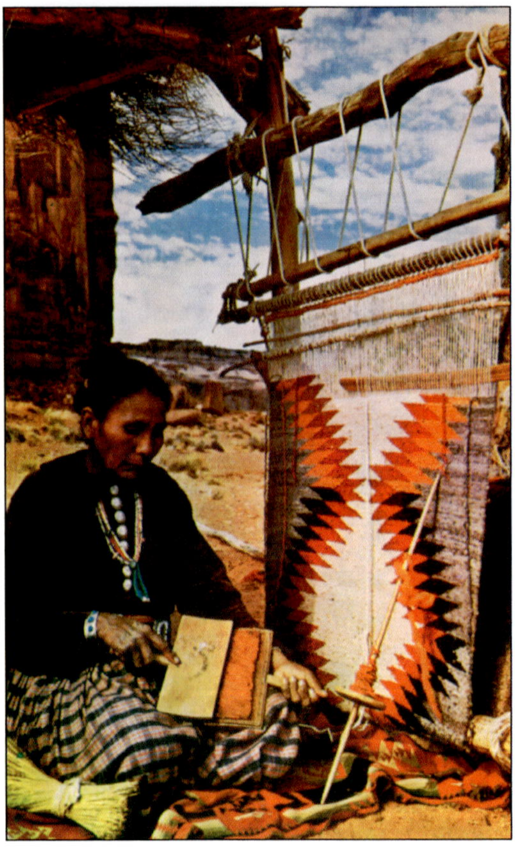

There are fewer than 12 inches yet to be woven on Happy Cly's loom in these images taken around 1956 by Josef Muench. Her rug is rolled underneath the bottom beam and extends up the backside. The zigzag rope at the top maintains an even tension on the warps and helps make an even, right-angled rug. As weaving progressed, she would untie and relax the upper rope, lowering the weaving to be within her reach. Some weavers still use such a rope, as it relates to the First Loom brought to the Diné by the Holy People and represents sacred zigzag lightning. Other weavers now use more efficient metal turnbuckles that replace the rope. (Both, NAU-CL, Josef Muench Collection. Above, PS; below, Mike Roberts.)

The loom's zigzag ropes, echoed in its shadow, emphasize a traditional tensioning system. A weaver can tighten or loosen the ropes, thereby adjusting the "pull" on her warps. As the rug grows on the loom, warp tension increases, so the ropes must be gradually released. The zigzag configuration allows for side-to-side adjustments and for lowering the work area toward the weaver. Although this postcard is labeled "Manuelito, New Mexico," other images in the same series record the location as "Navajo Reservation, Arizona." (FFS.)

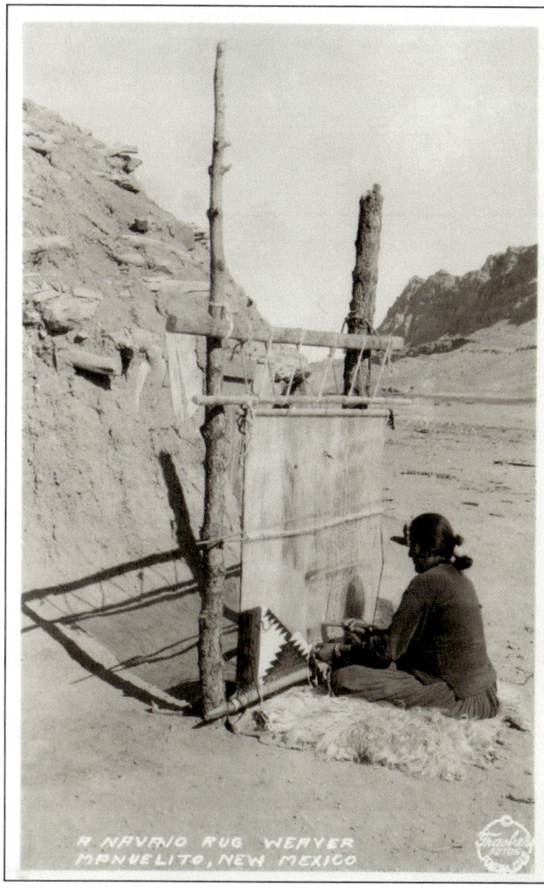

Silhouetted against the sky, zigzag tension ropes symbolize one sacred form of lightning in the Diné worldview. Some weavers view clouds, visible through the loom here, as another significant element. This postcard, although poorly tinted, reveals fine warps and an intricate "Eye Dazzler" pattern on one loom. The weavers work amidst kitchen utensils and household supplies without the artifice of a sanitized photo shoot. (W.H. Clune, Los Angeles.)

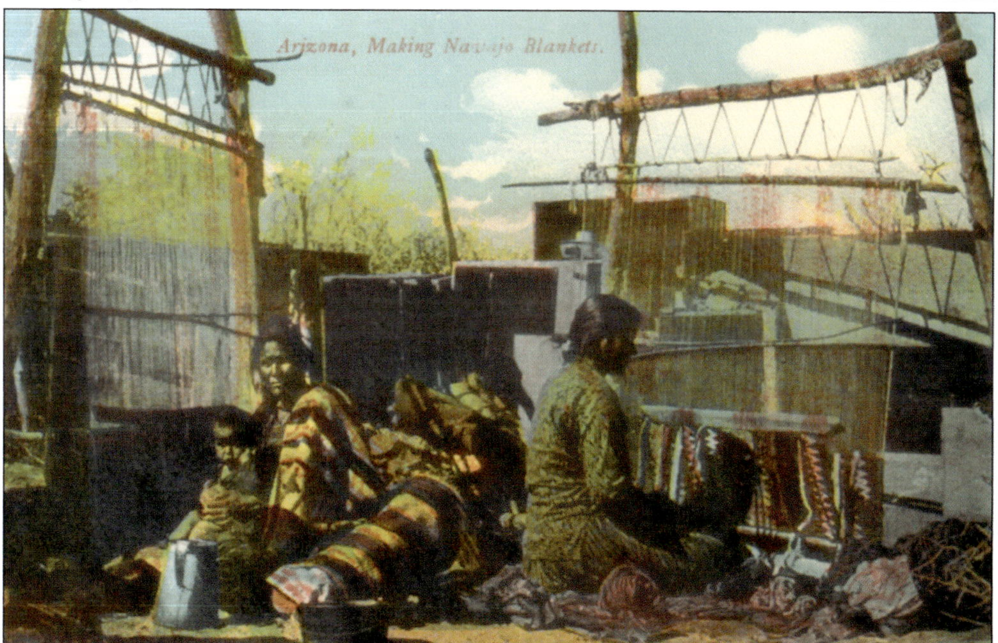

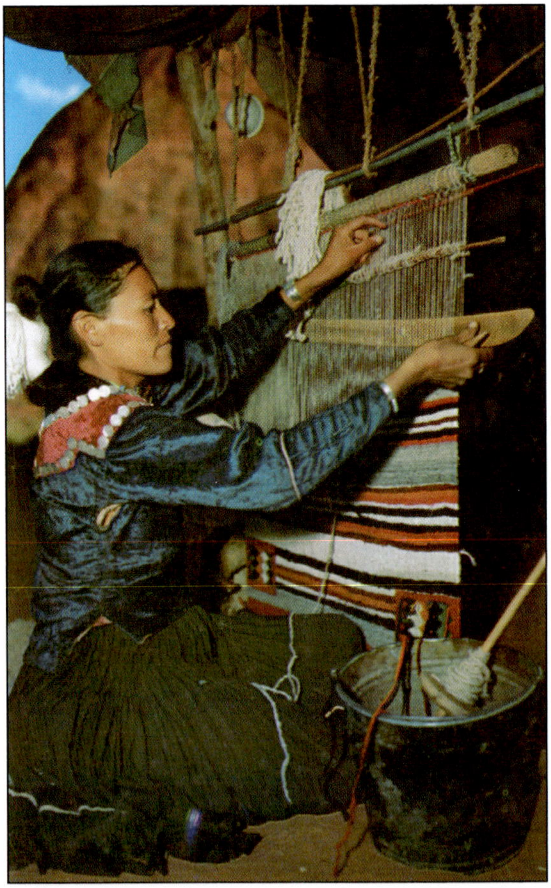

Making a coarse saddle blanket, the weaver inserts her wooden batten (also called a "sword") between every other warp string. Her left hand holds a "shed stick," and below that is the yarn-wrapped "heddle stick," which control the warps. She will turn the batten sideways to open a space ("shed") between the warps so that the weft yarn may be inserted. The photographer of this image was Jim Cagle, Sun Photograph Service, Salt Lake City.

Working in sections, the weaver focuses on her center pattern; above, her batten is placed sideways to hold open the "shed." Loose weft yarns are tucked into the warp on the left side. Her right hand holds a weaving comb used for beating the wefts into place; the batten is never used for this. This picture was taken by Ray Manley. (PS.)

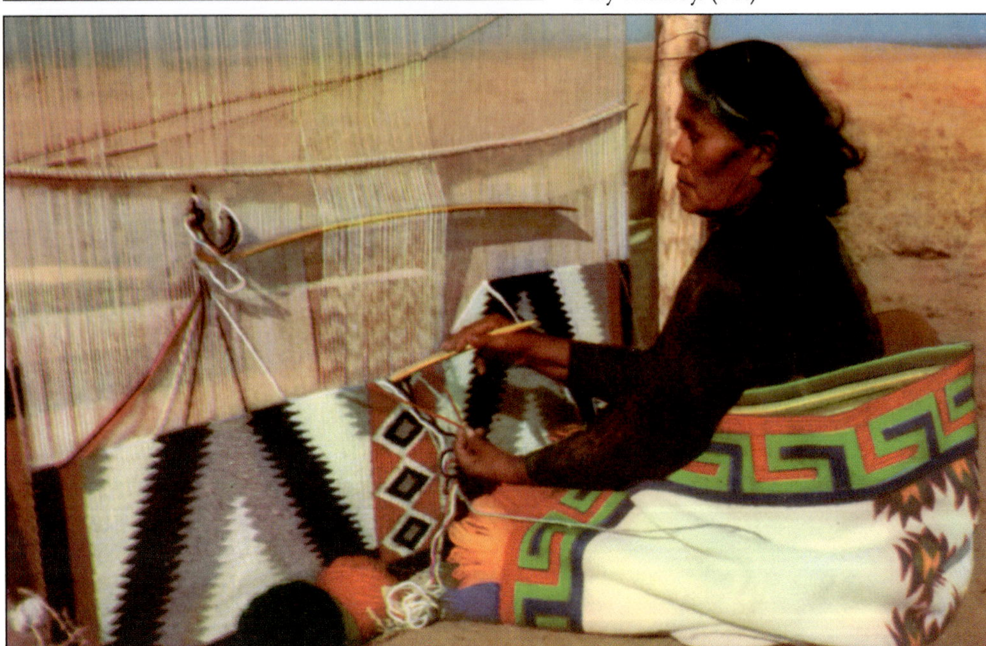

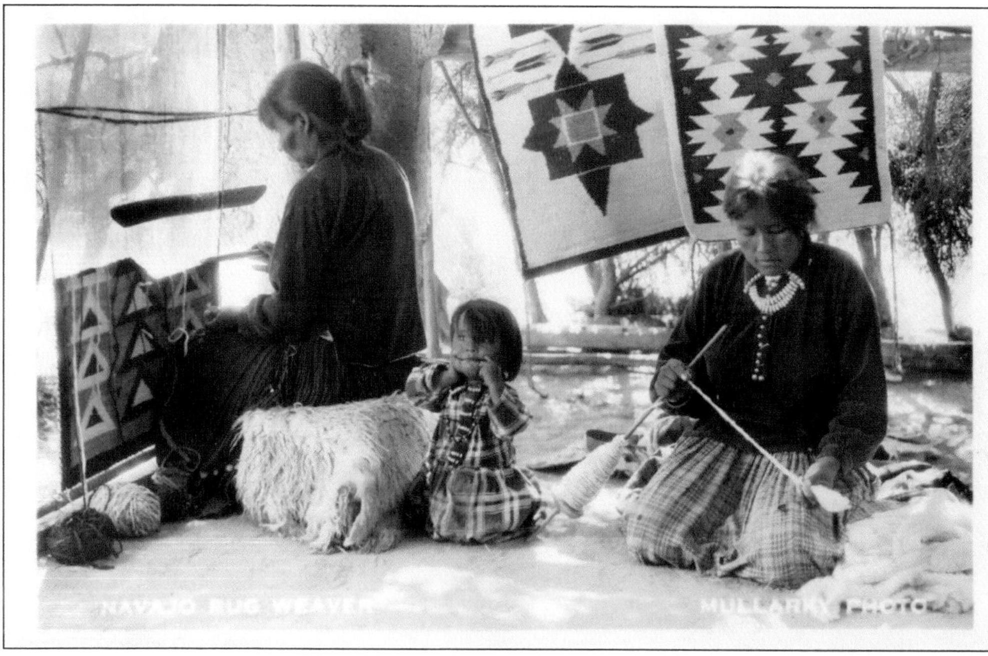

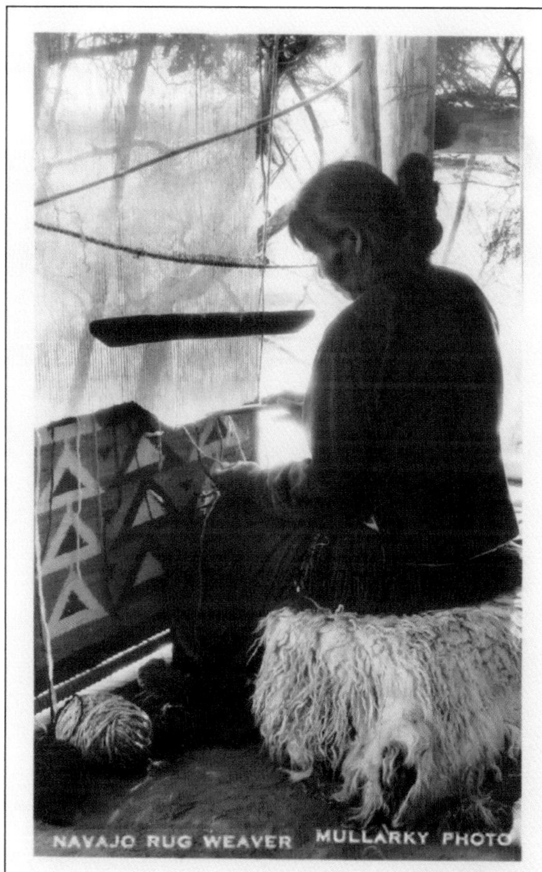

Said to represent a Diné rainbow, a batten (*bee ník'í'nítłish*) rests in place while the weaver uses her comb (*bee 'adzooí*), another form of rainbow, or "sundog," to pack down the interlaced weft yarns. Weavers often say, "You never put down the comb when you're weaving—hold it in your hand as you work with the batten, other tools, and yarn." Small bread-and-butter rugs produced for quick sale hang over a second loom. Several family members commonly work together in one space. Many Diné people fondly recall the sounds of a weaver's beating comb, fingers strumming the warps, batten flipping into place, and the soft whirring of a handspindle at work. (Both, MS.)

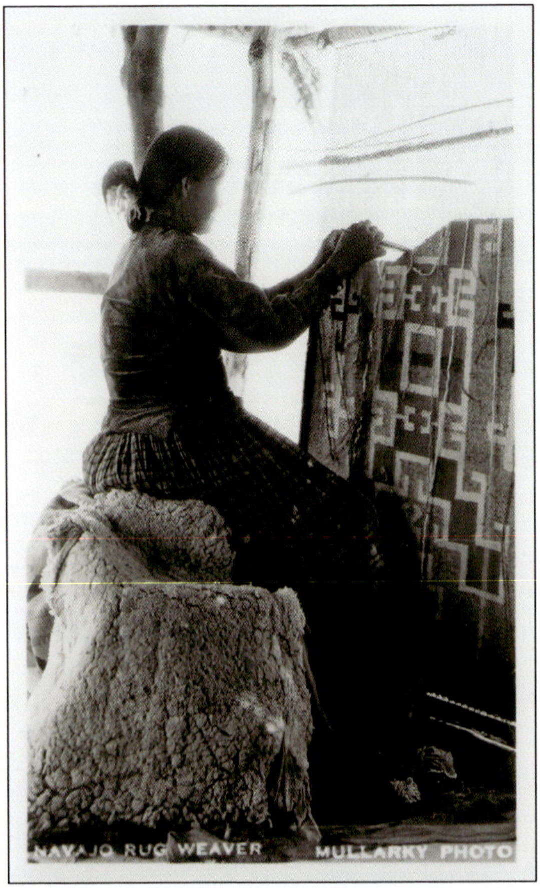

Some weavers sit directly on the ground or floor, often with a sheepskin for padding; others balance on boxes, chairs, or benches. This high, fleece-covered perch enables the woman to reach her work. She might even finish her "Storm Pattern" rug standing up. One woman places a chair on top of her kitchen table to complete large rugs! (MS.)

Sitting at ground level because she had recently started this blanket, the weaver holds her comb as she inserts weft yarns into the web, while the batten holds open the shed. She may use the pointed end of the comb to move wefts into proper position between the warps. Her wider-than-long blanket with three crosses will likely become a handsome manta (shawl) or shoulder blanket. (NPC.)

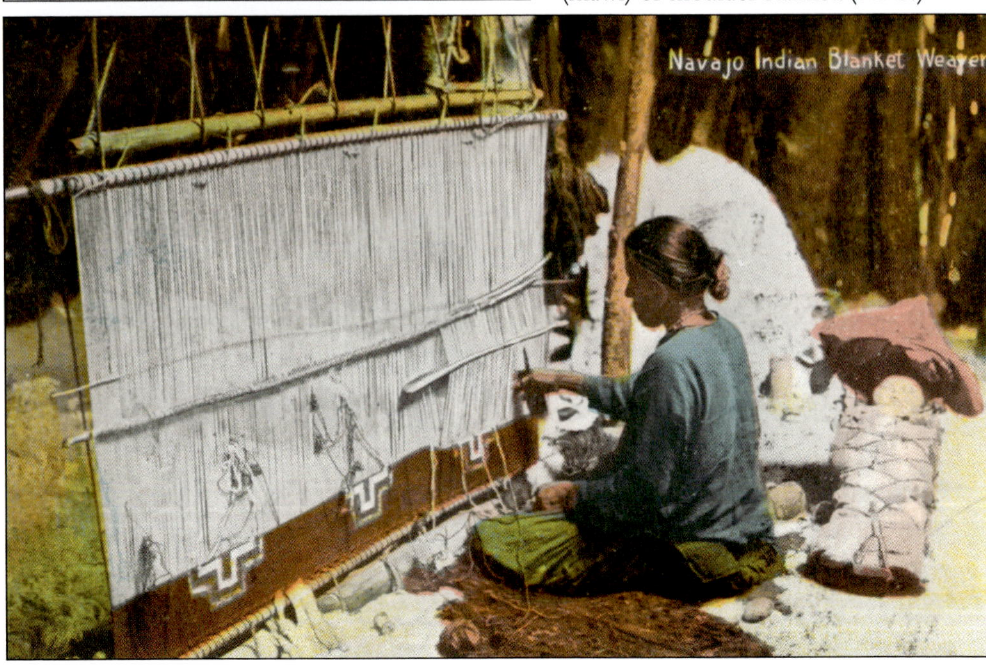

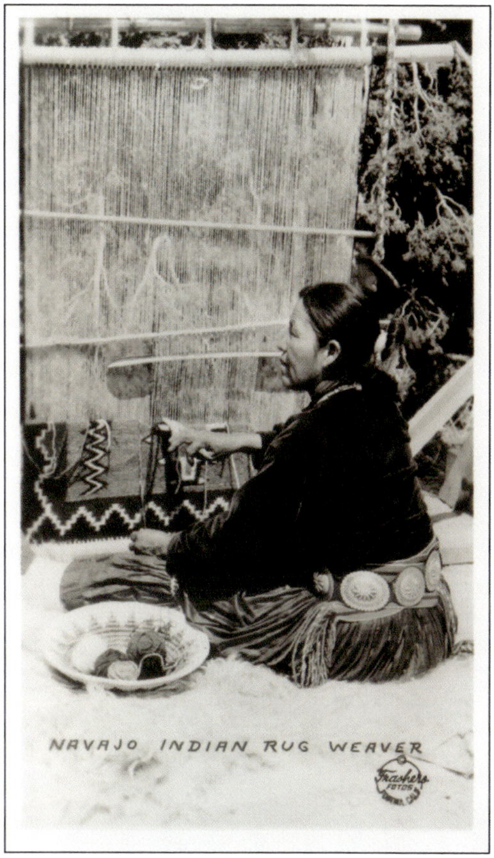

Everything about this weaver and her loom exudes skill and precision. The same woman appears with Tom of Ganado (in white pants) on page 34 and may be Elle of Ganado, "the best blanket weaver among the Navajos." She holds her comb precisely, using its teeth to beat or the point to position and pack the weft yarns. Her clothing, tidy yarn basket, loom's even tie-up, fine and regularly-spaced warps, and rug's detailed pattern reflect goals of perfection. Few Diné weavers rely on the maxim that one must weave an imperfection into their work; instead, they take pride in doing the best possible job. Postmarked from Gallup, New Mexico, to Philadelphia in 1946 (although photographed between 1915 and 1917), the hand-tinted postcard's handwritten message simply says, "Dear Bobby, This sure is a real western place. Love, Mother & Dad." (Both, FFS.)

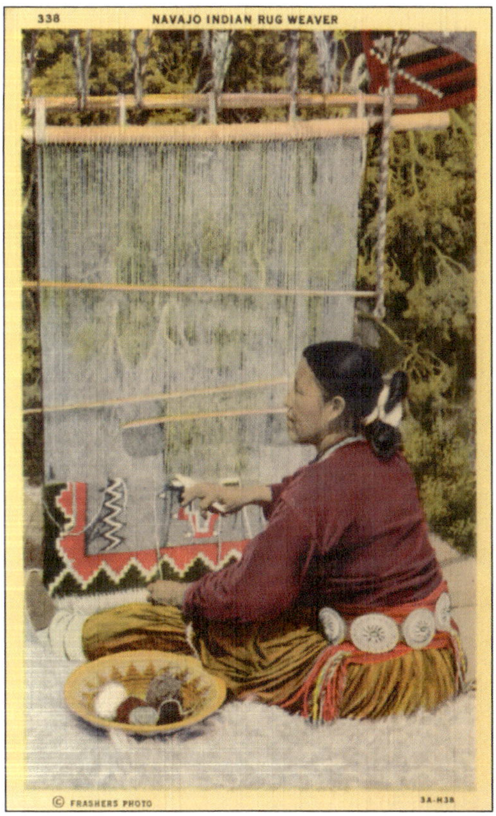

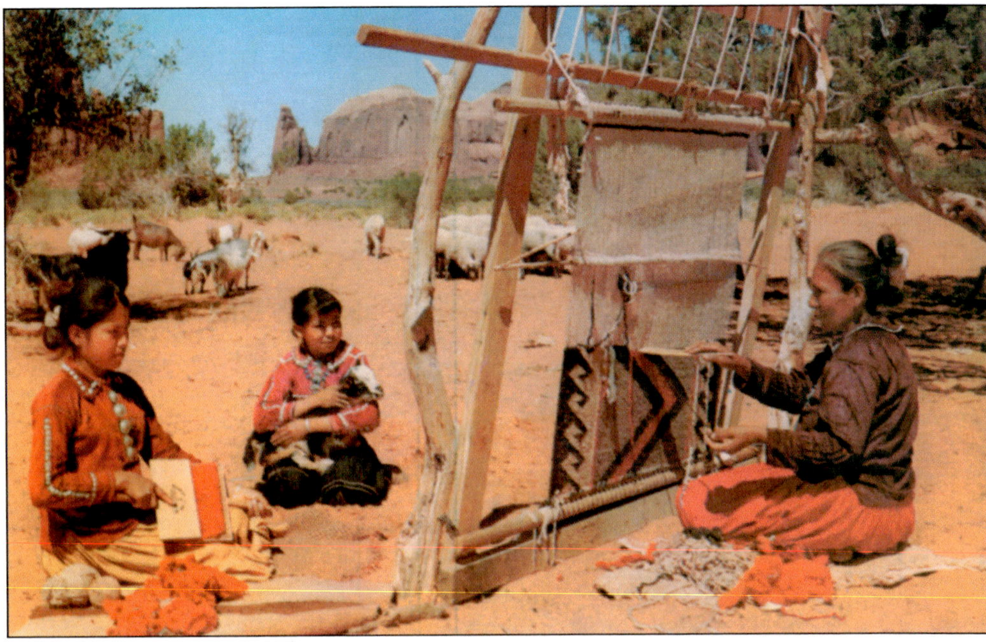

In the technique of "tapestry weave," which Navajos use for most blankets and rugs, the weft yarns form a design by completely covering the white or gray warp yarns, forming solid colored areas. Happy Cly had at least eight colored yarns running from edge to edge—black, white, gray, black, red, black, gray, white and black. She passed each weft over and under the warps in succession. (TB.)

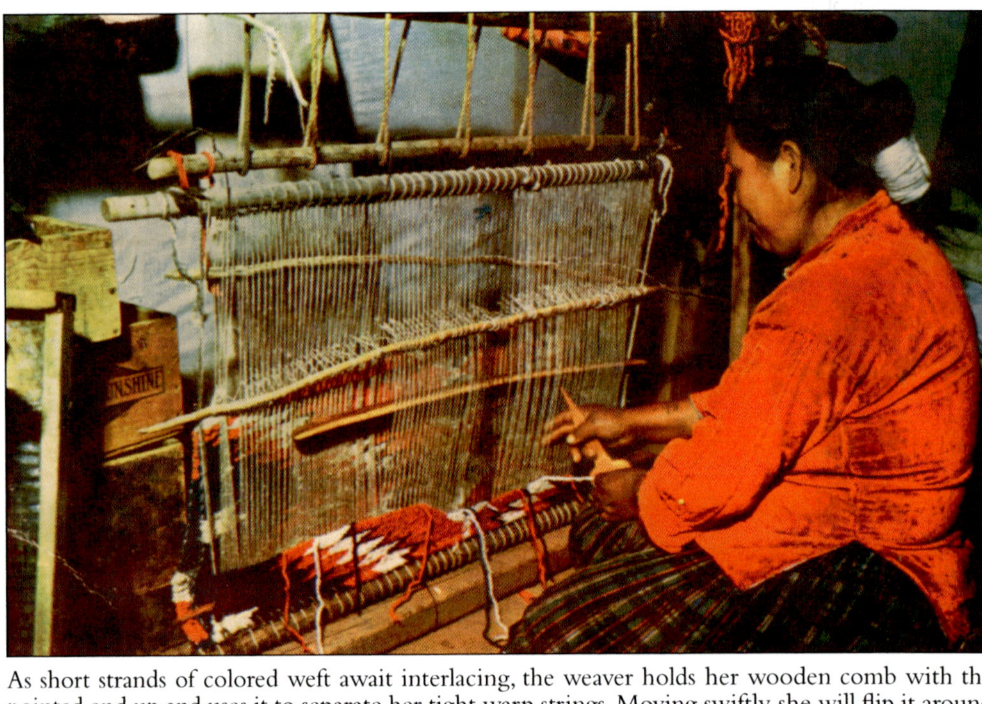

As short strands of colored weft await interlacing, the weaver holds her wooden comb with the pointed end up and uses it to separate her tight warp strings. Moving swiftly, she will flip it around to beat a weft yarn into place. Not all combs have pointed handles, but those that do are especially helpful. This card is postmarked 1963. (PS.)

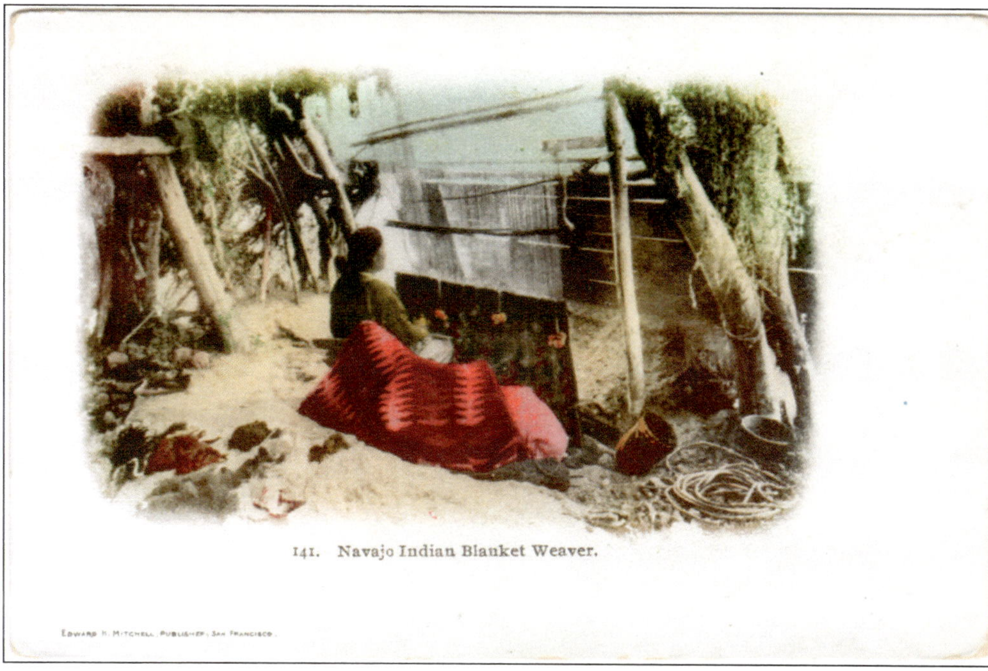

Small bundles of unwoven yarn hang from the loom's work area, ready as the weaver works across the textile. These are sometimes called "butterflies." A handwoven blanket enigmatically covers her seat, and a handmade Navajo ceramic jar, of the type used as peyote water drums, sits at the corner of her loom. (E.H. Mitchell.)

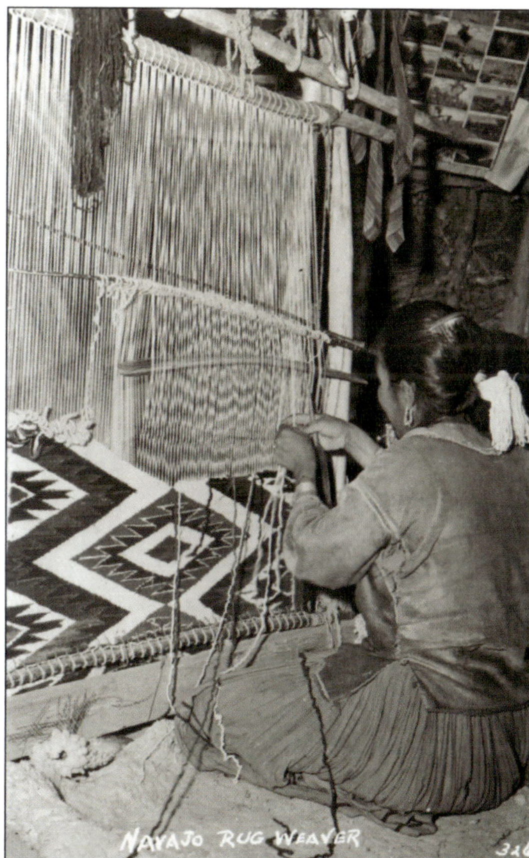

The environment in which an artist works is always interesting. At home, this weaver is making a "Red Mesa Outline" rug, a successor to earlier "Eye Dazzlers." Curiously, half the string loops are removed from her heddle stick, so only the right side functions. Hanging on the wall is a board mounted with rodeo pictures; several men's ties drape over the loom. (CSNM.)

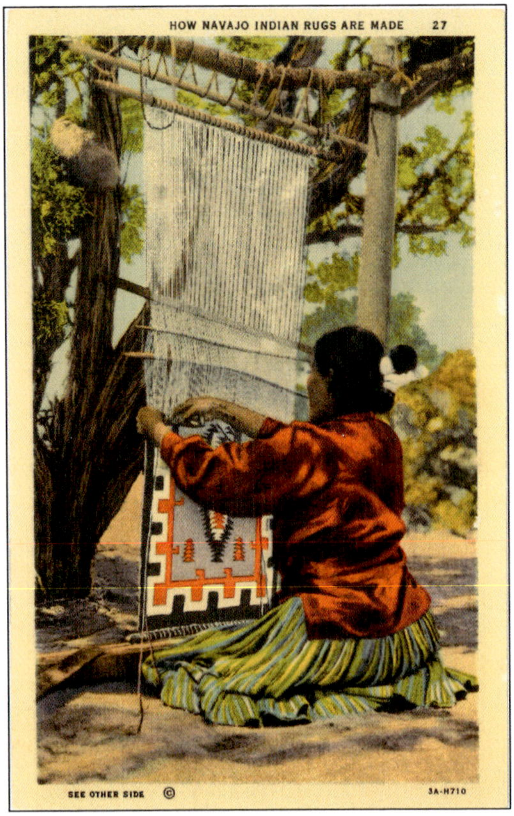

People often ask how much time it takes to make a Navajo rug. Given two views of this weaver working on the same rug, it would be great to know how much time intervened between them! Generally, weavers advance several inches on an average-sized rug each day, but the actual time depends on the size and fineness of the rug, the weaver's experience, and her other responsibilities, including children to tend, sheep to herd, household tasks, and jobs beyond the home. A rug of this size and quality probably took from 7 to 20 days for the weaver to finish after she had spent several weeks preparing and dyeing the wool. J.R. Willis took the photograph at left. (Left, FHC; below, US.)

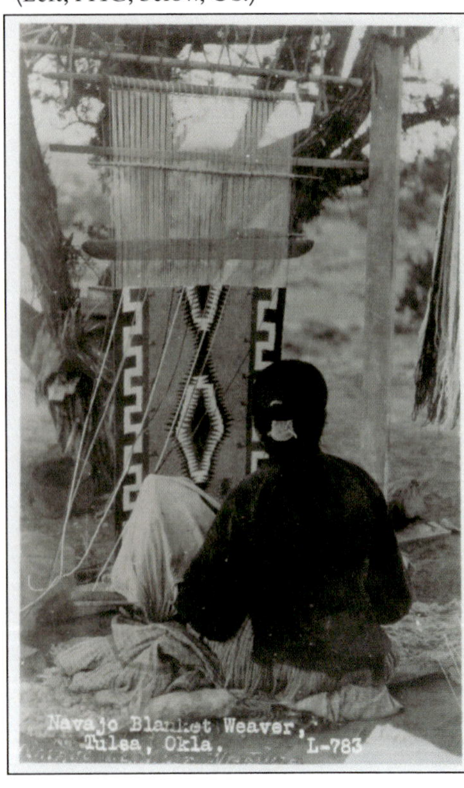

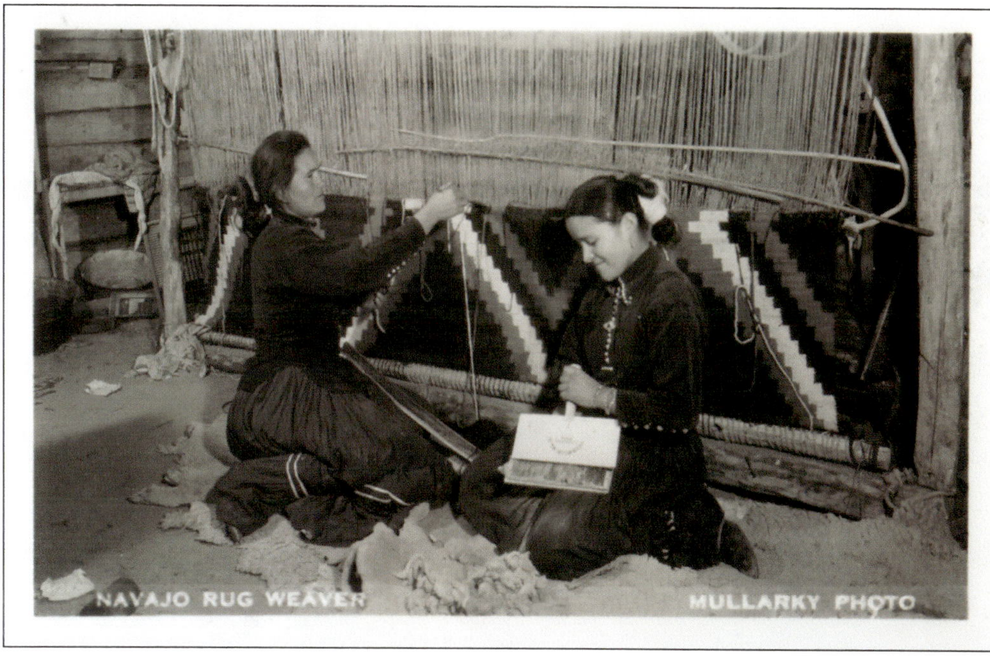

Although posing for a photographer, both women may have worked side by side on this large rug. Usually, one weaver makes design decisions, with the other following her lead. Where they meet in the middle may be joined with a darning needle. This classic revival blanket has a subtle banded background called "Moqui Stripe," named after the archaic name for the Hopi Indians. (MS.)

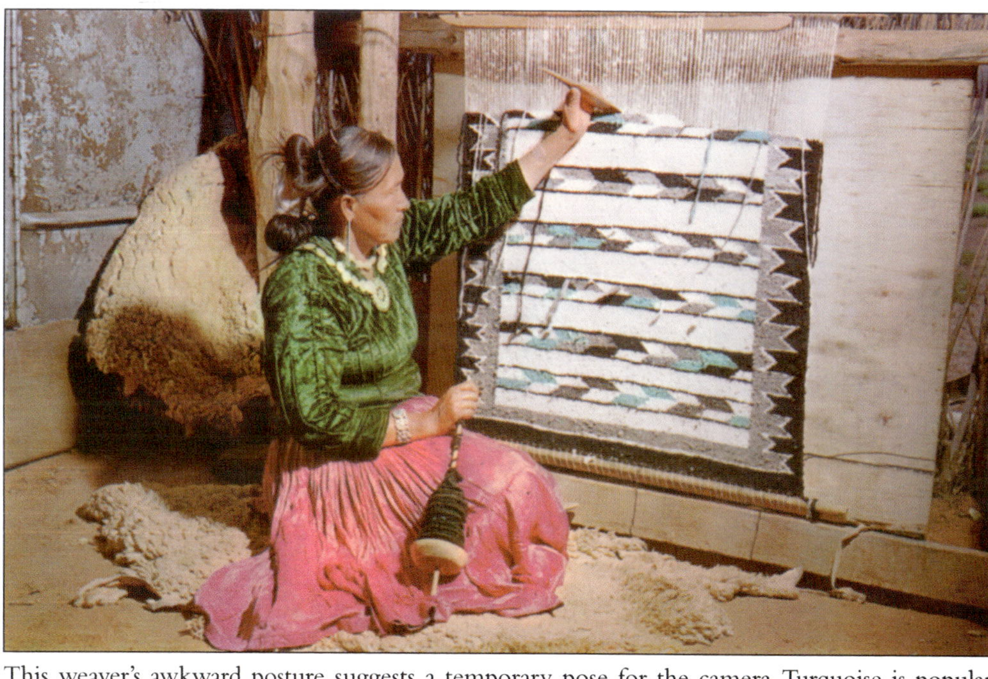

This weaver's awkward posture suggests a temporary pose for the camera. Turquoise is popular in Navajo jewelry but an uncommon color in rugs. While it is possible to obtain this color by combining indigo and yellow plant dyes, the time-consuming process is rarely used. This blue likely came from synthetic rather than natural dyes. The rug's other colors are natural sheep tones. (PS.)

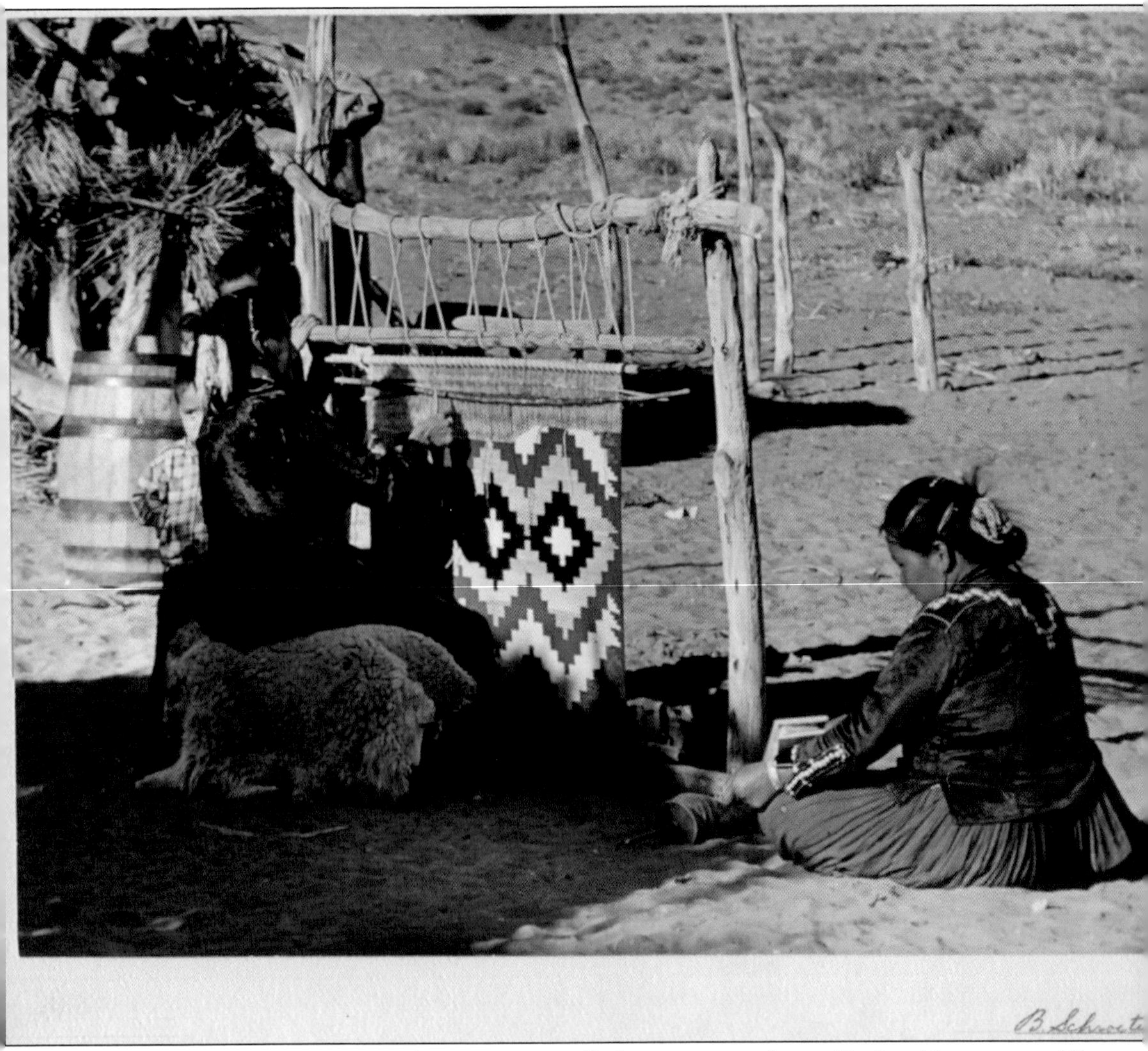

When a wide rug is woven, the weaver must find a way to work on side-by-side segments. The sections can be stitched together with a sacking needle or, more commonly, by using diagonal units called "lazy lines" that form one atop the other. In this photograph, signed and dated "B. Schroeter, '53" in pencil and originally measuring 10 by 13 inches, the weaver is about to weave on top of the angled white area to her right. Both women wear classic velvet shirts, patterned after Victorian blouses, with silver buttons on the yokes and cuffs. Although less common since the 1960s, some trading posts still keep bolts of the richly colored plush fabric for women who sew their own clothing, often using treadle sewing machines.

Narrow rugs do not require the use of "lazy lines," but weavers also use them to focus on one pattern area at a time. A diagonal woven piece appears just above the weaver's arm and awaits her attention while she completes the left-hand section. The audible beat of her weaving comb may have lulled this baby to sleep while it was snug in its cradleboard. (MS.)

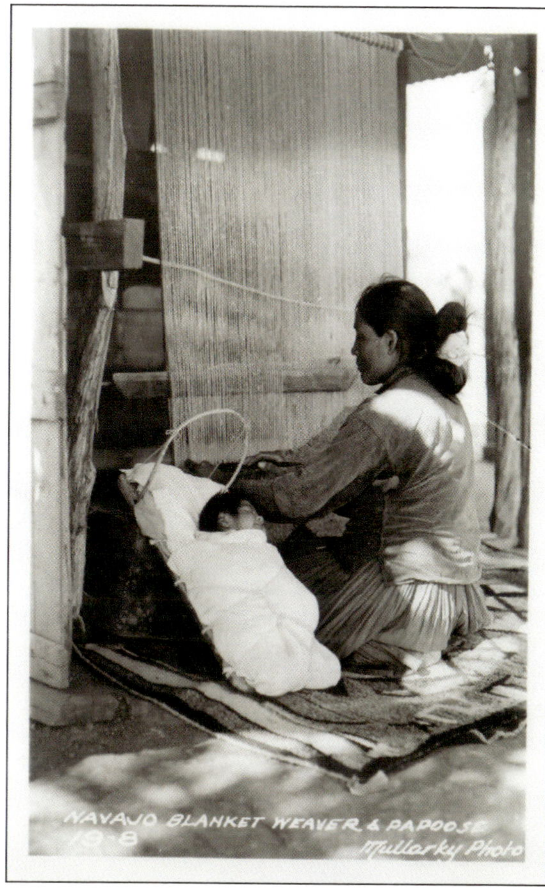

A diagonal "lazy line" is put to good use on this wide loom, where the weaver is seated on the left but will move to her right as the rug grows. Lazy lines result in a subtle network of almost-invisible diagonal lines across a rug and are common in late 19th and early 20th century rugs. Today, weavers use ingenious alternative methods to accommodate wide weaving. (US.)

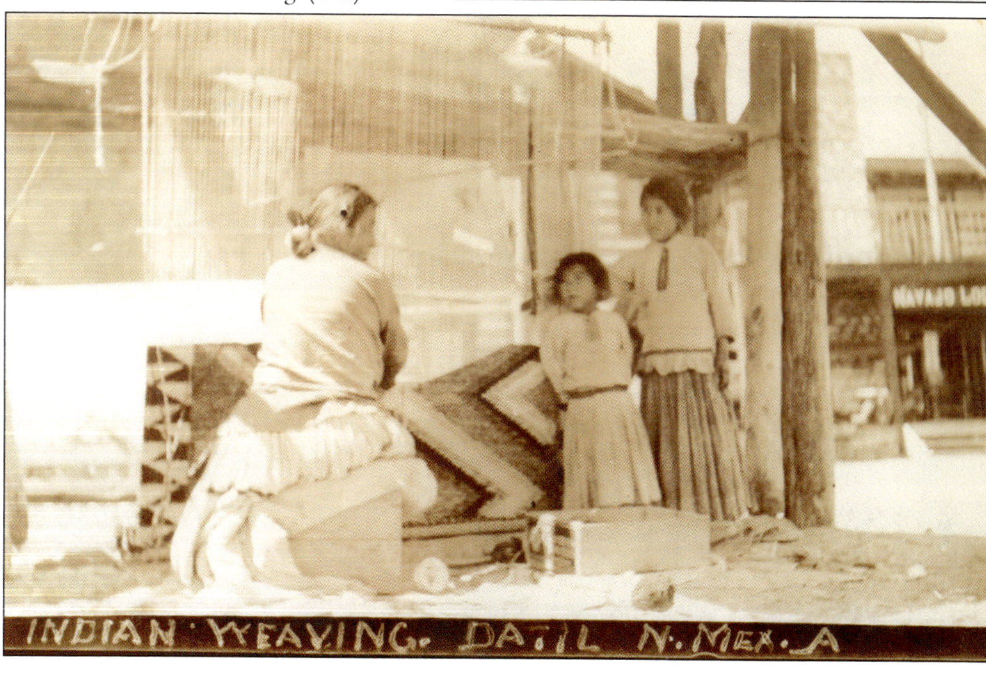

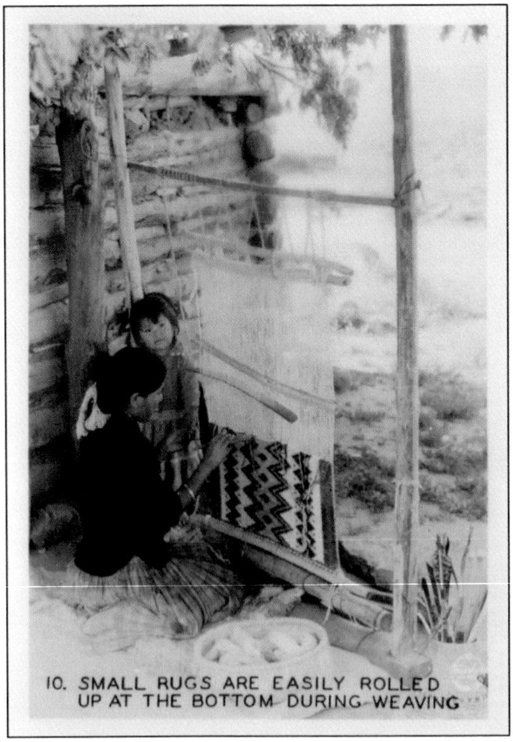

The rug's lower edge should have a dark border, but it was rolled under and stitched to the lower bar so the weaver can reach her work area. A rug in progress, such as this one, can be removed from its frame, rolled up, and moved to another location, making it quite portable. (FFS.)

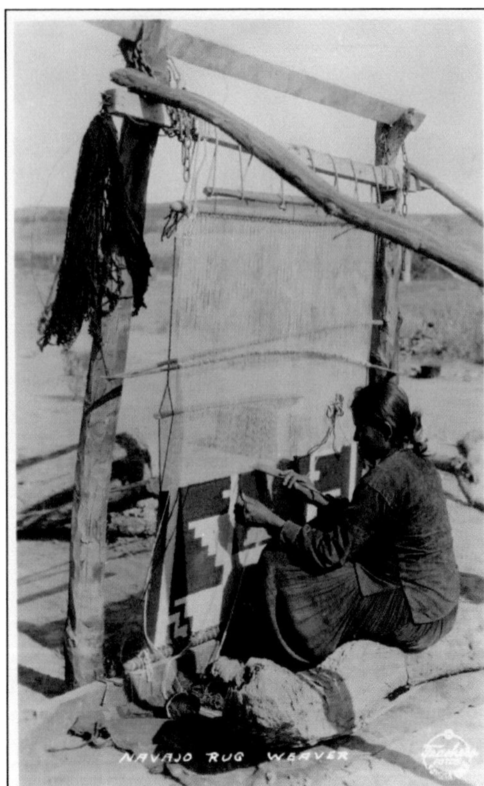

All looms shown on these two pages reveal the same "stitch-down" technique for reducing the weavers' upward reach. Sometimes this method left one or more rows of tiny telltale puckers across the textile. These are most commonly seen in 19th-century wearing blankets, but this 1930 photograph and the one above (from 1932) prove that stitching down continued at least into the 1930s. (FFS.)

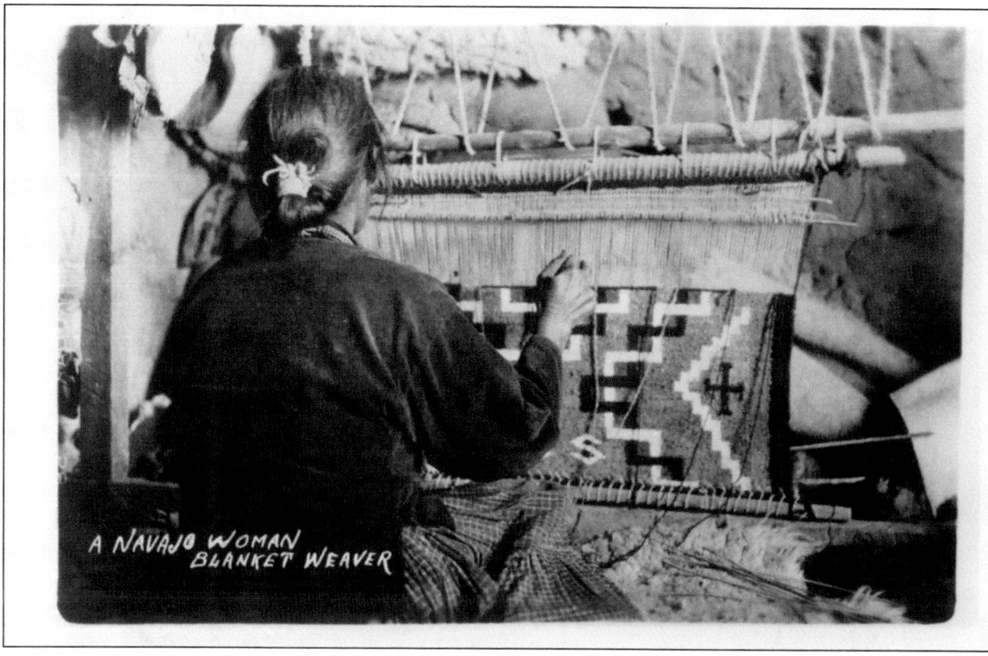

Well-woven Navajo rugs have carefully twined end and side cords (*tł'óółts'ósí*) that strengthen and beautify the rug's edges. Both these rugs show dark cords running vertically along their sides. The weaver integrates the heavier pairs or triplets of two- and three-ply cords into the fabric as her weaving progresses upward. (Above, US; below, NAU-CL, Leo Crane Collection, NAU. PH.658.218.)

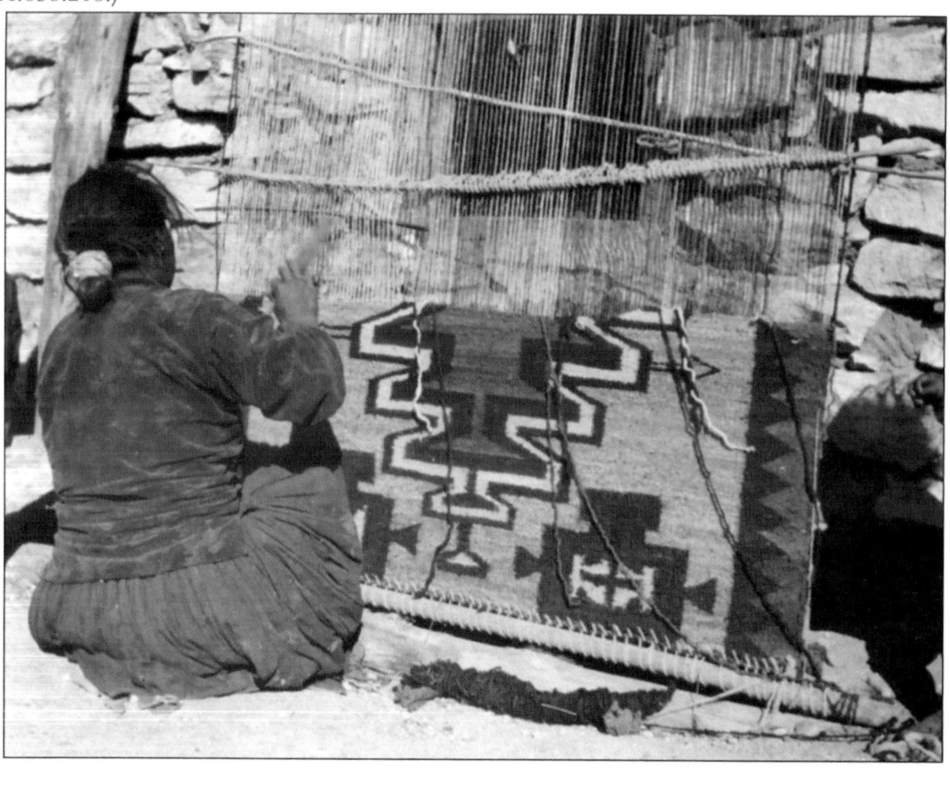

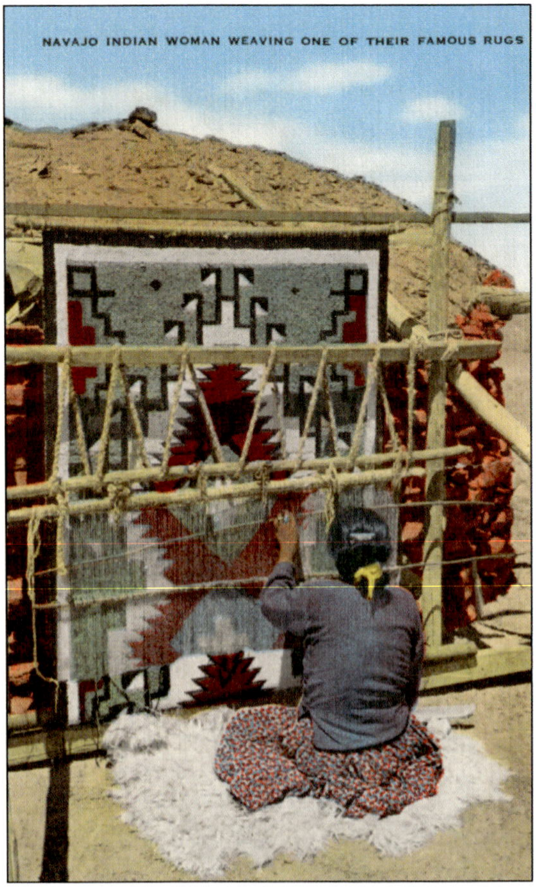

These weavers have mastered their loom's technology. Each is about two feet from finishing a large rug with bold geometric patterns in symmetrical layouts and enclosing double borders. The woven portion of their work is wrapped below the lower loom beam and extends up behind the unwoven warp threads and tension ropes. If it were simply rolled at the bottom, the design would be hidden and unavailable for comparison with the work ahead. In the image at left, a long, diagonally-placed pole (on the right, possibly one of a pair) rests on the hogan's roof and supports the loom's upper tension beam; below, a similar pole is used where a living tree is not available for support. The living tree, also shown below, appears to support a second loom with an equally ambitious rug. (Left, NMST; below, US.)

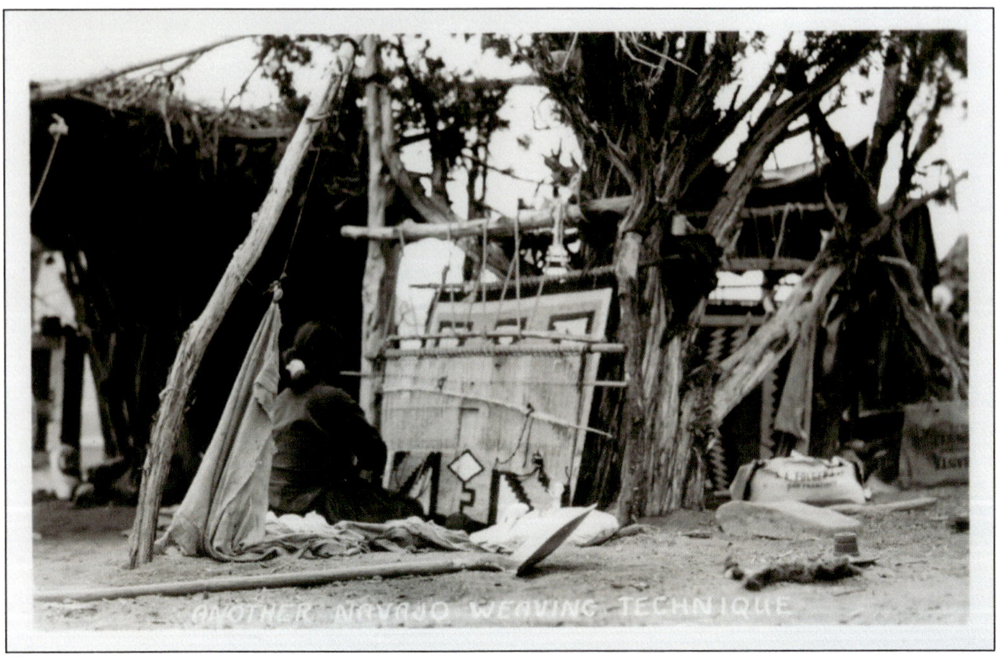

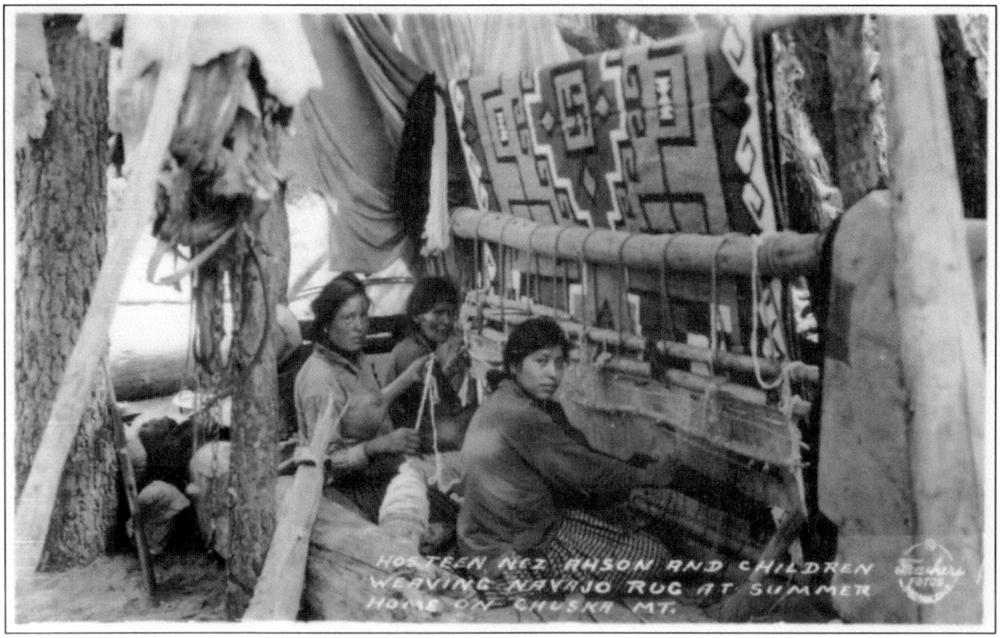

Representing two or three generations in 1932, these women probably worked together on this large rug and have about 12 more inches to finish. The woven part is wrapped under the lower beam and then folded over a second time at the loom's top bar before hanging down the back. The design is a geometric "Old Crystal" style, like Plate XXVII in J.B. Moore's 1911 catalogue for Crystal Trading Post. Canvas tarps are draped around the oversize loom, likely in defense of the high country's summer rains. One woman is identified as "Hosteen Nez Ahson," which translates as "Tall Man's Wife" (or "wife of Mr. Nez"). (Both, FFS.)

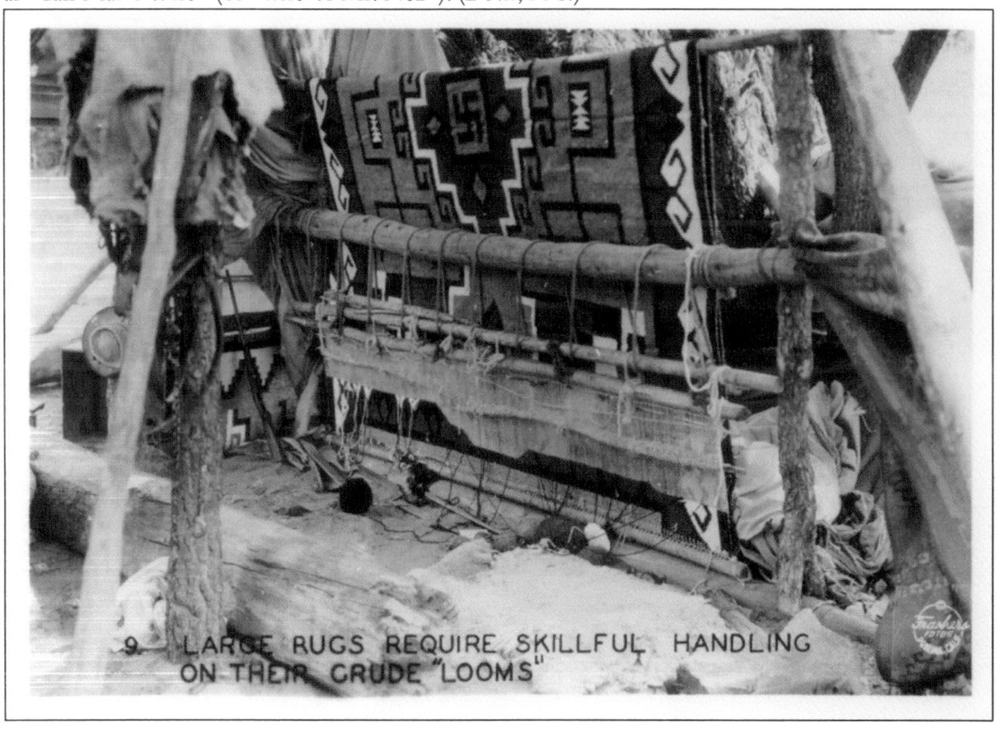

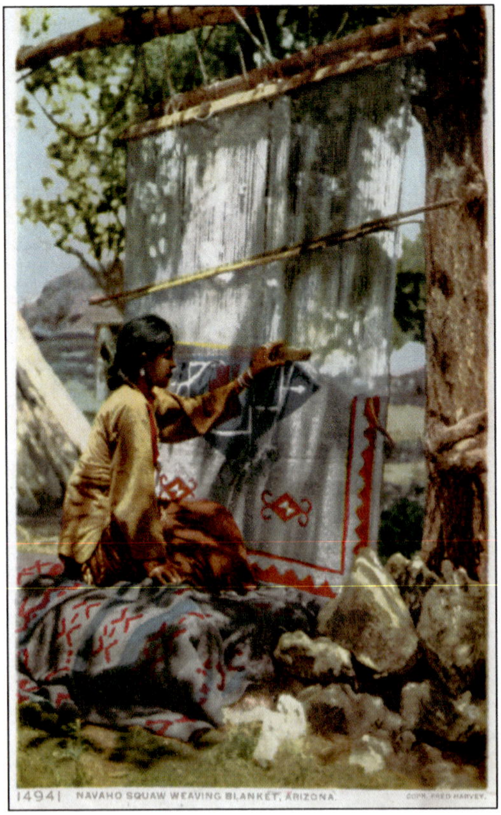

This idyllic image reveals a frontal view of the loom, rug, and unwoven warps. The young woman could weave directly to the top by either raising her seat or lowering the web to within reach. Alternatively, she might remove the entire web from the loom frame, turn it around, and reattach it upside down. She would then start again from the bottom and weave to the middle. (FHC.)

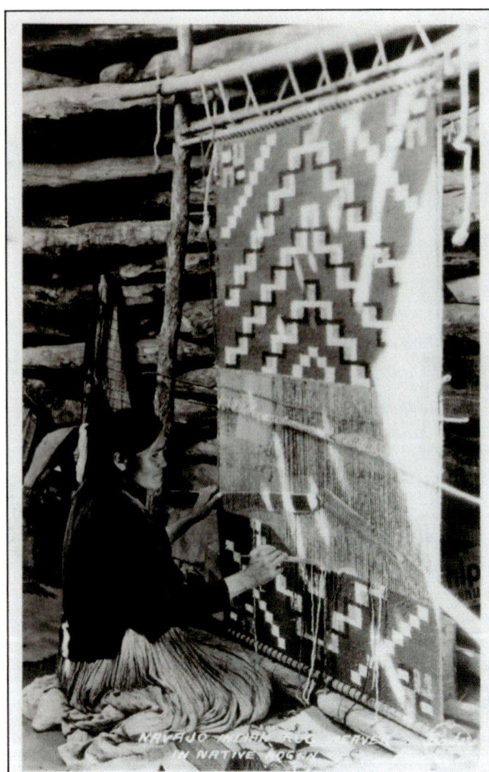

The upper half of this rug was woven first in reversed position; it was removed, turned around in the loom frame, and relashed into place. The woman is now weaving toward the middle, where her work will meet the first half. Achieving quadrilateral symmetry within the fixed frame of the Navajo loom represents a remarkable feat skillfully repeated by many Navajo weavers. (FFS.)

Six

What's on the Loom?

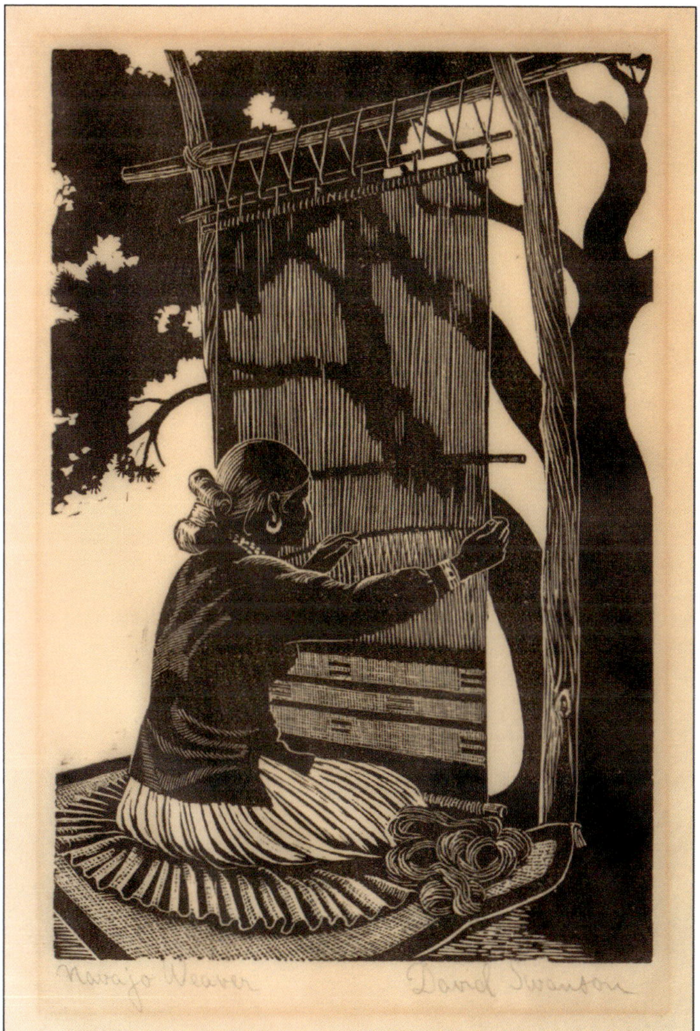

The Navajo upright loom provides a "canvas" where a weaver can depict many styles—from basic stripes to elaborate geometry to stylized and realistic pictures. Tapestry weave provides the "brush" and wool yarns the "paint" for Diné woven artistry. In David Swanson's linocut print, which is titled "Navajo Weaver" and originally measured nine by six inches, the banded rug on the loom reflects a mid–20th century "revival" of striped designs without borders.

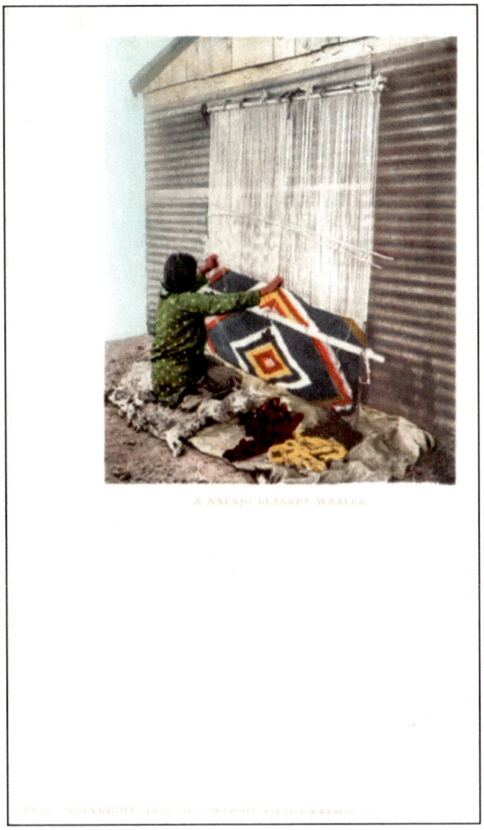

The large size and soft texture of this weaving attest to it being an old-style blanket rather than a floor rug, but it was made for the growing tourist trade of the early 1900s. The dark indigo-dyed blue and natural white were either handspun wool or commercial yarns. The red could have been handspun or commercial yarn or perhaps the famous "bayeta" yarn that was unraveled from commercial trade cloth, respun, and rewoven. To show off her pattern, the weaver has unrolled the bottom portion and brought it forward, overlapping her work area. This design of concentric serrated diamonds shows the influence of the Mexican "Saltillo" style on Navajo weavers. Known for its strong colors and sharp zigzags, the trend began during the late 1870s and continued well into the 20th century. (Both, US.)

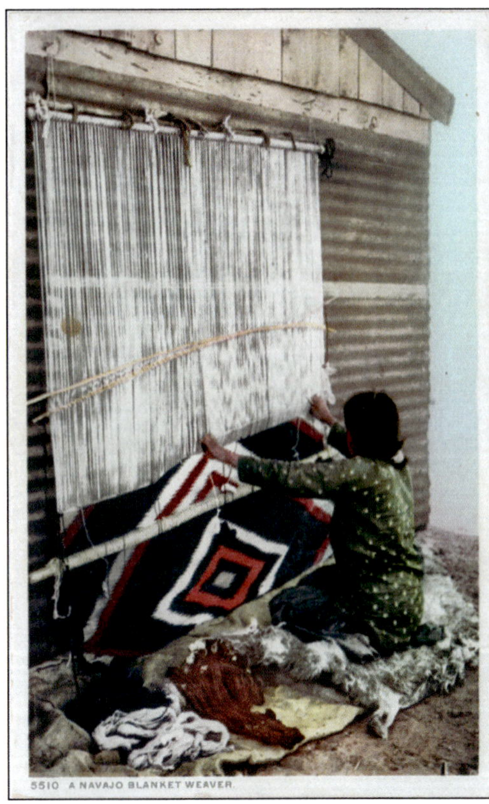

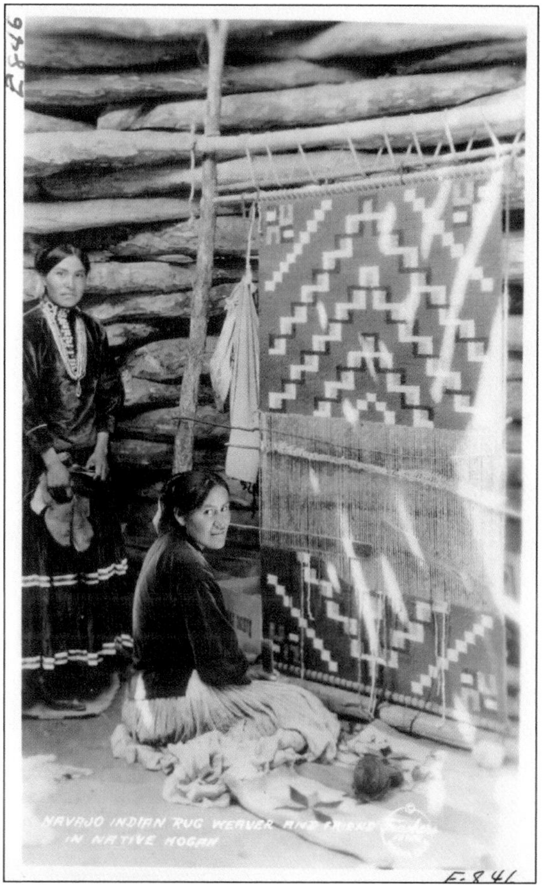

The elaborate pattern on this 1930s rug reflects both old traditions and new trends. Like earlier classic blankets of the mid-19th century, it contains stepped elements, not diagonal serrations, and a simple palette of four contrasting colors. The design layout extends from edge to edge without an enclosing, or entrapping, border like those of later regional rug styles. In contrast to older blankets, and more common in 20th-century rugs, are the intricately interlaced lines and curious corner motifs. Similar lines, almost an optical illusion, appear as an all-over rug pattern in Plate V of trader J.B. Moore's 1903 catalogue for Crystal Trading Post. (Both, FFS.)

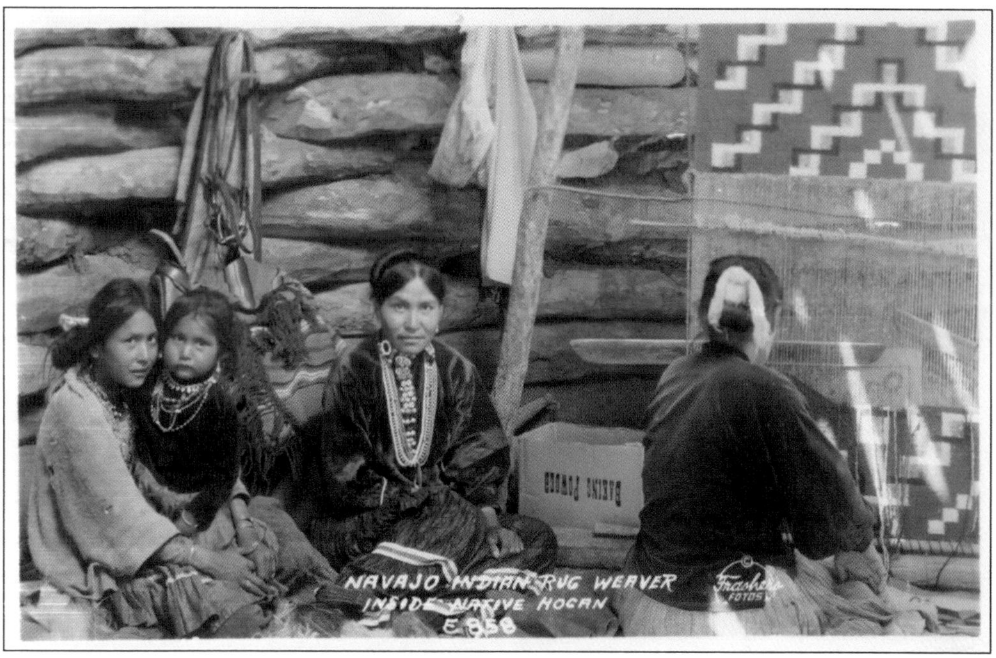

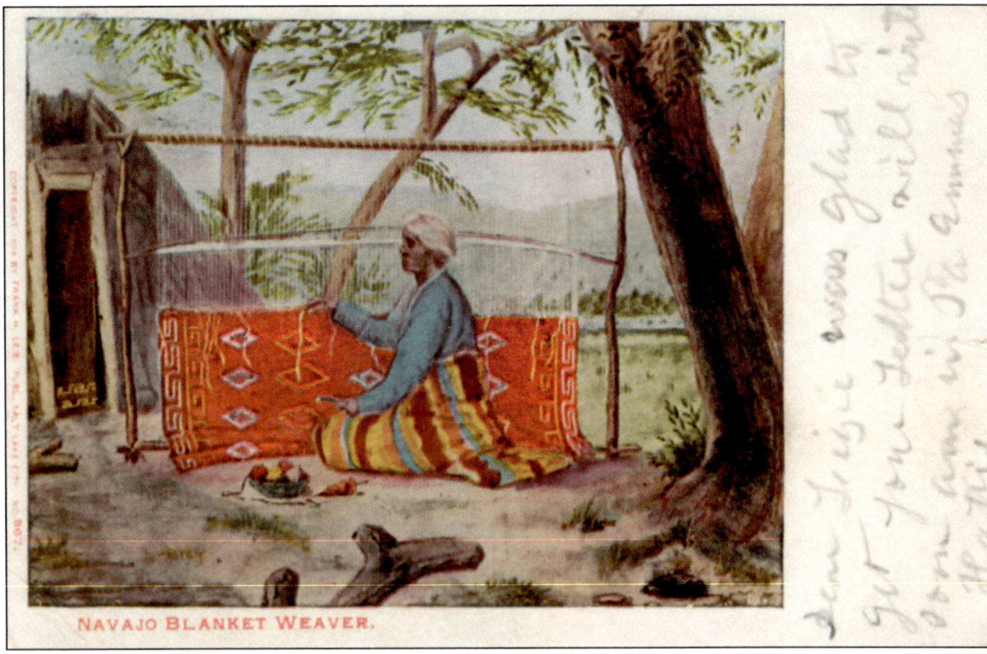

Using artistic license, the painter inaccurately portrayed this loom—it is impossibly delicate for a large weaving and is missing its tension ropes and beams. Nevertheless, both blankets are interesting. The weaver's striped "robe" was either handwoven or store-bought. Her patterned "Germantown blanket" harks back to the 1890s (like that of the one shown at left). Such fancy borders were occasionally documented as early as the 1860s. This card is postmarked 1909 and has a copyright date of 1904. (Frank H. Leib.)

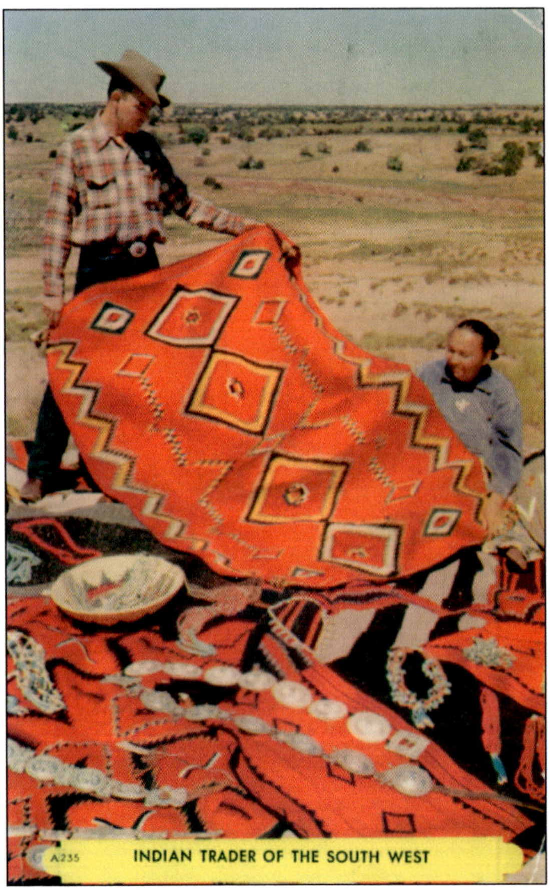

An unidentified trader shows off a beautiful old blanket of the 1890s (like the one pictured on the postcard above). This was most likely woven with commercial yarns imported from mills in Germantown, Pennsylvania, and popular from the 1880s through the 1910s. A traditional two-panel dress and several other old weavings appear underneath the classic Southwestern jewelry and Diné basketry bowl. (RWEN.)

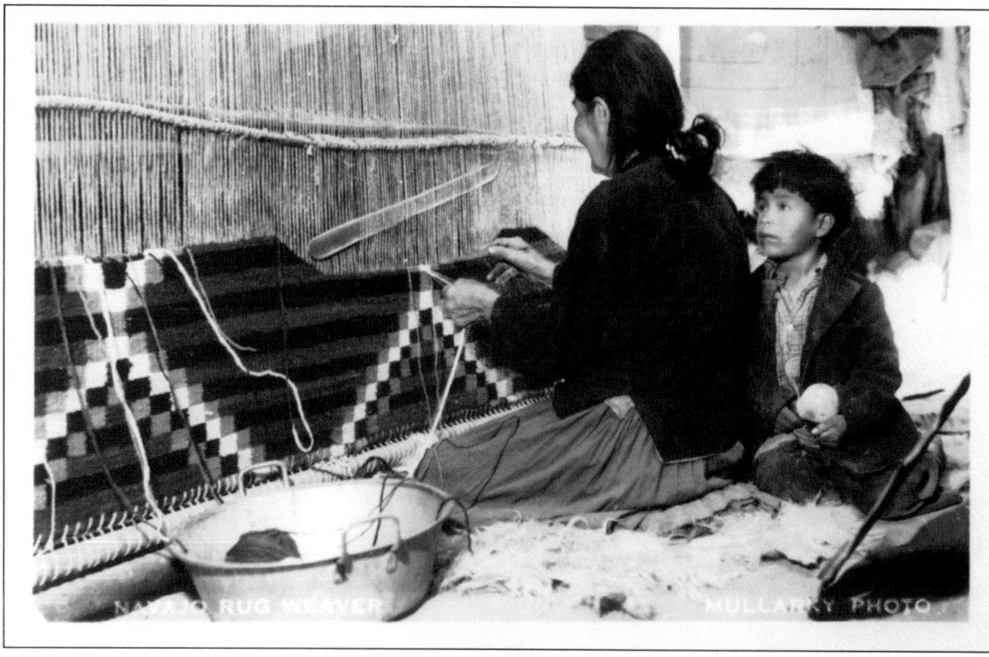

The revival of older blanket styles was popularized by Hubbell Trading Post during the 1890s and continues today. Depending on coloration, the pattern might be called a "woman's wearing blanket" if the stripes are black and gray or a "Moqui striped blanket" if they are black and dark blue. The boy holds a small gourd rattle. (MS.)

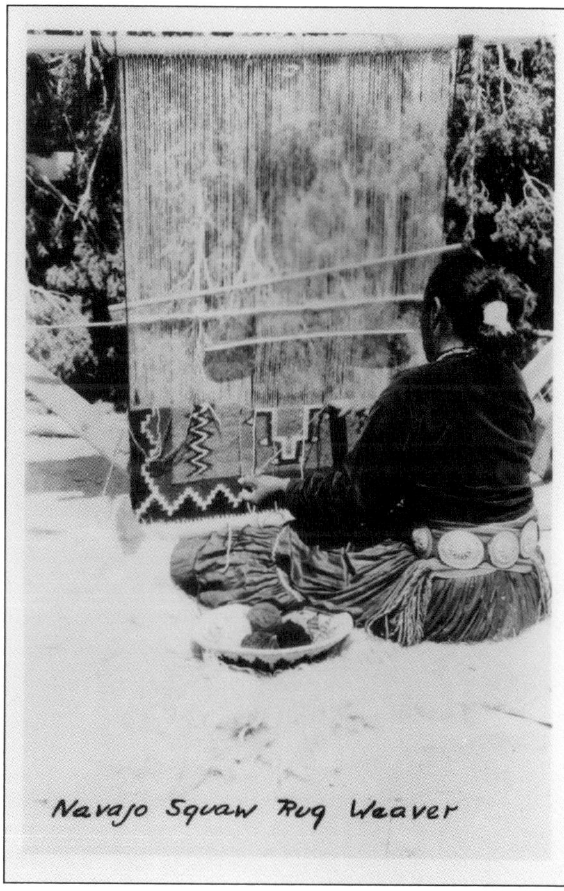

A transition from creating wearing blankets to making floor rugs occurred during the 1880s. During the early rug period (1890–1935), weavers focused on rugs with central diamonds or double diamonds, zigzag filler motifs, and fancy borders. The tiny appendages at the diamond's corners are playfully called *bijaatł'óól* (its earrings.) For colored versions of this rug that suggest an early "Ganado Red" style, see pages 34 and 91. (FFS.)

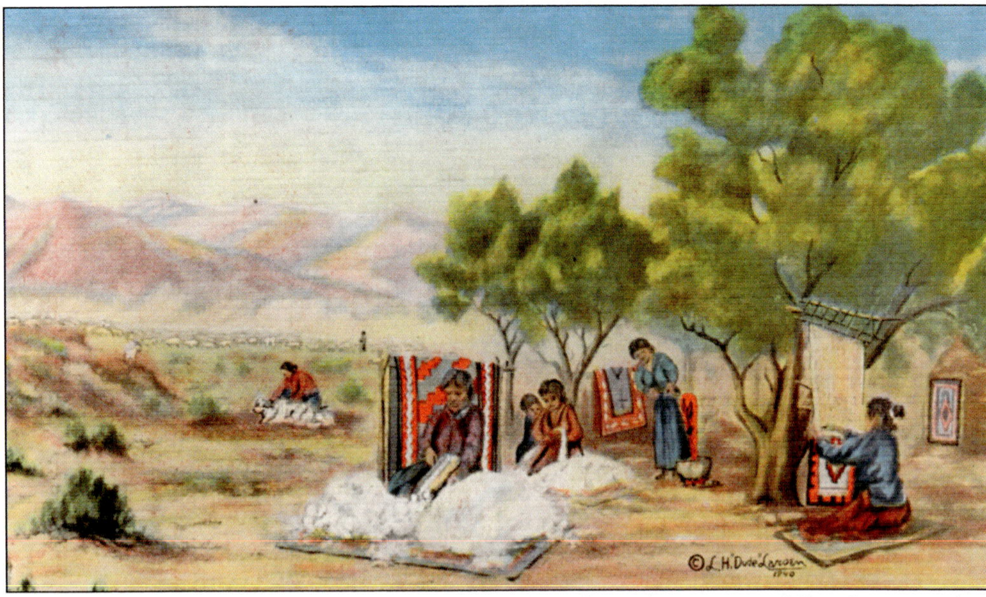

Some Navajo weavers persist in utilizing one style throughout their career, while others vary their designs. Cowboy poet and artist L.H. ("Dude") Larsen's oil painting, "The Navajo" (1940), shows a variety of earlier rug styles presumably made by a single family or individual. Each has a fancy border and similar color palette, but no two are alike. (LHL.)

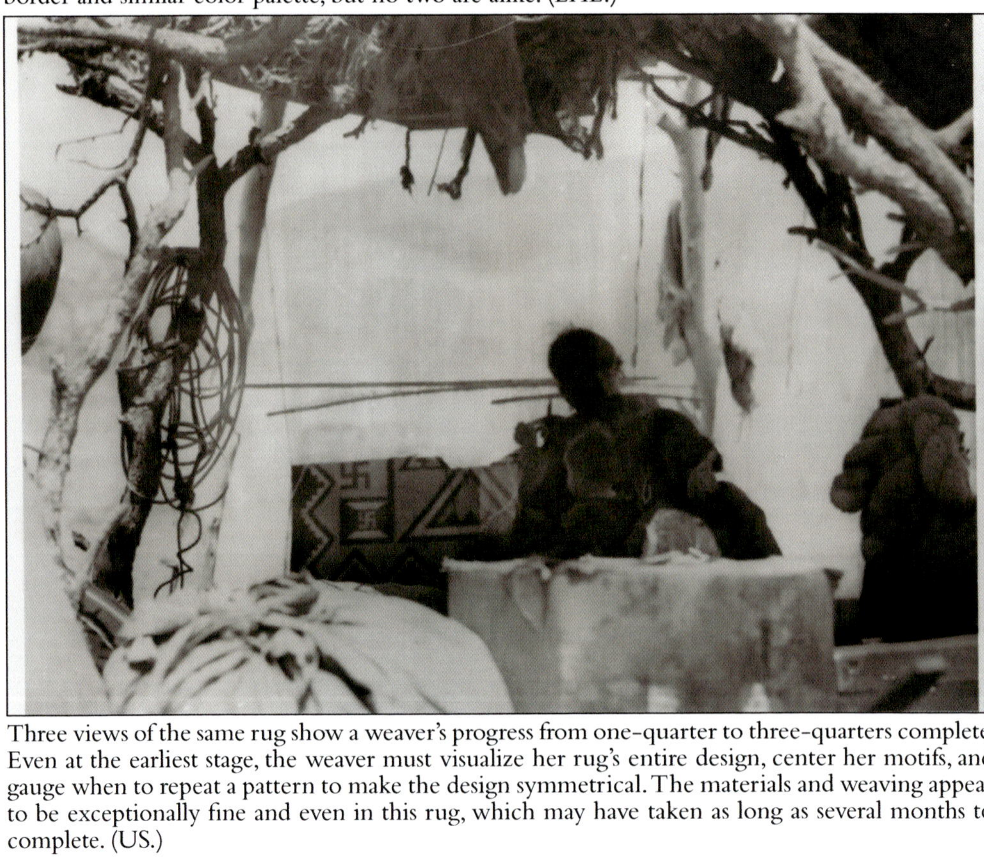

Three views of the same rug show a weaver's progress from one-quarter to three-quarters complete. Even at the earliest stage, the weaver must visualize her rug's entire design, center her motifs, and gauge when to repeat a pattern to make the design symmetrical. The materials and weaving appear to be exceptionally fine and even in this rug, which may have taken as long as several months to complete. (US.)

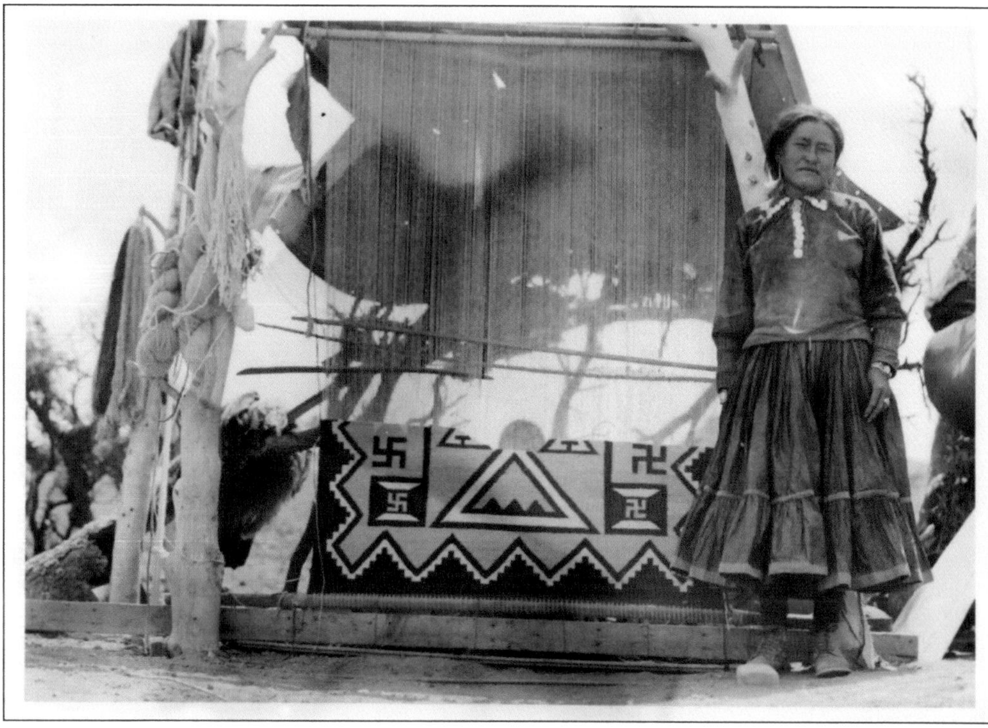

The rug style shown in these photographs (and the previous one on page 108), which originally measured five by seven inches, is known as a "Storm Pattern," depicted in plate XXVIII of J.B. Moore's 1911 catalogue and described as "one of the really legendary designs embodying a portion of the Navajo mythology." Six stepped lines (symbolizing zigzag lightning) radiate from a central rectangle (central fire, hogan, lake, or storm house); four extend to the rug's corners (sacred mountains, winds, or cardinal directions). Swastikas serve as filler motifs and refer to the "whirling logs" design from Diné sandpaintings, with no connection to the Nazi symbol. For another Storm rug, see page 66. A second weaving peeks out from the far left side of one photograph. Handspun yarns, a lariat, and spurs hang from the loom; a Navajo saddle and dark fleece in the foreground complete the tableau. (Both, US.)

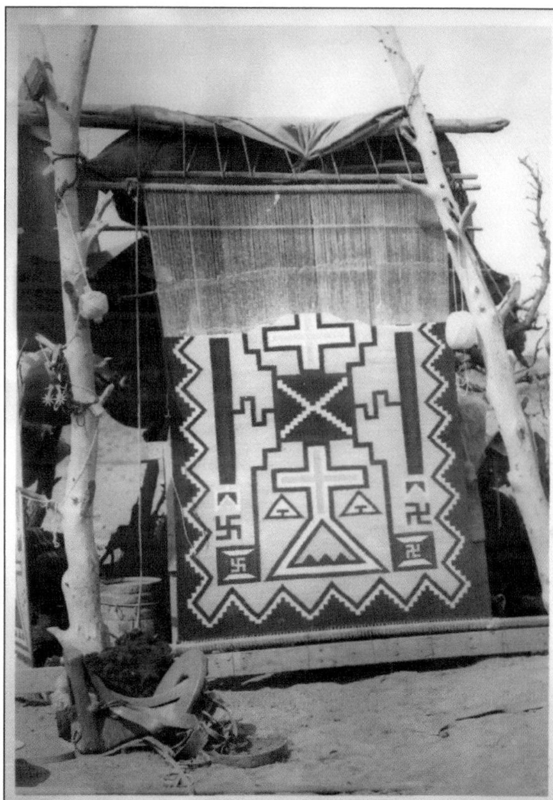

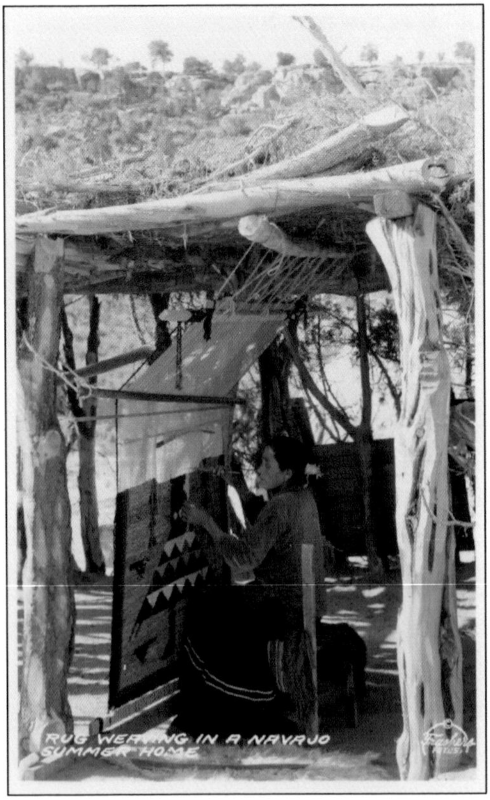

Figurative imagery, especially isolated birds and pictorial elements, began appearing in Diné weaving in the 1860s. In this 1930s scene, the moccasin-clad feet, fancy kilt, belted torso and feathered arm streamers of a ceremonial *yé'ii* figure emerge as the weaving progresses. Two birds appear on the left. The loom is ingeniously angled inside a shady ramada, and the weaver's chair is adapted to her needs. (FFS.)

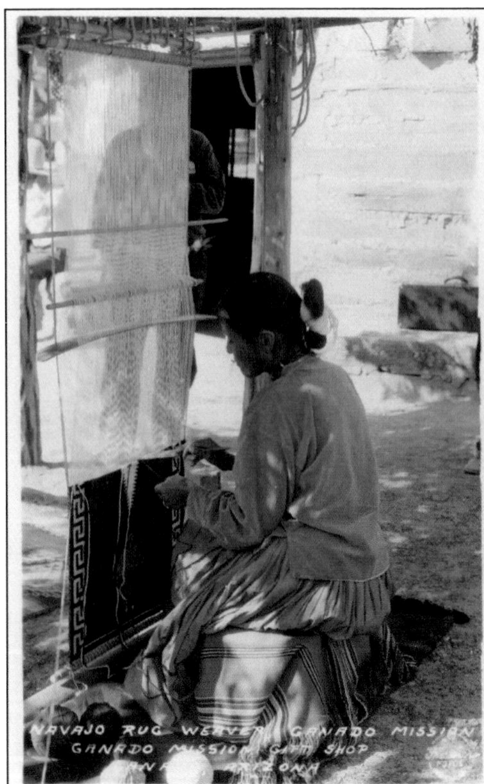

On this long runner, a single figure appears below the beginnings of a narrow, serrated diamond. The figure appears to have a bird's head, wings, and three tail feathers, possibly representing a Diné eagle or "thunderbird." Possibly commissioned by a client, the runner has a fancy "Greek key" border. Wearing a concho belt, the man behind the loom adds an element of mystery. (FFS.)

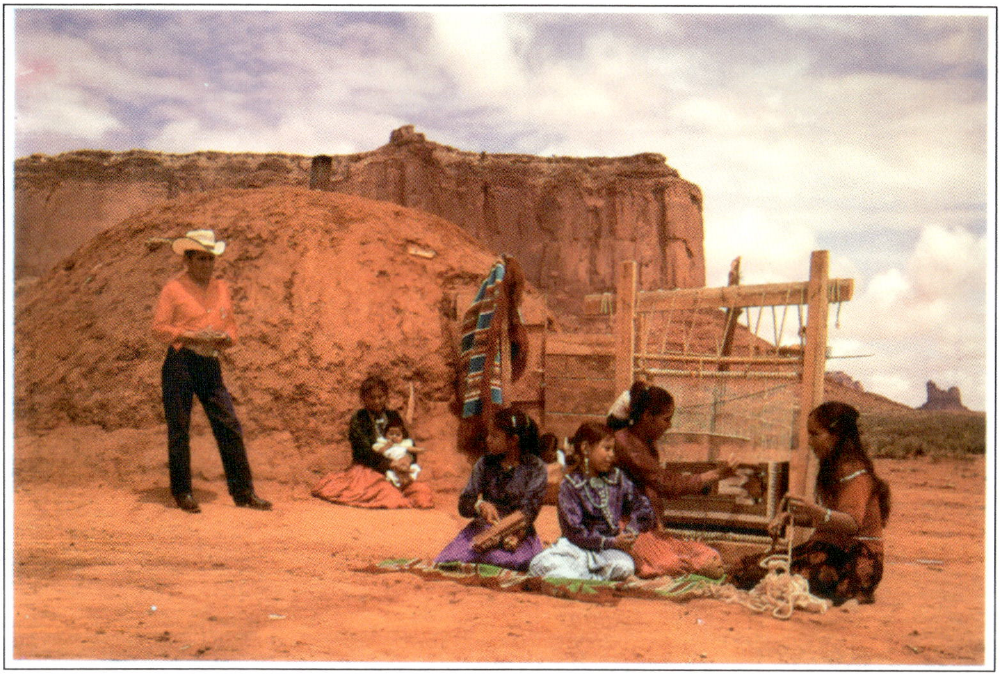

Above, a father, grandmother, and baby observe as a mother and girls demonstrate their skills for photographer Josef Muench. On the rug and woven sideways (as European tapestries are also made), the figure with upraised arms is a ceremonial dancer, likely impersonating a female *yé'ii* (supernatural being). This is probably the first in a row of similar figures yet to be woven. Below, the start of this 1962 pictorial rug features a pair of basketry jars with the traditional Diné "wedding basket" pattern in black and red. A skinny pair of moccasin-clad legs appears between the baskets—where will the weaver take this design? The wave-like reciprocating border adds a bold touch and demonstrates her skill in making curved forms. (Both, NAU-CL, Josef Muench Collection.)

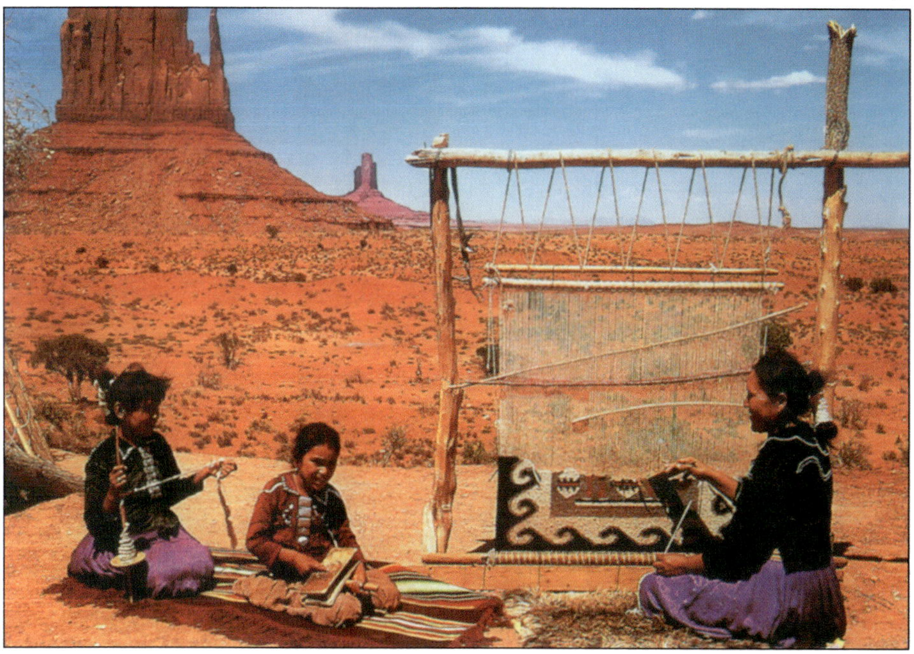

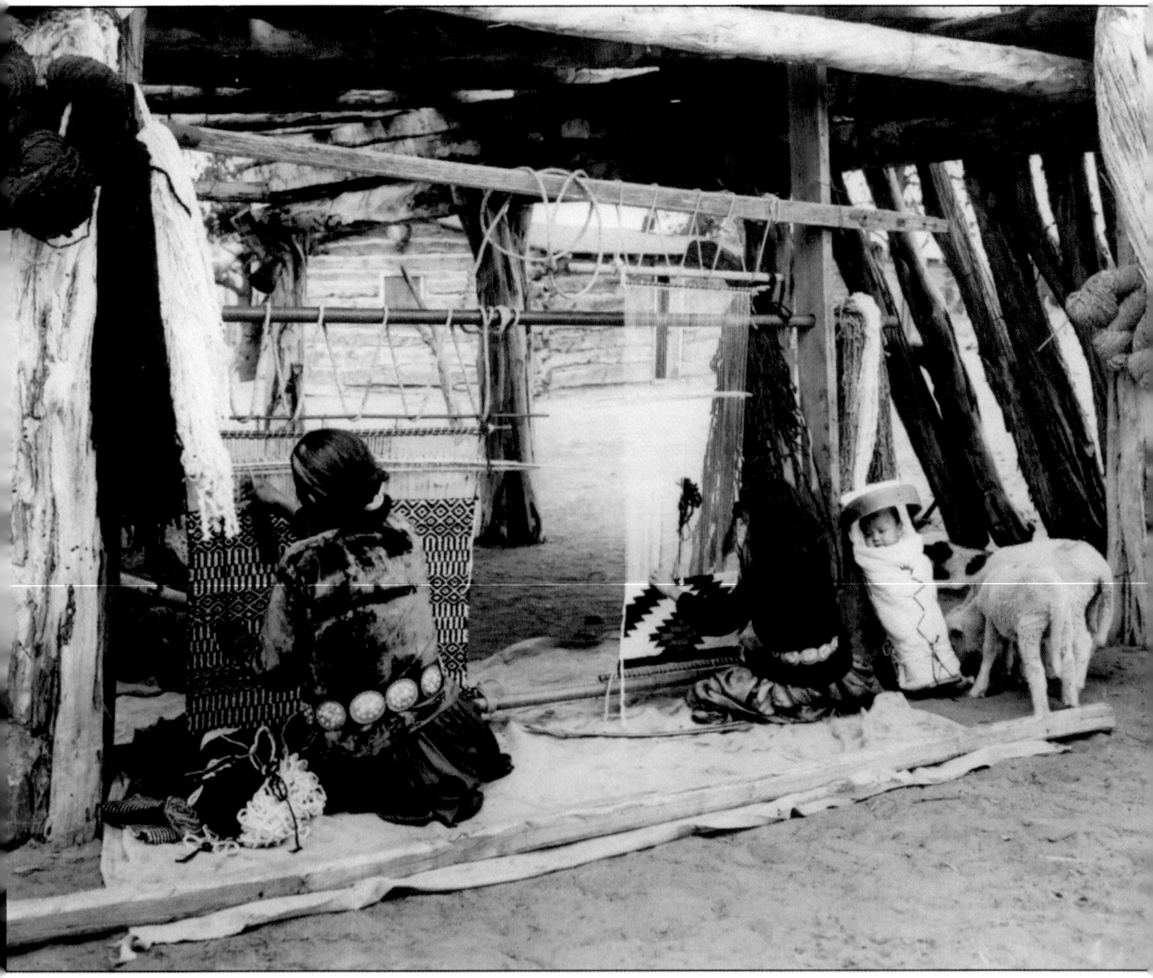

A spacious shade house with a wide loom accommodates two weavers. Coauthor Ramona Sakiestewa comments, "I have taught many weaving workshops where my students' husbands believed they could improve upon the weaving technology and set about making new looms. The only positive innovation I have seen is a loom made with two-by-12-inch side beams that are drilled with large holes. These holes support metal pipes, create an adjustable loom to accommodate different weaving sizes, and give strength and consistency to the warps' tension." This loom has such side supports, with metal pipes inserted as lower and upper beams. Beginning in the 1970s, local work programs across the Navajo Nation built even more elaborate looms with "Swiss cheese" side supports, adding more holes for increased flexibility. The photographer inscribed the original eight-by-ten-inch card: "8-15-01 To Peter Hiller, with best wishes, George C. Hight." This photograph is reproduced with permission from Matthew Hayes.

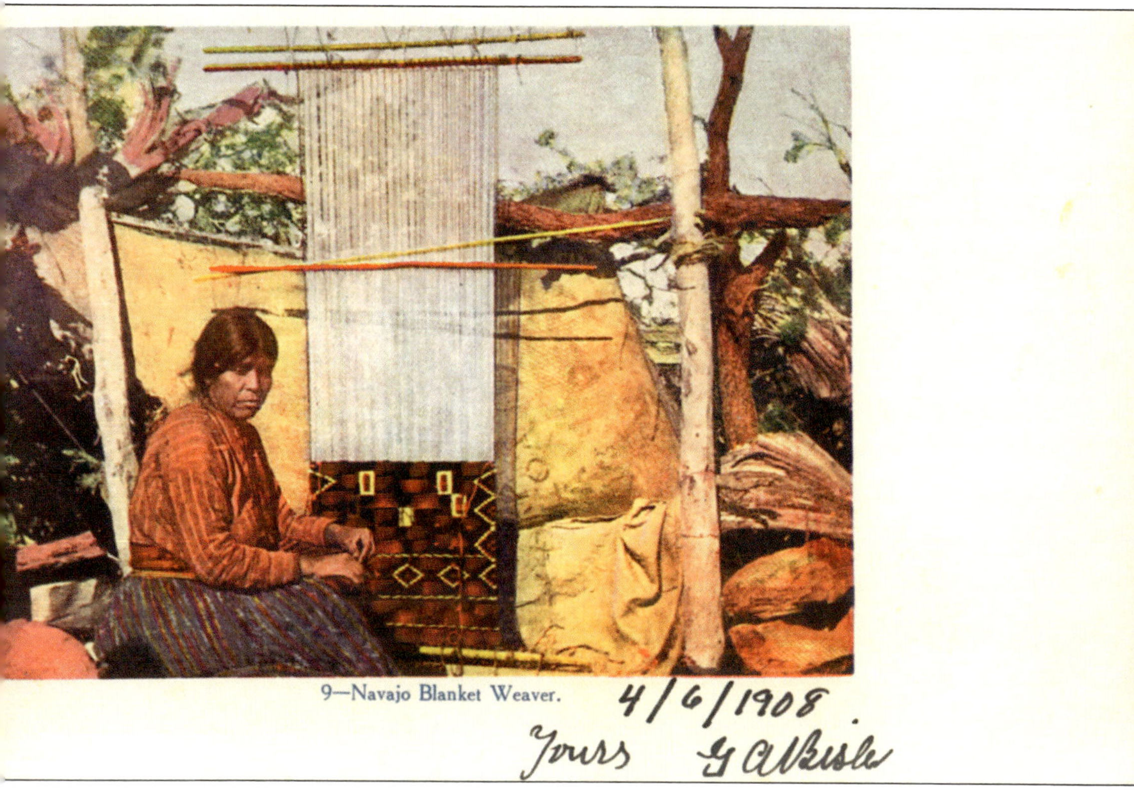

Like most Diné weavers, this woman is using tapestry weave, in which the yarns are interlaced throughout over-one, under-one. When finished, her long narrow piece perhaps became a fancy saddle cover, a floor or table runner, or a pair of pillow covers—popular curio items during the early 1900s. Runners were favored in East Coast homes, where central hallways were a common architectural feature. In the photograph on page 112, the young weaver on the right is making a runner with serrated diamonds, also in tapestry weave. The weaver on the left has nearly completed a rug using twill weave with an overall pattern of "bird's-eye" diamonds (*'i'íí'mas*) and standing bars (*'i'íí'mas naazíní* or *niidz'į*). Twill patterns have over-two, under-two interlacing and variations. Woven with three alternating colors (often black/white/gray or red/white/gray), Diné twill weaves are called "saddle blanket weaves" due to their thick, durable nature and use as extra padding between a saddle and a horse's back. (W-H.)

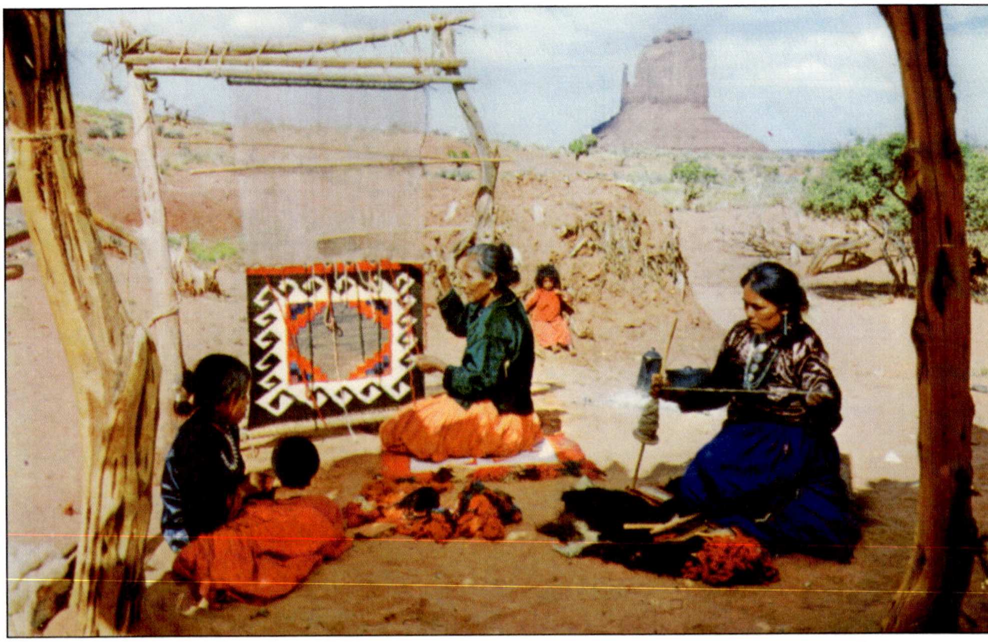

Single saddle blankets measure roughly 30 by 30 inches, roughly what appears to be woven on this loom so far. Double saddle blankets are 60 by 30 inches and designed to fold in half, creating an extra cushion. Sometimes, each half has a different pattern. This weaver, Happy Cly, could have chosen to repeat her design or weave something different on the second half. (RWEN.)

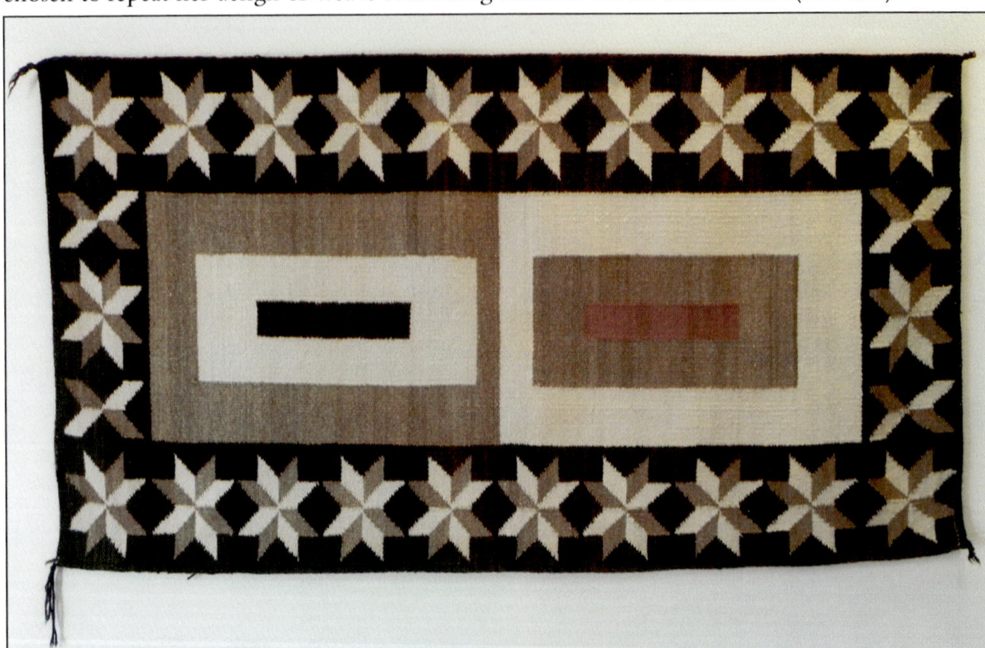

This double saddle blanket, which measures 58 by 32 inches, is from the 1940s and features a border with "Vallero Stars," a motif possibly derived from early American quilt patterns and also woven into Spanish American blankets. ("Vallero" refers to the valley of the Rio Grande.) Folded in half, it would look handsome on a horse's back; otherwise, it makes a charming floor rug or modern version of a saddle blanket—a seat cover for a pickup truck!

The saddle blanket on this loom has a "ribbon" pattern with a checkered border. Today, handwoven saddle blankets are sold as small rugs. Navajos usually buy Mexican or other cheaper commercial products for their own horses. This patient steed has a rainbow-hued Mexican blanket on its back. The weaver sits on a fancy Pendleton blanket with red fringed edges. The photographer of this image was Bob Bradshaw of Sedona, Arizona. (Roben Co.)

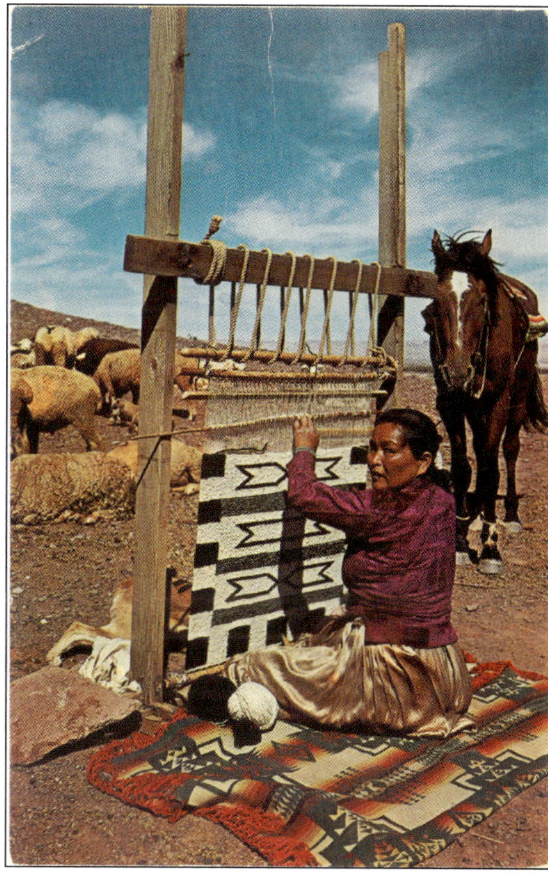

The postcard's reverse side reveals a glimpse at Southwest tourism in 1973—"The Ray Manleys are superb tour hosts – We took picture[s] similar to this card – had better model. She later made fried bread on which we put honey. The road 25 miles in Canyon de Chelly in water in big army trucks – New adventure. Najove [*sic*] drivers excellent and humorous. Lush motel and grounds . . . unusual in this arid area."

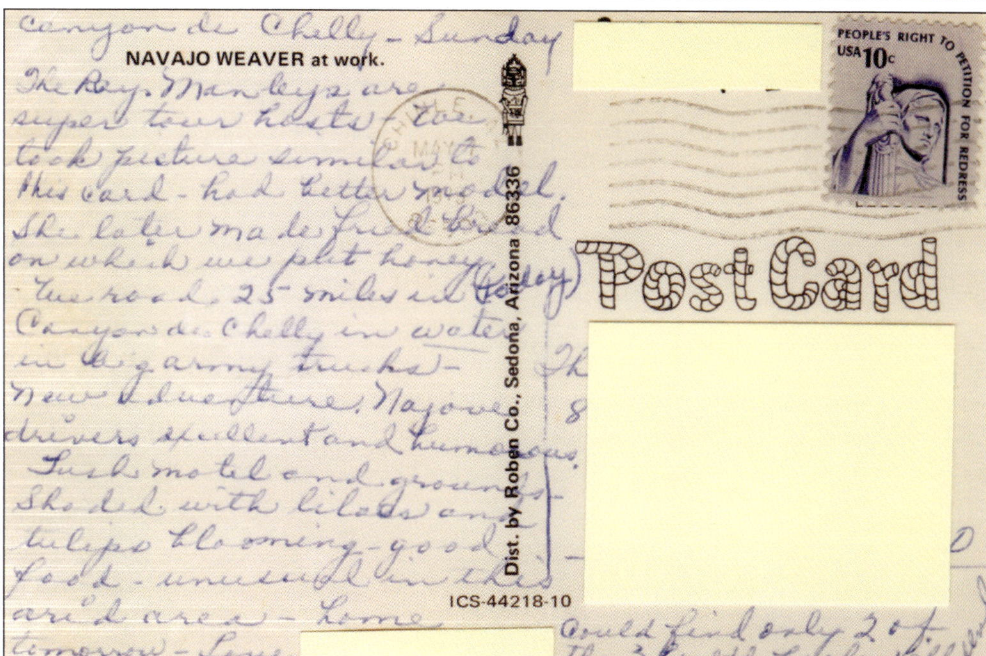

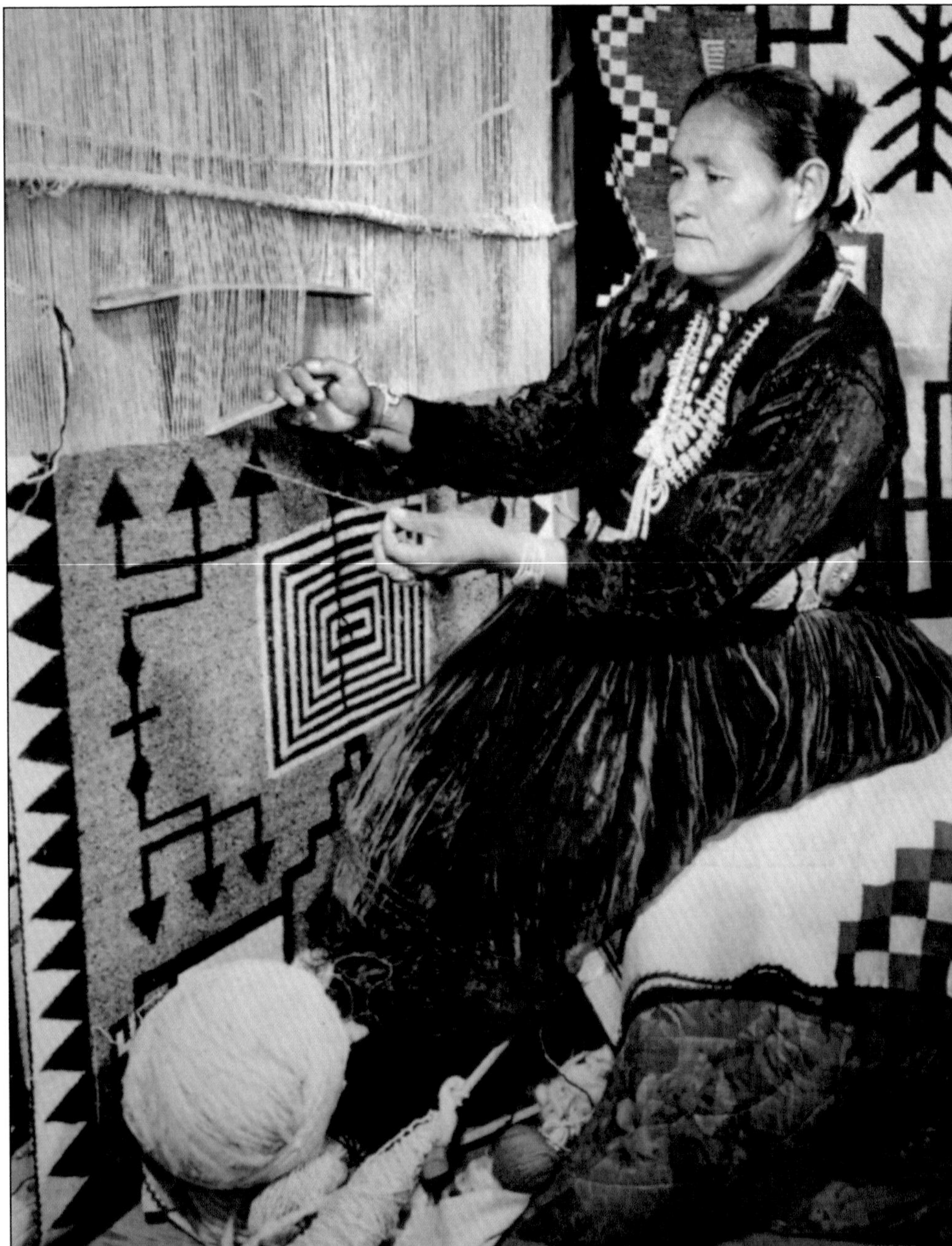

While regional rug styles developed around Ganado, Two Grey Hills, Wide Ruins, and other Navajo communities, some weavers developed their own unique styles that are difficult to name or classify. None of the three rugs visible in this image belong to a standard stylistic category. This highly skilled weaver is working on a large rug with multiple design elements that present technical challenges that are difficult to execute in a symmetrical pattern. She has succeeded in weaving the central concentric squares and radiating elements in an even, well-spaced fashion. The outer border of horizontal triangles, difficult to pack uniformly, is precisely controlled. (US.)

Seven

Card Sets and Curios

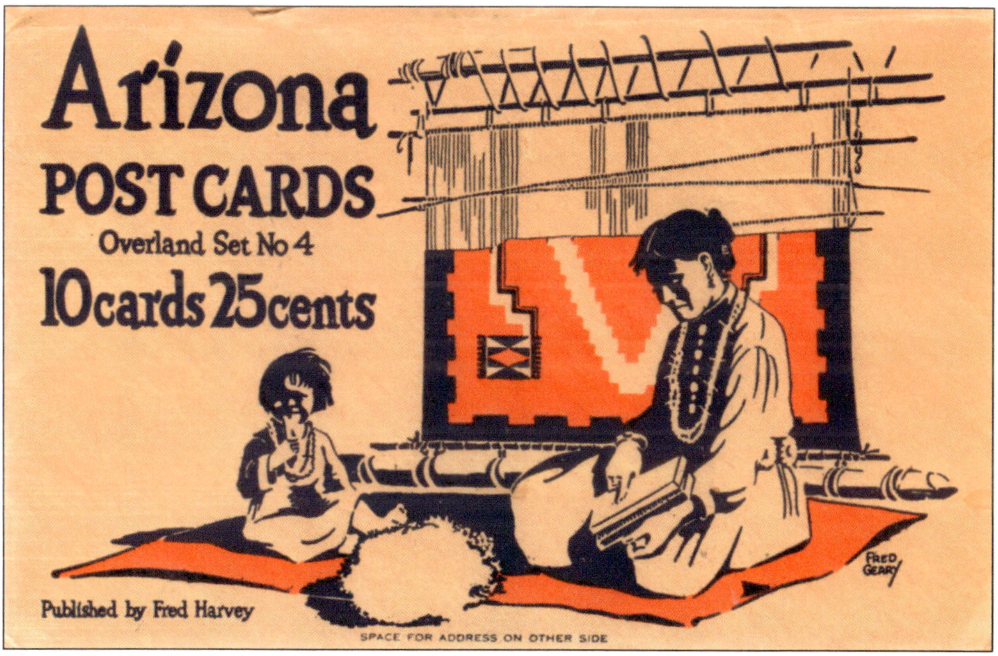

The commercialization of Navajo weaving imagery forms a cornerstone in the branding of the Southwest. Some products, such as this postcard wrapper, appropriately represent their subjects. Others have adopted images in culturally insensitive or inaccurate ways, often to appeal to consumers as funny, charming, or exotic. Today, tribal agencies, public museums, scholarly organizations, and other institutions decry such marketplace abuses. (FHC.)

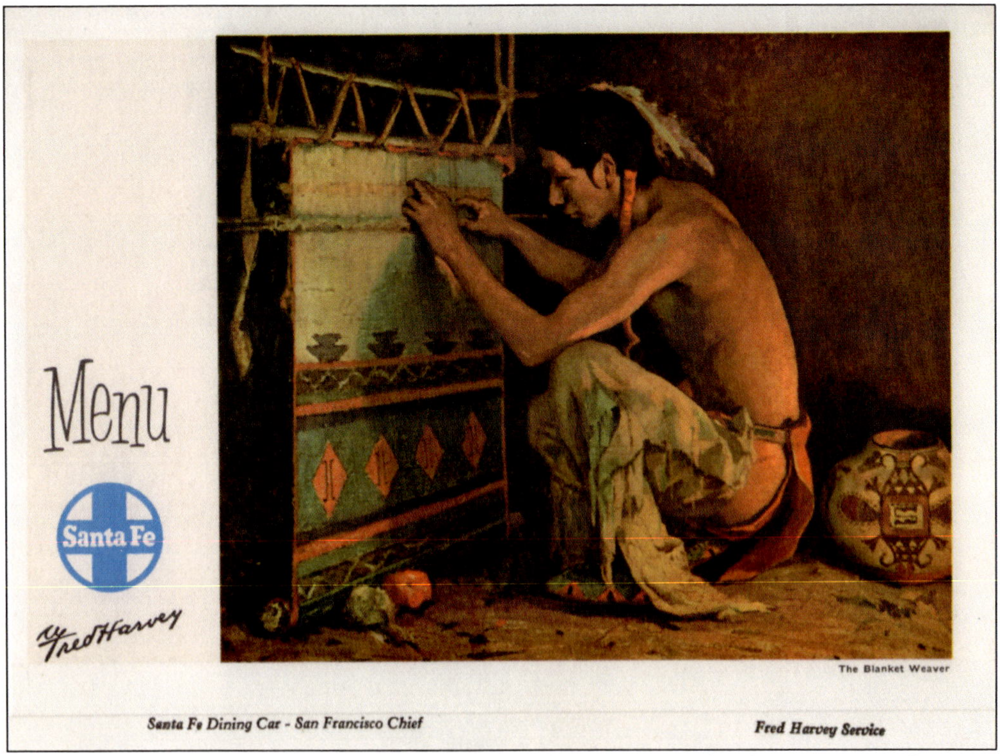

The Fred Harvey Company excelled in promoting all things Indian for the Santa Fe Railway. An oil painting by E.I. Couse titled "The Blanket Weaver" adorns the cover of this train restaurant menu. The caption on the reverse seems to refer to Navajo weaving customs: "Few crafts of the Southwest Indian combine more skill and artistic ability than blanket weaving. . . . No two blankets are designed exactly alike, for the weaver makes up his design as the blanket is being woven. It is unique and original designs of Indian blankets that make them appealing to travelers visiting the Southwest." Yet the weaver is a Rio Grande Pueblo man who is posed as though weaving an outsized Pueblo-style ceremonial dance sash with traditional designs that are often repeated with this exact patterning. The painting is reproduced with permission from Virginia Couse Leavitt and the Couse Foundation. (SFR and FHC.)

Dinner

Price of Entree Determines Cost of Dinner

Cucumber Rings

Cream of Chicken a la Reine
or
Consomme en Tasse, Hot or Jellied

Grilled Lake Superior Whitefish, Maitre d'Hotel 2.90
Omelette with Fresh Strawberries 2.20
Young Guinea Hen, Canadienne 2.90
Roast Ribs of Prime Beef au Jus 3.65

Mashed Potatoes — Fresh Asparagus, Drawn Butter

Lettuce with 1000 Island Dressing
(Salad Served with Above Meals 25c. Additional)

Dinner Rolls

Maple Nut Sundae — Vanilla Ice Cream with Cookies — Cherry Pie
Layer Cake
Stewed Rhubarb
Blue Cheese

Coffee — Tea — Milk

SPECIAL SIRLOIN STEAK DINNER $4.25
Charcoal Broiled Sirloin Steak
French Fried Potatoes — Fresh Asparagus
Chef's Salad
Dinner Rolls
Coffee — Tea — Milk

CHEF'S SUGGESTION - READY TO SERVE $1.65
Hot Roast Beef Sandwich, Mashed Potatoes and Gravy
Ice Cream or Layer Cake
Coffee — Tea — Milk

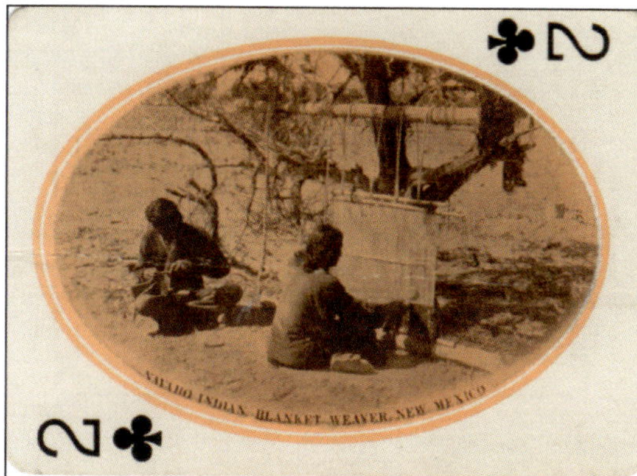

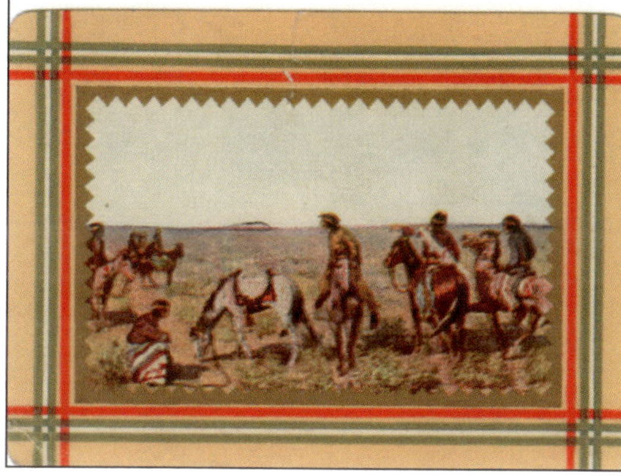

In 1911, the Fred Harvey Company produced commercial playing cards with a series of Southwest scenes. The two of clubs features a blanket weaver possibly accompanied by a moccasin-maker. Each deck included 52 cards plus a joker that shows a Zuni "Knife Wing" personage flanked by two stylized bears with sacred heart-lines; a rainbow deity arches overhead. The reverse of each card shows men with their horses.

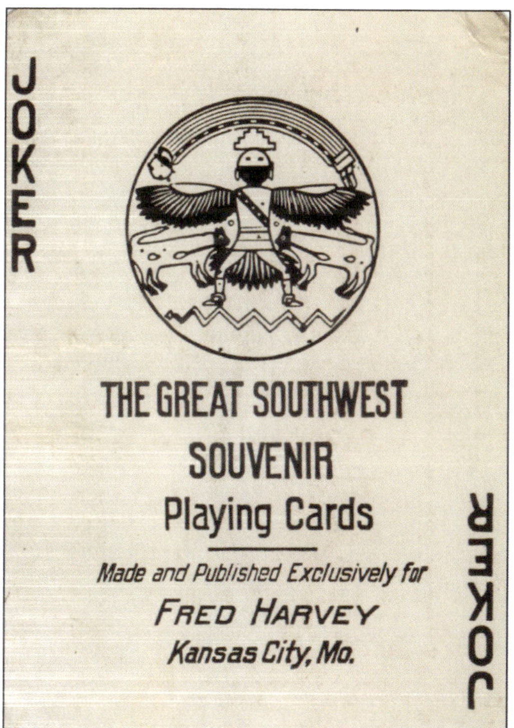

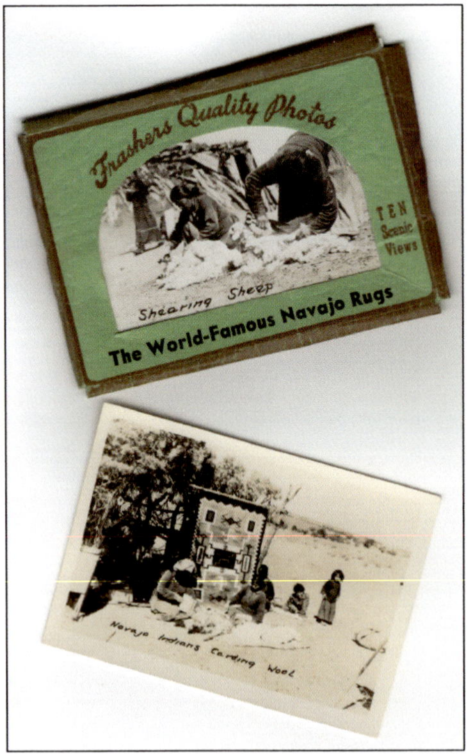

In addition to standard picture postcards and eight-by-ten-inch black-and-white prints, the Frashers Fotos studio reproduced at least two types of boxed sets of miniature photographs, each showing 10 different views of the weaving process. Like the postcards, early versions of the small cards had handwritten legends; later forms included typescript captions. (All, FFS.)

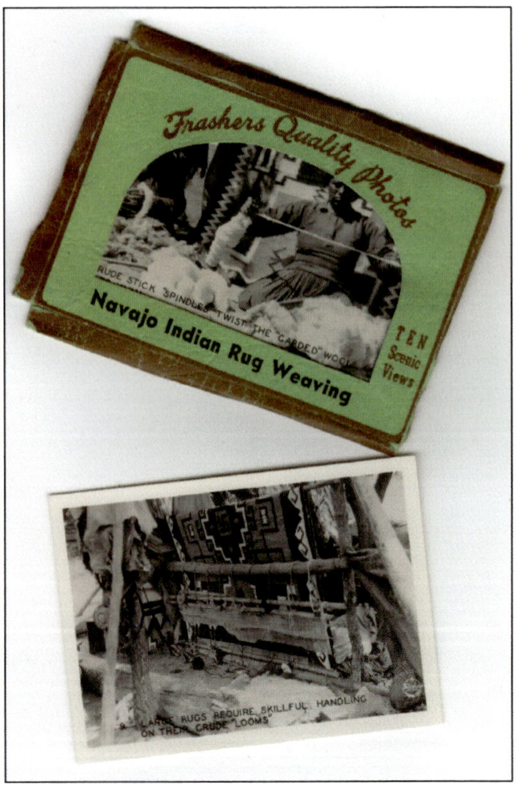

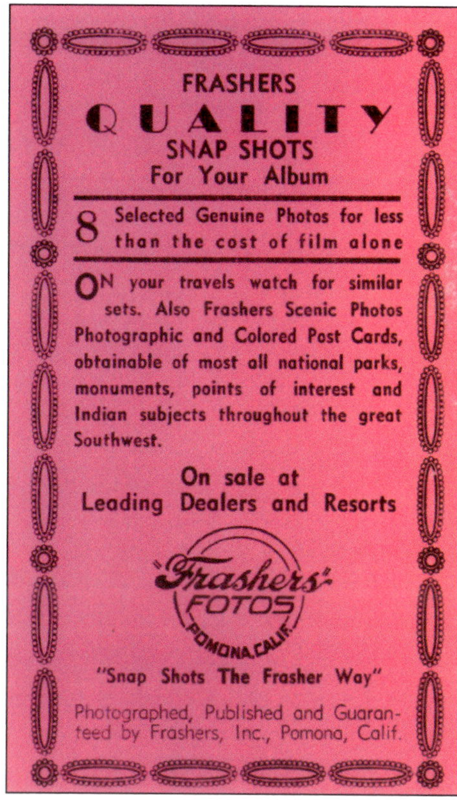
FRASHERS
QUALITY
SNAP SHOTS
For Your Album

8 Selected Genuine Photos for less than the cost of film alone

ON your travels watch for similar sets. Also Frashers Scenic Photos Photographic and Colored Post Cards, obtainable at most all national parks, monuments, points of interest and Indian subjects throughout the great Southwest.

On sale at
Leading Dealers and Resorts

Frashers' FOTOS POMONA, CALIF.

"Snap Shots The Frasher Way"

Photographed, Published and Guaranteed by Frashers, Inc., Pomona, Calif.

Burton Frasher Sr. traveled with a portable darkroom and produced photographs on demand for local shops that readily sold postcards and "instant snapshots" to visitors. According to the enclosure accompanying a set of eight "Genuine" photographs, some Frashers Fotos images were intended as lasting mementos to be added to tourists' personal photograph albums. (All, FFS.)

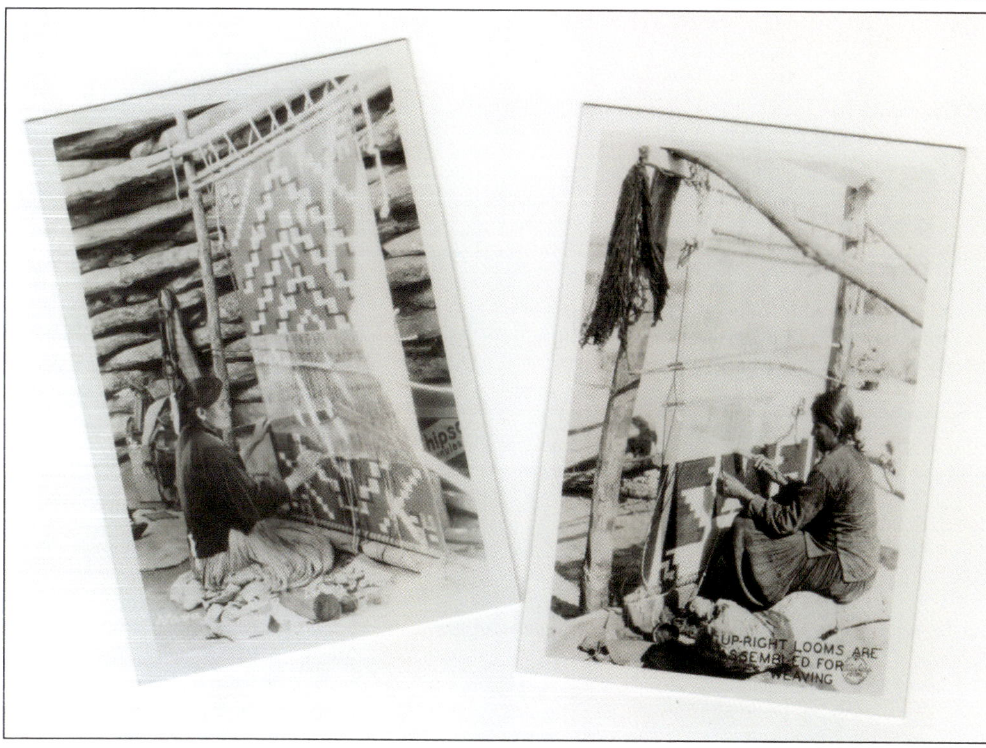

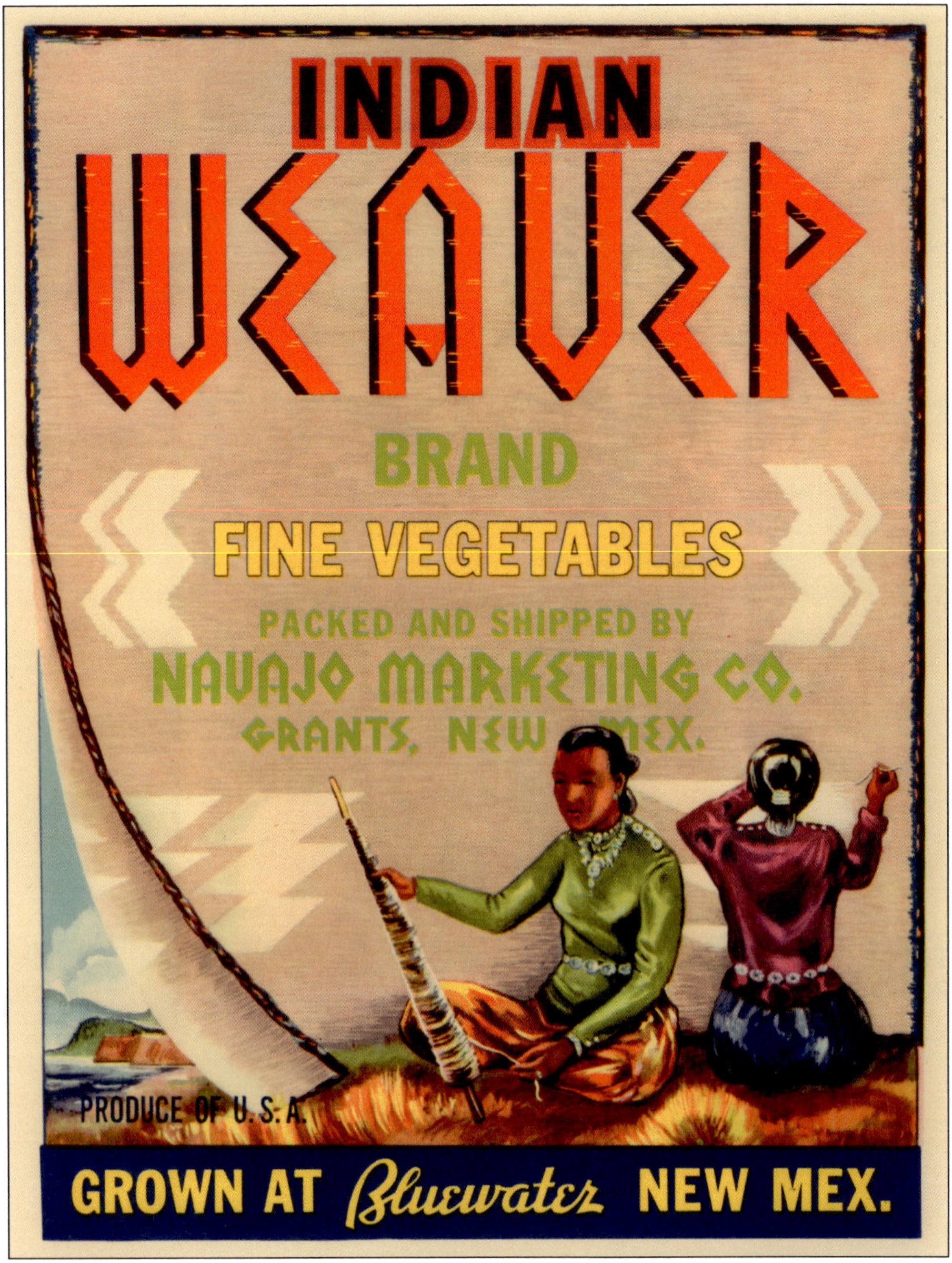

This 1940s produce box label came from the Navajo Marketing Company, headquartered near the Navajo Nation's southeastern corner. The cleverly stylized scene shows two Navajo women—one winding yarn on an oversized handspindle and one presumably weaving on an improbably large rug, ready to sail away on the wind. The original label measures nine by seven inches. (NMC.)

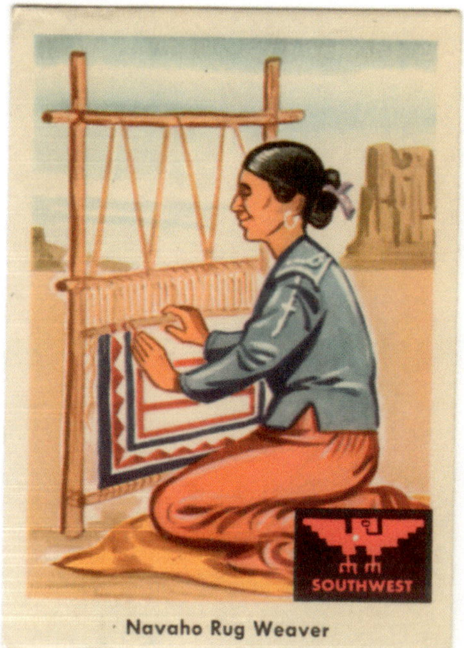

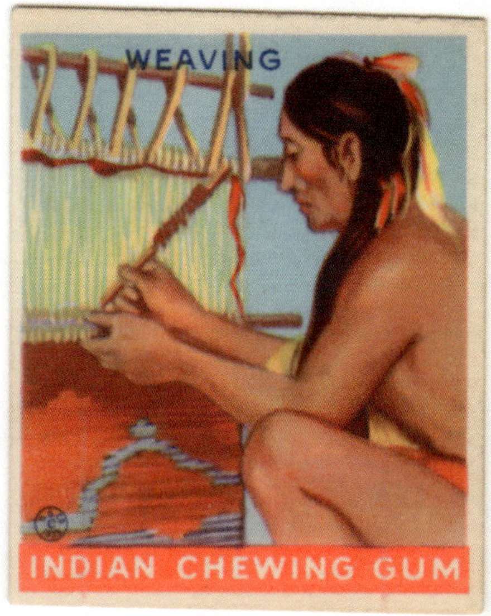

Vintage curios with simplistic, stereotypical, exaggerated, or otherwise incorrect images and captions are a product of earlier times and perspectives. Although no longer regarded as entertaining or socially acceptable, items such as these trading cards have become historical documents that reflect attitudes and values from the past. (Above, F.H. Fleer; below, Goudey Gum.)

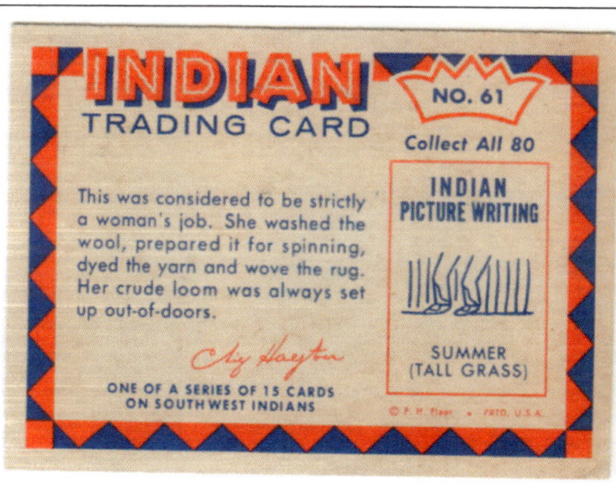

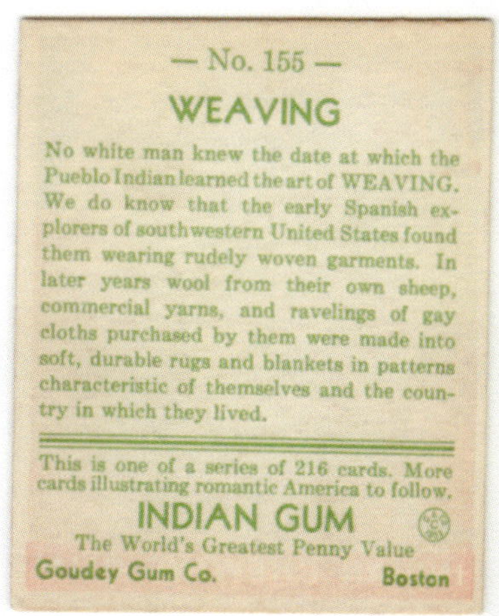

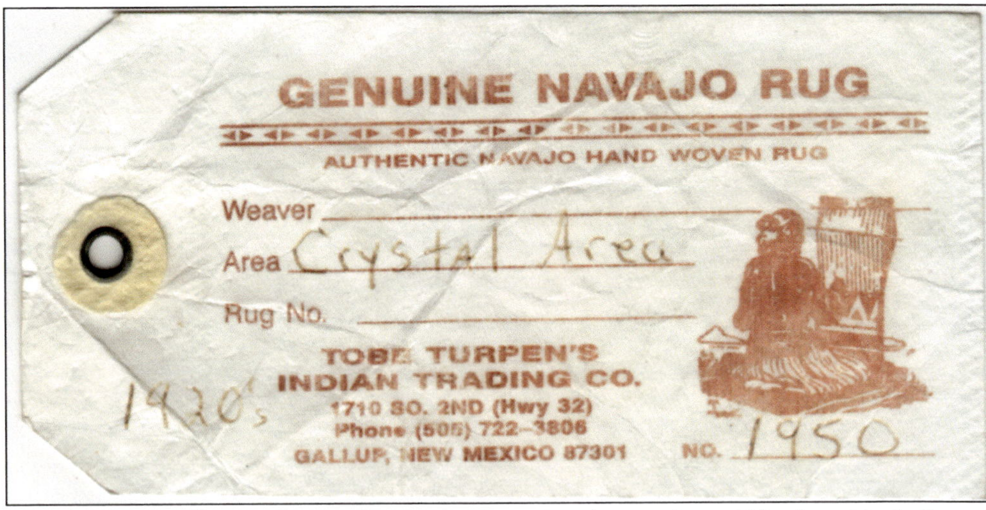

Coauthor Peter Hiller sought Navajo weaving imagery wherever it could be found, including on this "Genuine Navajo Rug" sales tag from a well-known trading post and pawn shop. Such labels were adopted by many shops and reflect a trend, common since the 1960s, to record the weaver's name and home community. Often, a Polaroid photograph of the weaver with the just-sold rug accompanies the tag. (Tobe Turpen's Trading Company.)

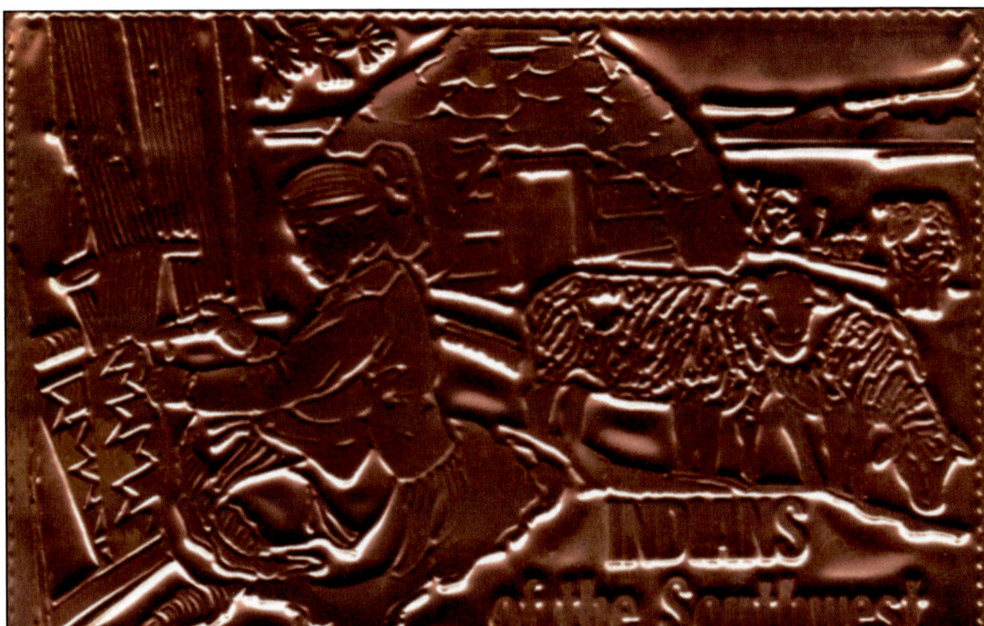

A weaver's image, with sheep and hogan, is embossed onto copper foil on this novelty postcard. A paper backing provides a writing surface and a caption that tries to connect modern Native Americans and their past: "The Indians of the Southwest come from a vast history that includes the places they live, the lands they occupy, the ruins that are protected, and the customs they practice." (Kopper Kard Co.)

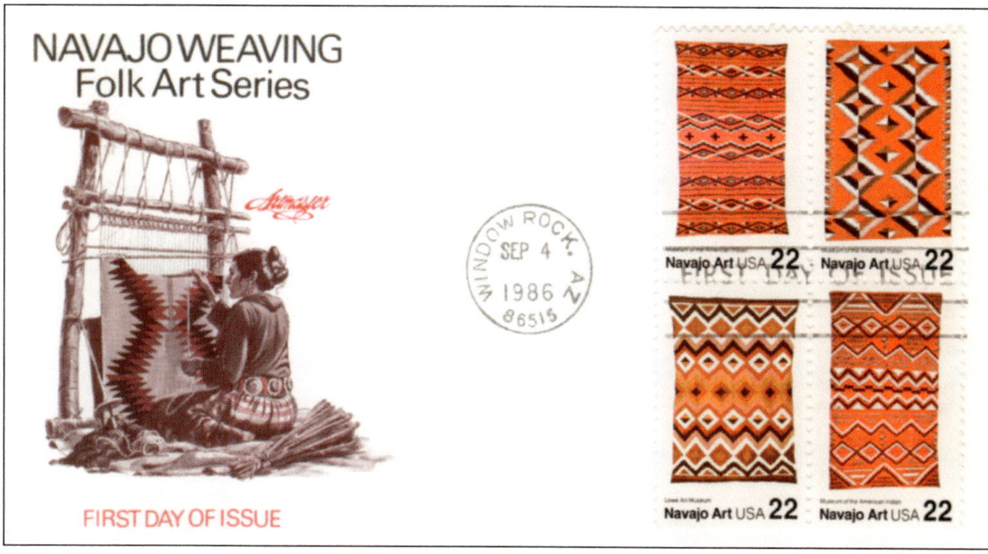

This commemorative postcard and four stamps were designed by Derry Noyes, a graphic designer and art director for the US Postal Service in Washington, DC. The stamps represent four classic Diné wearing blankets of the 19th century, now in the collections of the Smithsonian and the Lowe Art Museum. The Navajo Weaving Folk Art Series was first issued during the Navajo Nation Fair in Window Rock, Arizona, in 1986.

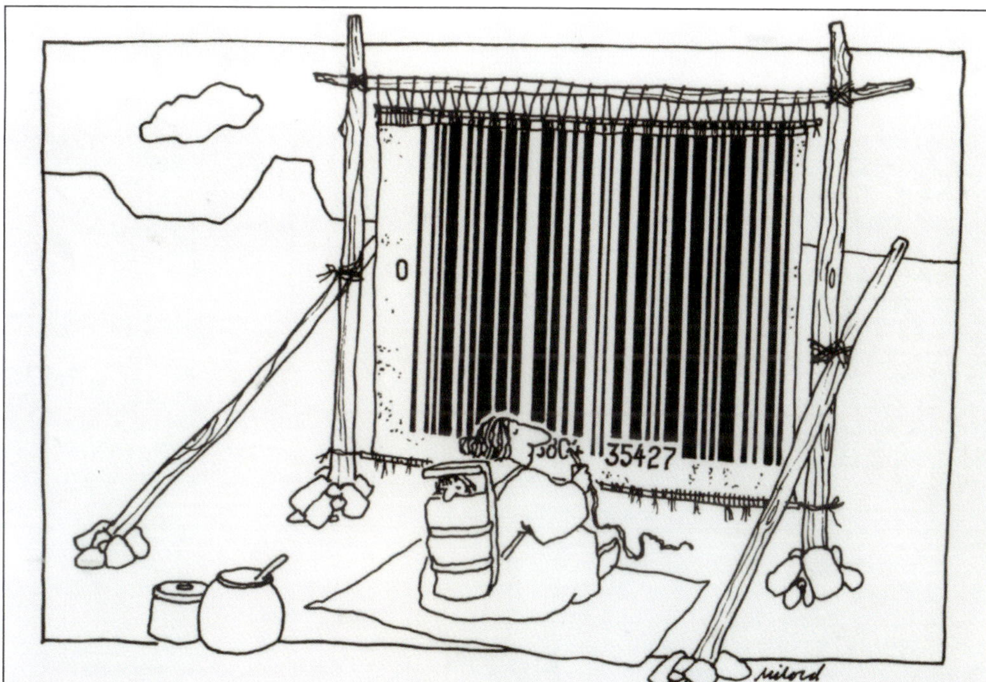

Laughter is ever-present when Navajo weavers gather. Humor emerges in puns, word games, gossip, and joke-telling. In weaving, visual puns and 3-D optical illusions appear. One artist has worked silicon chip imagery into her commissioned rugs; another wove beads to form a QR code for smartphones. The "Bar Code Weaver," designed by New Mexico artist Jerome E. Milord, takes this approach in a good-natured way. This card, copyrighted by the artist in 1989, is reproduced with permission from Christian Milord.

Bibliography

Batkin, Jonathan. *The Native American Curio Trade in New Mexico*. Santa Fe, NM: Wheelwright Museum of the American Indian. 2008.

Bernardin, Susan, Melody Graulich, Lisa MacFarlane, and Nicole Tonkovich, with an Afterword by Louis Owens. *Euro-American Women Photographers and Native North Americans, 1880–1940*. New Brunswick, NJ: Rutgers University Press. 2003.

Binkley, David A. "Artists Under Glass: The Nelson-Atkins Museum of Art's Native American Dioramas." In *The Great Southwest of the Fred Harvey Company and the Santa Fe Railway*, edited by Marta Weigle and Barbara A. Babcock, pp. 176–186. Phoenix, AZ: Heard Museum. 1996.

Blomberg, Nancy. *Navajo Textiles: The William Randolph Hearst Collection*. Tucson, AZ: University of Arizona Press. 1988.

Curtis, Edward S. *The North American Indian*, 20 volumes. 1907-1930.

Faris, James C. *Navajo and Photography, A Critical History of the Representation of an American People*. Albuquerque, NM: University of New Mexico Press, 2003.

Gilpin, Laura. *The Enduring Navaho*. Austin, Texas: University of Texas Press. 1968.

Hedlund, Ann Lane. *Navajo Weaving in the Late 20th Century: Kin, Community, and Collectors*. Tucson, AZ: University of Arizona Press. 2003.

———. "Beyond Beauty: Exploring the Ethnoaesthetics of Navajo Weaving." *American Indian Art Magazine* (40)3: 44-59. Summer 2015.

Howard, Kathleen L., and Diana F. Pardue. *Inventing the Southwest: The Fred Harvey Company and Native American Art*. Flagstaff, AZ: Northland Press. 1996.

James, George Wharton. *Indian Blankets and Their Makers*. Chicago: A.C. McClurg. 1914.

Jett, Stephen C., and Virginia Spencer. *Navajo Architecture: Forms, History, Distribution*. Tucson, AZ: University of Arizona Press. 1981.

Klein, James B. "Preserving our Western Natural and Historical Heritage: The Enduring Legacy of S. J. Holsinger." *The Smoke Signal* (Tucson Corral of the Westerners) no. 84. 2008.

Leadabrand, Russ. "Photographer of the Desert [Burton Frasher Sr.]." In *Los Angeles Corral Brand Book No. 1*, edited by Russ Leadabrand, pp. 48-76. Los Angeles, CA: Westerners. 1964.

Margolis, Eric, and Jeremy Rowe. "Manufacturing Assimilation: Photographs of Indian Schools in Arizona." http://www.public.asu.edu/~jeremy/indianschool/paper.htm. 2002.

Matthews, Washington. "Navajo Weavers." *Third Annual Report of the Bureau of American Ethnology*, 1881-1882, pp. 375-391. Washington DC: US GPO. 1884.

Moore, J. B. *The Catalogues of Fine Blankets, Rugs, Ceremonial Baskets, Silverware, Jewelry & Curios, originally published between 1903 and 1911*. Albuquerque, NM: Avanyu Press. 1987.

Regan, Margaret. "Paper Faces: Photographs of Navajos and Hopis. In *Picturing Arizona: The Photographic Record of the 1930s*, edited by Katherine G. Morrissey and Kirsten M. Jensen. Pp.125–143. Tucson, AZ: University of Arizona Press. 2005.

Reichard, Gladys. *Navajo Shepherd and Weaver*. New York: J. J. Augustin. 1936.

Valette, Rebecca M., and Jean Paul Valette. *Navajo Weavings with Ceremonial Themes: A Historical Overview of a Secular Art Form*. Atglen, PA: Schiffer. 2018.

Wheat, Joe Ben. *Blanket Weaving in the Southwest*, edited by Ann Lane Hedlund. Tucson, AZ: University of Arizona Press. 2003.

Young, Robert W., and William Morgan. *The Navajo Language: A Grammar and Colloquial Dictionary*. Albuquerque, NM: University of New Mexico Press. 1980.

Index

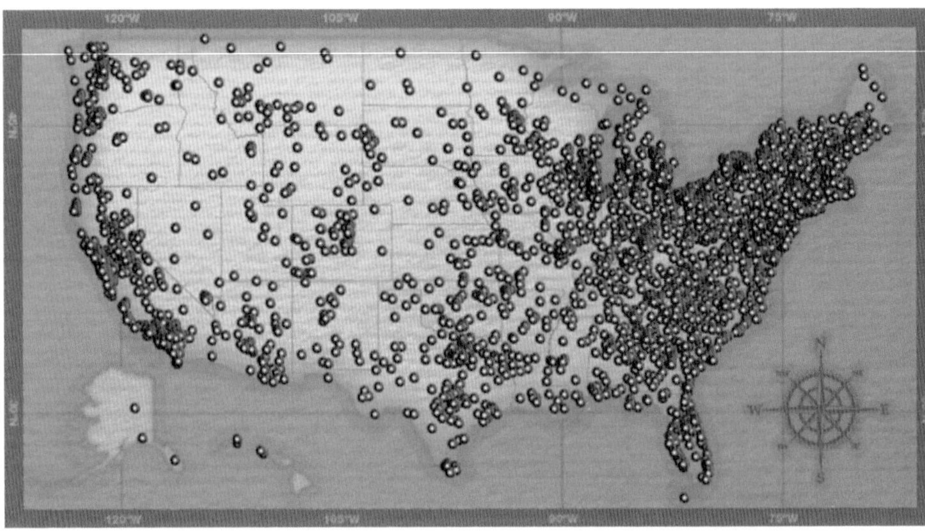

Consistent with our mission to preserve history on a local level, this book was printed in South Carolina on American-made paper and manufactured entirely in the United States. Products carrying the accredited Forest Stewardship Council (FSC) label are printed on 100 percent FSC-certified paper.

MADE IN THE USA